EFFICIENCY ANALYSIS BY PRODUCTION FRONTIERS
THE NONPARAMETRIC APPROACH

THEORY AND DECISION LIBRARY

General Editors: W. Leinfellner and G. Eberlein

Series A: Philosophy and Methodology of the Social Sciences
Editors: W. Leinfellner (Technical Universtiy of Vienna)
G. Eberlein (Technical University of Munich)

Series B: Mathematical and Statistical Methods
Editor: H. Skala (University of Paderborn)

Series C: Game Theory, Mathematical Programming and
Operations Research
Editor: S. H. Tijs (University of Nijmegen)

Series D: System Theory, Knowledge Engineering and Problem
Solving
Editor: W. Janko (University of Vienna)

SERIES B: MATHEMATICAL AND STATISTICAL METHODS

Editor: H. Skala (Paderborn)

Editorial Board

Scope

The series focuses on the application of methods and ideas of logic, mathematics and
statistics to the social sciences. In particular, formal treatment of social phenomena, the
analysis of decision making, information theory and problems of inference will be
central themes of this part of the library. Besides theoretical results, empirical investiga-
tions and the testing of theoretical models of real world problems will be subjects of
interest. In addition to emphasizing interdisciplinary communication, the series will
seek to support the rapid dissemination of recent results.

For a list of titles published in this series, see final page.

EFFICIENCY ANALYSIS BY PRODUCTION FRONTIERS
THE NONPARAMETRIC APPROACH

by

JATI K. SENGUPTA

Professor of Economics and Operations Research,
University of California, Santa Barbara, CA, U.S.A.

KLUWER ACADEMIC PUBLISHERS

DORDRECHT / BOSTON / LONDON

Library of Congress Cataloging in Publication Data

Sengupta, Jatikumar.
    Efficiency analysis by production frontiers : the nonparametric
approach / Jati K. Sengupta.
        p.   cm. -- (Theory and decision library. Series B,
Mathematical and statistical methods.)
    Includes indexes.
    ISBN 0-7923-0028-9
    1. Production functions (Economic theory) 2. Parameter
estimation.   I. Title. II. Series: Theory and decision library.
III. Series: Theory and decision library. Series B, Mathematical
and statistical methods.
HB241.S37 1989
338.5--dc19   88-7634
                                                                CIP

ISBN 0-7923-0028-9

Published by Kluwer Academic Publishers,
P.O. Box 17, 3300 AA Dordrecht, The Netherlands.

Kluwer Academic Publishers incorporates
the publishing programmes of
D. Reidel, Martinus Nijhoff, Dr W. Junk and MTP Press.

Sold and distributed in the U.S.A. and Canada
by Kluwer Academic Publishers,
101 Philip Drive, Norwell, MA 02061, U.S.A.

In all other countries, sold and distributed
by Kluwer Academic Publishers Group,
P.O. Box 322, 3300 AH Dordrecht, The Netherlands.

Printed in The Netherlands

To
Sri Thakur and Sreema
with
all my devotion

TABLE OF CONTENTS

PREFACE

Measuring productive efficiency for nonprofit organizations has posed a great challenge to applied researchers today. The problem has many facets and diverse implications for a number of disciplines such as economics, applied statistics, management science and information theory. This monograph discusses four major areas, which emphasize the applied economic and econometric aspects of the production frontier analysis:

A. Stochastic frontier theory,
B. Data envelopment analysis,
C. Clustering and estimation theory,
D. Economic and managerial applications

Besides containing an up-to-date survey of the most recent developments in the field, the monograph presents several new results and theorems from my own research. These include but are not limited to the following: (1) interface with parametric theory, (2) minimax and robust concepts of production frontier, (3) game-theoretic extension of the Farrell and Johansen models, (4) optimal clustering techniques for data envelopment analysis and (5) the dynamic and stochastic generalizations of the efficiency frontier at the micro and macro levels.

In my research work in this field I have received great support and inspiration from Professor Abraham Charnes of the University of Texas at Austin, who has basically founded the technique of data envelopment analysis, developed it and is still expanding it. My interactions with him have been most fruitful and productive. I am deeply grateful to him.

Finally, I must record my deep appreciation to my wife and two children for their loving and enduring support. But for their support this work would not have been completed.

University of California
Santa Barbara, California
August 15, 1988

Jati K. Sengupta
Professor of Economics and
  Operations Research

Chapter 1

EFFICIENCY ANALYSIS IN PRODUCTION

In the current microeconomic theory of production, characterizing efficiency, estimating it and analyzing its policy implications have posed new challenges for the economists. These challenges are at several levels: (1) a nonparametric class of approaches has been proposed against production functions or production frontiers which are usually specified in parametric forms e.g., Cobb-Douglas functions, (2) the econometric estimation of efficiency in nonparametric contexts raises new issues, (3) the distribution of input-output data may have significant impact on the measurement and estimation of efficiency in a nonparametric context, and (4) finally, the method of aggregation employed in generating efficiency measures at the industry level is more important in dynamic contexts than so far recognized. Our objective in this chapter is to present a broad overview of the recent developments in the nonparametric approach to measuring and estimating efficiency through production frontiers.

Farrell [1] is perhaps the first to introduce a nonparametric approach to measure productive efficiency. Instead of estimating conventional production functions, he starts out from the observed input-output coefficients of a set of firms and as a standard for measuring the efficiency of the firms he fits a frontier function to the points as a piecewise linear function. This frontier function is called "the efficient production function", which is used as a reference for comparing the efficiency (or inefficiency) of various firms relatively to the frontier surface. Farrell introduced three major efficiency concepts, two at the firm level and one at the industry level. "Technical efficiency", which is measured by the distance of an observed input-output point of a firm from the frontier curve and "the price efficiency" which measures the degree of correctness in the adaptation of factor proportions to current input prices are the two measures at the individual firm or, unit level. Then we have the "structural efficiency" as a measure for the whole industry, which indicates in a broad sense the degree to which an industry

1

keeps up with the performance of its own best firms. Thus, two or more industries can be compared in terms of structural efficiency e.g., industry A may be said to be more efficient structurally than industry B, if the distribution of its best firms is more concentrated near to its frontier for industry A than for B. Clearly, if the industries are viewed as 'sectors' as in Leontief input-output models, then the concept of structural efficiency can be easily applied at the sectoral level. This shows that the efficiency concept of Farrell though developed in a partial equilibrium framework of individual firms can be easily related to a general equilibrium context.

1.1   Partial and General Equilibrium Models

Unlike Farrell, Johansen [2] developed a linear programming (LP) approach with its major thrust on deriving an industry production frontier from the stochastic input-output data of individual firms. Thus he introduced explicitly the notions of a statistical distribution of the input coefficients when plants are used at full capacity (i.e., the capacity distribution) and a capacity utilization function. He derived the mathematical conditions under which the aggregate production frontier will have some conventional functional forms such as Cobb-Douglas, which specifies a log-linear form. The second major contribution of Johansen is in relating his efficiency concept to (a) short vs. long run production, (b) technological change through factor-augmenting processes, and (c) above all, to the dynamics of the macro-economic process of growth in the tradition of the neoclassical models of growth.

The emphasis on the general equilibrium structure in Johansen's approach is of particular importance to economic theory due to its future research implications. First of all, this approach can be easily related to the whole class of computable general equilibrium models, which have recently attracted much attention in development planning and large-scale economic modeling. Secondly, the dynamic component of Johansen's efficiency can be directly utilized in the open-dynamic version of Leontief's input-output model; it can also be synthesized with the von Neumann model of optimal economic growth. Thirdly, one could easily generalize the Johansen model in nonlinear programming terms by allowing nonlinear specification of the technology used in the model.

In the partial equilibrium framework, the Johansen model specifically distinguished between (a) the *ex ante* and *ex post* frontiers, (b) the short (when some inputs are fixed) and the long run (when all inputs are free to vary) function, and (c) the different rules of aggregating the individual units to industry-level production frontiers depending on the form of the capacity distribution and the capacity utilization function.

Besides Farrell's and Johansen's contributions one has to mention three other major contributions in recent times. One is the attempt by Afriat [3] to apply a nonparametric method for testing whether a finite body of input-output data is consistent with an optimal production behavior. His characterization associates a production function with a given input-output data set subject to the limitation that the production function has some specified economic properties e.g., quasi-concavity, monotonicity and that it is efficient in the sense of a production frontier. This has opened up a whole new line of research to test if a given (or observed) data set satisfies the efficiency hypothesis above along with other properties like monotonicity and quasi-concavity. This line of economic and econometric consistency tests has been followed up by several authors in recent times e.g., Hanoch and Rothschild [4], Diewert and Parkan [5] and Varian [6].

The second major contribution is by Charnes, Cooper and Rhodes [7], who developed a nonparametric method of efficiency measurement of a set of decision making units (DMUs) or, firms for each of which the only data available are the multiple inputs and multiple outputs without any knowledge of their prices. This approach termed "data envelopment analysis" (DEA) has been shown to be a significant generalization of the Farrell method of efficiency measurement and also equivalent to the concept of Pareto efficiency. This DEA model has been very widely applied in management science and operations research particularly to pubic sector organizations where the data on input and output prices are frequently unavailable and the profit maximization principle frequently inapplicable. This line of research has been actively followed up in recent times by several authors [8-10].

A third development is in the area of econometric estimation of stochastic production frontiers. Unlike the parametric approach to the estimation of a stochastic production frontier, it applies a nonparametric regression approach. Thus in the parametric approach e.g., we may estimate the production frontier from the specification

$$y_j = \mu(x_j) - e_j, \qquad\qquad\qquad e_j \geq 0$$

$$\mu(x_j) = \sum_{i=1}^{m} \beta_i x_{ij}; \qquad\qquad i = 1, 2, \ldots, m; j = 1, 2, \ldots, n$$

$$\hspace{10cm} (1.1)$$

where x_j's are m inputs, y_j is output for unit (firm) j and e_j denotes nonnegative errors for which n observations are available. In parametric regression we assume that the form of $\mu = \mu(x_j)$ is known e.g., $\mu = x'_j\beta$ is assumed here as a linear form, although log-linear or other nonlinear forms can also be tried if they are suitable. A nonparametric regression model however assumes only that μ belongs to some collection of functions e.g., it may be assumed to be only concave. Thus one has to rely more heavily on the characteristics of the observed data points, because one has to choose an appropriate function space to which μ is believed to belong. Two aspects of this nonparametric approach deserve some comments. First of all, this approach can utilize some of the recent methods of nonparametric estimation [11] of the probability density of the error term e_j in (1.1), which does not assume any specific form of the probability distribution. Secondly, the DEA model mentioned before can be viewed as a two-stage estimation procedure [12], where the nonparametric regression can be applied at the second stage after the efficient units are determined at the first stage of the DEA model, which compares each DMU relative to the overall constraint set $C(\beta)$ by solving n linear programming (LP) models one for each DMU i.e.,

$$\operatorname*{Min}_{\beta'(k) \in C(\beta)} g_k = \beta'(k) x_k = \sum_{i=1}^{m} \beta_i(k) x_{ki}$$

$$\hspace{10cm} (1.2)$$

where

$C(\beta) = \{\beta | X\beta - y \geq 0, \beta \geq 0\}$

$x_k = (x_{ki})$: m-eement input vector for k-th DMU

$y = (y_j)$: n-element output vector.

1.2   Production Frontier as Flexible Production Functions

The flexibility of the production frontier approach in a nonparametric context can be indicated in several ways e.g., (a) by comparing it with average production functions where both efficient and inefficient units are included, (b) by considering clusters of different units with different degrees of closeness to the frontier and (c) by comparing the nonparametric frontier with a parametric production function in econometric terms. Farrell's approach characterized the optimal isoquant associated with the production frontier for any given set of observed input-output data and the distance of any observed point from the optimal isoquant when suitably defined is used to measure inefficiency.

For the single output (y_j) and m input (x_{ij}) case let the observed data set be D = (y,X) comprising the n-element vector y and the m by n input-output matrix X. Firm k is then compared relative to the industry of n firms (units) by solving for the optimal input price vector β in the linear programming (LP) model:

$$\text{Min}_{\beta} \; g_k = \sum_{j=1}^{m} \beta_i x_{ik} = \beta' x_k \qquad (1.3)$$

subject to (s.t.)

$R = \{\beta | \beta'X \geq y', \beta \geq 0\}$

Farrell used its dual:

$$\text{Max}_{\lambda} \ z_k = \sum_{j=1}^{n} \lambda_j y_j = \lambda' y$$

s.t. $\qquad\qquad\qquad\qquad\qquad\qquad\qquad\qquad$ (1.4)

$$\lambda \ \varepsilon \ C = \{\lambda \mid X\lambda \leq x_k, \lambda \geq 0\}$$

where prime denotes transpose and $\beta = \beta(k)$, $\lambda = \lambda(k)$ since we are solving for the efficiency of firm k relative to the industry comprising n firms. Assuming all outputs positive and all inputs nonnegative, the dual problem can also be written as

$$\text{Max}_{\lambda} \ z_k = \sum_{j=1}^{n} \lambda_j = \lambda' e$$

s.t. $\qquad\qquad\qquad\qquad\qquad\qquad\qquad\qquad$ (1.5)

$$A\lambda \leq x_k, \lambda \geq 0$$

where $A = (a_{ij})$, $a_{ij} = x_{ij}/y_j$ is the input coefficient matrix and e is an n-element column vector with each element unity. Farrell used this standard model (1.5) to compare the efficiency of firm k relative to the industry. Three features of the Farrell model are to be noted. First of all, the dual variables $\beta = (\beta_i)$ and $\lambda = (\lambda_j)$ are the shadow prices of inputs and outputs at the optimum; hence if market prices are not available, these shadow prices β^*, λ^* could be interpreted as market prices. Second, the efficiency of each firm k is compared in relation to the industry sets R and C defined above. Thus the k-th firm is said to be *efficient* in the Farrell sense, if it satisfies the following two conditions of maximum output and minimum inputs:

(max. output): $\quad y_k^* = \sum_{i=1}^{m} \beta_i^*(k) \ x_{ik} = y_k$

$$\text{and } s_k^* = y_k^* - y_k = 0 \qquad\qquad\qquad\qquad (1.6)$$

(min. inputs): $\quad x^*_{ik} = \sum_{j=1}^{n} x_{ij} \, \lambda^*_j(k) = x_{ik}$

$$\text{and } w^*_{ik} = x_{ik} - x^*_{ik} = 0, \text{ all } i \tag{1.7}$$

These two conditions for efficiency say that for the efficient firm there is no shortfall in output from its maximal level and no input surplus above the minimal level. Let K be the number of firms (or units) which are thus efficient and let $Y^* = \{y^*_k, k \in K\}$ be the set of all efficient outputs. The corresponding set of efficiency prices of inputs and output are then $B^* = \{\beta^*(k), k \in K\}$ and $L^* = \{\lambda^* = \lambda^*(k), k \in K\}$ respectively. Clearly, the efficient output set Y^* is supported by the two sets B^*, L^* of efficiency prices. By the principle of duality one set Y^* cannot exist without the other (B^*, L^*). Hence if we consider any arbitrary set Y of positive outputs, none of which are efficient in the Farrell sense, then the distance between the two sets Y and Y^* and hence between B and B^* or, between L and L^* can be used to characterize inefficiency in the industry, provided of course the distance concept is suitably defined. Third, the efficiency surface B^* above may be viewed as a set of efficiency facets, one for each k where $k \in K$. Thus two measures of technical efficiency can be obtained e.g., one is firm-specific (i.e., each unit or firm k is either Farrell efficient or not) and the other is an average over the whole industry. The parametric theory of frontier estimation only provides an industry average measure of efficiency, since it specifies a particular one-sided probability distribution (e.g. half-normal) and defines the expected value of this distribution as the measure of technical efficiency.

Now consider some aspects of the single output Farrell model which relate it to the Pareto-Koopmans concept of efficiency under decentralization. First of all, note that the otpimal shadow prices λ^*_j are m in number where it is assumed that $m < n$ but for a single output this is discriminatory pricing and not competitive pricing. If the industry were competitive, the only price $p_0 = p_0 e$ could prevail for the single output for all efficient firms $k \in K$. Two cases are now possible: either the law of one price $\lambda^* = p^*_0 e$

holds for the efficient firms where p_0^* is a positive scalar or it does not. In the former case the set (β^*, p_0^*) of efficiency prices possesses the decentralization property of competitive equilibrium i.e. the industry equilibrium of K efficient firms can be decomposed into K individual efficient equiilbria. In the latter case the decentralization property does not ordinarily hold. Two options are nevertheless available. One is to introduce the notion of a representative firm and use its optimal output price as p_0^*. In this case the crucial question is how to specify the representative firm. An alternative approach which avoids the problem of locating the representative firm is to directly formulate an industry model:

$$\text{Max } \pi = p_0 \, e'y \quad \text{s.t. } Ay \le v, \, y \ge 0 \tag{1.8}$$

This is Johansen's approach [2], where the input coefficient matrix $A = (a_{ij})$ and the aggregate inputs $v = (v_i)$ are observed and the optimal values y* of the output vector are solved for. Here a_{ij} are input coefficients at full capacity outputs. Since p_0 has no role in optimization, it may be dropped. The dual of this reduced model is

$$\text{Min } g = \beta'v \quad \text{s.t.} \quad \beta'A \ge e', \, \beta \ge 0 \tag{1.9}$$

where the objective function can also be written as

$g = n\beta'\bar{x} = \sum_{i=1}^{m} \beta_i \bar{x}_i, \; \bar{x}_i = (1/n) \sum_{j=1}^{n} x_{ij} = v_i/n$. Hence this is equivalent to

$$\text{Min } \bar{g} = \beta'\bar{x} \quad \text{s. t.} \quad \beta'A \ge e', \, \beta \ge 0 \tag{1.10}$$

By comparing (1.10) with (1.3) it is clear that if the input vector x_k of firm k is very close to the mean vector $\bar{x}$, then the optimal solutions of the two LPs would be identical. This provides a basis for the following theorem.

Theorem 1.

Let $N(x_k)$ be the neighborhood of x_k throughout which the optimal nondegenerate solution $\beta^*(k)$ of (1.3) remains optimal and likewise for $N(\bar{x})$ associated with the optimal nondegenerate solution β^{**} of (1.10). If the set $N(x_k; \bar{x})$ of intersections of the two sets $N(x_k)$ and $N(\bar{x})$ is not empty, then $\beta^*(k) = \beta^{**}$ for all $k \in N(x_k; \bar{x})$. For all such k the macro production frontier is identical with the micro frontier.

Proof.

Since $\beta^*(k)$ and β^{**} are nondegenerate optimal solutions satisfying the respective simplex criteria $\Delta^*(k) \geq 0$, $\Delta^{**} \geq 0$, the two neighborhoods $N(x_k)$, $N(\bar{x})$ cannot be empty. Let $N(\bar{x})$ defined by $\{x_k \mid x_k = \bar{x} + e_k\}$ where e_k may be sufficiently small. Such a point must exist by the condition hypothesized. Hence the result.

This result is useful for two reasons: (a) it provides a method of screening the data set for determining points which are close to the mean input levels of the industry model, and (b) the closeness of x_k to $\bar{x}$ may be statistically tested by a suitable distance function when e.g., x_k follows a normal distribution around $\bar{x}$.

Now we can consider the multiple output generalization of the Farrell model. Following our development above we present several lines of generalization as follows:

Case A: Composite Output Model

Here we replace each output y_j by the composite output $y_j^c = \sum\limits_{r=1}^{s} \alpha_r y_{rj}$ where each firm is assumed to produce s outputs ($s \geq 2$). The LP model (1.3) now becomes

$$\underset{\alpha, \beta}{\text{Max }} J_k = \alpha' y_k - \beta' x_k$$

$$\text{s.t.} \tag{1.11}$$

$$X'\beta \geq y^c; \quad \alpha, \beta \geq 0$$

The aggregate industry version is, subject to the same constraints

$$\text{Max}_{\alpha,\,\beta} \ J = n(\alpha' \ \bar{y} - \beta' \ \bar{x})$$

$$(1.12)$$

where $\bar{y} = (\bar{y}_r), \bar{y}_r = (1/n) \sum\limits_{j=1}^{n} y_{rj}$ and $\bar{x} = (\bar{x}_i)$ as before. Clearly this model

(1.11) would be identical with the one output case (1.3) of the Farrell model if we

assume the nonnegative weights α_r to be given or known. When the weights $\alpha = (\alpha_r)$

assume the nonnegative weights α_r to be given or known. When the weights $\alpha = (\alpha_r)$

are not known there exist several choices. One is to choose by solving the LP model

(1.11), where one may impose an additional requirement i.e. $\sum\limits_{r=1}^{s} \alpha_r = 1$. This makes

the composite output y^c a convex combination of different outputs. Secondly, one may

choose α_r by the Laplace criterion by interpreting that α_r is the probability of the state of

nature y_r, where all states of nature are equally likely.

Case B: Efficiency Ratio Model

The approach of data envelopment analysis minimizes the efficiency ratio h_k for

firm k i.e.

$$\text{Min}_{\alpha,\,\beta} \ h_k = (\sum\limits_{i=1}^{m} \beta_i x_{ik}) / (\sum\limits_{r=1}^{s} \alpha_r y_{rk})$$

$$\text{s.t. } h_j \geq 1, \quad j = 1,2,...,n \tag{1.13}$$

$$\alpha, \beta \geq 0$$

This leads to the LP model:

$$\text{Min}_{\alpha,\,\beta} \ g_k = \beta' x_k$$

$$\text{s.t. } X'\beta \geq Y'\alpha \tag{1.14}$$

$$\alpha' y_k = 1; \quad \alpha, \beta \geq 0$$

Note that the last condition i.e. $\alpha' y_k = 1$ is nothing but the numeraire condition of the Walrasian system. But since the numeraire condition should not vary from firm to firm it is more appropriate to apply it to the whole industry i.e. to replace the condition $\alpha' y_k = 1$

by $\alpha' \bar{y} = \sum\limits_{r=1}^{s} \alpha_r \bar{y}_r = 1$, where $\bar{y}_r = (1/n) \sum\limits_{j=1}^{n} \bar{y}_{rj} =$ is the mean level of r-th out-

put. The industry version of this model is

$$\text{Min} \quad g = n\beta' \bar{x}$$
$$\text{s. t.} \quad X'\beta - Y'\alpha \geq 0, \ \alpha' \bar{y} = 1 \tag{1.15}$$
$$\alpha, \beta \geq 0$$

Case C: Vector Efficiency

Here we extend the Johansen model (1.8) in terms of a vector objective function.

Let $u_r = \sum\limits_{j=1}^{n} \bar{y}_{rj}$ and $v_i = \sum\limits_{j=1}^{n} x_{ij}$ be the aggregate output (type r) and input (type i) respectively. Let $F(u)$ denote the s-element column vector with a typical element u_r (r = 1,2,...,s). We then set up the vector optimization problem:

$$\text{Max } F(u) \quad \text{s.t.} \quad A u \leq v, u \geq 0 \tag{1.16}$$

where $A = (a_{ir})$ is the input coefficient matrix and $u' = (u_1, u_2, ..., u_s)$ is the aggregate output vector. Here we have set $F(u) = u$ to keep the same framework as Johansen's, although we may have used a more general representation i.e. $F'(u) = (f_1(u_1), f_2(u_2), ..., f_s(u_s))$ where each $f_r(u_r)$ is a continuous concave function of output u_r. In terms of the model (1.16) an output vector $u^* = F^*(u)$ is called *Pareto-optimal* or vector-efficient if it satisfies the constraint of (1.16) and there exists no other vector u which satisfies $u_r > u_r^*$ for all r, the strict inequality holding for at least one r (r=1,2,...,s). Alternatively, we may consider a weighted sum of outputs (or utilities)

$$U = \sum_{r=1}^{s} w_r f_r(u_r) = \sum_{r=1}^{s} w_r u_r$$

(1.17)

with weights $w_r \geq 0$, $\sum_{r=1}^{s} w_r = 1$ as a social welfare function representing consumer's viewpoint. For a given weight vector $w \in W$, where $W \{w \geq 0, w'e = 1\}$ let u^{**} be the maximizing output vector for the LP model

Max $U = w'u$ s.t. $Au \leq v$, $u \geq 0$ (1.18)

and U^{**} be the associated welfare maximum. Then we can state some results linking the welfare maximum and the Pareto optimal solution.

Theorem 2.

For any set of weights $w \in W$ there exists a welfare maximum U^{**} and its associated output vector $u^{**} = u^{**}(w)$, if the input coefficients in A are nonnegative and the input vector v is positive. Furthermore, if all weights are positive, then there exists a Pareto-optimal output vector u^* for every welfare maximum U^{**}.

Proof.

Since the input coefficients are nonnegative and the aggregate inputs v_i are all positive, the Slater condition is satisfied and the restriction set $R: \{u \mid A u \leq v, u \geq 0\}$ is compact and nonempty; also not all w_r can be zero since $\Sigma w_r = 1$. Hence the welfare maximum $U^{**} = U^{**}(w)$ exists along with its associated maximizing vector $u^{**} = u^{**}(w)$. Suppose all w_r's are positive and the welfare maximum (U^{**}, u^{**}) is not Pareto optimal. Then there must exist a feasible output vector $\hat{u}$ such that $\hat{u}_r \geq u_r^{**}$ for all r and $\hat{u}_r > u_r^{**}$ for some $r = 1,2,...,s$. This means $\Sigma w_r \hat{u}_r > \Sigma w_r u_r^{**}$ which is a contradiction. Hence the result.

Two comments are in order. First of all, if w_r's are interpreted as "prices" $p_r(u)$ such that $p_r(u) = p_r$ i.e. independent of output then the output vector u^{**} can be interpreted as profit maximizing under a competitive market. However if p depends on vector u then we have the discriminatory pricing model of monopolistic competition. Secondly, it is also known from Kuhn-Tucker theorem on nonlinear programming that for every Pareto-optimal output vector u* of the LP model (1.18) there exist some positive vector w > 0 of weights such that u** solves the vector optimum problem (1.16). One may impose additional regularity conditions to obtain u* = u**.

Case D: Dominant Technology Model

In this case the input-output coefficient $a_{ir}(j) = x_{ir}(j)/y_r(j)$, $(i=1,2,...,m; r=1,2,...,n)$ of each firm j is viewed as a particular technology as in activity analysis model and the objective of the industry manager is to obtain one or a subset of firms which is in some sense the optimum. This follows the idea of Manning [13] who has applied a similar concept in the context of Leontief's input-output model and called the optimum set of firms as having a "dominant technology set". Let $x(j)$, $y(j)$ be the input and output vectors of firm j and $A(j)$ be the input coefficient matrix of order m by s. Following Johansen we assume that these input coefficients indicate that current inputs are required in the same proportions to output as they would be at full capacity utilization; these are variables *ex ante* rather than fixed and subject to specific utilization patterns chosen by firms. Johansen has called this pattern the capacity utilization function which determines the effective levels of aggregate inputs and outputs. Let p be the s-element competitive price vector of all outputs $y(j)$, $j=1,2,...,n$ and β be the m-element competitive price vector of all inputs $x(j)$, $j=1,2,...,n$ then the industry manager solves for the optimal values (p^*, β^*) from the LP model:

$$\text{Max} \ z = \sum_{j=1}^{n} p' y(j) - \sum_{j=1}^{n} \beta' x(j)$$

$$\text{s.t.} \ A'(j)\beta \geq p; \ j=1,2,...,n \qquad (1.19)$$

$$\beta \geq 0, p \geq 0$$

where the outputs y(j) and inputs x(j) of all firms are observed. This is the industry version of Farrell model with multiple outputs. Next consider the industry version of the Johansen model e.g. let w and q be the output and input prices (or weights) preassigned by the industry manager, who now seeks to determine the optimal levels of outputs y(j) and inputs x(j) so as to maximize total profits π:

$$\text{Max } \pi = \sum_{j=1}^{n} w' y(j) - \sum_{j=1}^{n} q' x(j)$$

$$\text{s. t. } \sum_{j=1}^{n} A(j)y(j) \leq \sum_{j=1}^{n} x(j) \tag{1.20}$$

$$y(j), x(j) \geq 0; \quad j=1,2,\ldots,n$$

Theorem 3.

Let $\lambda^*(j)$ and b^* be the optimal dual variables of (1.19) and (1.20) respectively, such that $\lambda^*(j) = y^*(j)$, $b^* = q = \beta^*$ and $p^* = w$, then the two LP models are equivalent.

Proof.

The optimal vectors (p^*, β^*) and $(y^*(j), x^*(j))$ must satisfy the necessary conditions of the Kuhn-Tucker theorem:

$$\sum_{j=1}^{n} [y(j) - \lambda^*(j)] \leq 0, \lambda^*(j) \geq 0$$

$$\sum_{j=1}^{n} A(j)\lambda^*(j) \leq \sum_{j=1}^{n} x(j), \lambda(j) \geq 0$$

and

$$w - A'(j) b^* \leq 0, b^* \geq 0$$

-q + b* $\leq$ 0, b* $\geq$ 0

Under the given conditions it follows that the optimal input-output vectors [y*(j), x*(j)] are supported by their dual prices (p*, β*). Hence the result.

Note that if A = [A(1),A(2),...,A(K)] is the technology set associated with the K efficient firms, then this defines a dominant technology set, since it dominates all other technologies A(j) not belonging to A.

Several policy implications of these competitive allocation models may be derived here e.g., (a) if some resources are nontransferable, then second best optimal solutions will result, (b) if the information about the dominant technology set is not freely available, then the optimal frontier cannot be attained by all firms and (c) finally, the competitive solution can be viewed as a two-stage planning process between the individual units and the aggregate.

1.3 Parametric Forms and their Econometric Estimation

Consider a firm producing a single output y with m inputs $x = (x_1, x_2, ..., x_m)'$. A frontier production function characterizing an efficient transformation of inputs into output may then be specified by a function f(x), which shows the maximum output obtainable from various input vectors. The specification $\{y \leq f(x), x \geq 0\}$ may be estimated from the data set for n units (firms) as:

$$y = f(x) e^{-u}, \quad u \geq 0 \tag{1.21}$$

where u is the error term. Since $u \geq 0$ implies $0 \leq e^{-u} \leq 1$ we have f(x) as the maximum output. Thus we have in (1.21) an example of technical efficiency or a production frontier. If f(x) is specified as a parametric function of the inputs i.e. $f(x) = f(x,\theta)$ we have a parametric production frontier e.g., $f(x, \theta) = Ax_1^{\theta_1} x_2^{\theta_2}$ may be a Cobb-Douglas function. Once the frontier (1.21) is estimated econometrically, the efficiency of the individual units can be easily assessed on the basis of the shortfall in output from the estimated frontier. If the data on input prices (i.e. vector q) and output price (p) are available, then the efficient production technology can be specified by the cost and profit frontiers in an equivalent formulation: thus $c(y, q) = \underset{x}{\text{Min}} \ \{q' x \mid f(x) \geq 0, x \geq 0\}$ is the cost frontier i.e. it indicates the minimum expenditure needed to produce output at the input prices q. The profit frontier is $\pi(p, q) = \underset{x, y}{\text{Max}} \ \{py - q' x \mid f(x) \geq y, x \geq 0\}$.

Now consider a firm with an input-output plan (x^0, y^0). Since $f(x^0)$ is the production frontier, the firm is said to be technically efficient if $y^0 = f(x^0)$ and technically inefficient if $y^0 < f(x^0)$ i.e. the observed output is less than the efficient output. If the input and output price data are available and the firms are assumed to maximize profits in a competitive market, then one can define allocative efficiency as follows: the observed plan (x^0, y^0) is said to be allocatively efficient if $f_i(x^0)/f_j(x^0) = q_i/q_j$ and allocatively inefficient if $f_i(x^0)/f_j(x^0) \neq q_i/q_j$ assuming $f(x)$ to be differentiable such that $f_i(x^0)$ is the marginal product of input x_i evaluated at the vector point x^0. Clearly the allocative inefficiency is due to using inputs in the wrong proportions i.e. profit is not maximized or, cost is not minimized. Hence it follows that the observed expenditure $q'x^0$ equals minimum cost $c(y^0, q)$ if and only if the firm is both technically and allocatively efficient [14-15].

On the estimation of technical efficiency by a parametric production frontier, four general methods are propsoed in the current literature: A. Deterministic frontiers, B. Stochastic frontiers, C. Composed error model and D. Mixed parametric frontiers. All these methods share one common feature: either the shape of the frontier function is of a specific functional form, or the statistical distribution of the error term is of a specific form or both.

A.   Deterministic Frontiers

Consider the frontier equation (1.21) in logarithmic terms as a Cobb-Douglas function:

$$\ln y = \ln f(x) - u, \quad u \geq 0$$

$$= \alpha_0 + \sum_{i=1}^{m} \alpha_i \ln x_i - u, \quad u \geq 0 \tag{1.22}$$

Aigner and Chu [16] first showed that the parameter vector $\alpha = (\alpha_0, \alpha_1, ..., \alpha_m)'$ may be estimated either by linear programming (i.e. minimizing the sum of the absolute values of the residuals) or by quadratic programming (i.e. minimizing the sum of squared residuals). However they did not introduce any specific form of the distribution of the error term u. Later Schmidt [17] showed that if u is exponentially distributed, then Aigner and Chu's LP procedure is maximum likelihood (ML), while their quadratic programming procedure is ML if u is half-normally distributed. Several other forms of distribution of u have been used in the literature with corresponding ML estimates e.g., (a) a two-parameter beta distribution due to Afriat [3], (b) one parameter gamma due to Richmond [18] and (c) a two parameter gamma distribution due to Greene [19]. The choice of any particular distribution for u, which determines the different ML estimates of α involves the problem that the range of the dependent variable (i.e. output) depends on the parameters to be estimated. This violates one of the regularity conditions invoked to prove the general result that ML estimators are consistent and asymptotically efficient.

As an alternative to ML method one could apply the method of corrected ordinary least squares (COLS) which is due to Richmond [18]. For example, consider the log-linear case of the Cobb-Douglas model (1.22) and let μ be the mean of u; then we can write

$$\ln y = (\alpha_0 - \mu) + \sum_{i=1}^{m} \alpha_i \ln x_i - (u - \mu)$$

where the new error term (u-μ) satisfies all the standard OLS conditions e.g. zero mean, constant variance, except of course normality. Hence this equation may now be estimated by the OLS method to obtain best linear unbiased estimates of (α_0-μ) and of the

α_i. When any specific distribution e.g., beta or gamma is assumed for u, then we can estimate these parameters from the moments of the distribution of the OLS residuals. Since μ is a function of these parameters, it too can be estimated consistently and this estimate can be used to 'correct' the OLS constant term, which is a consistent estimate of $(\alpha_0-\mu)$. But this type of 'correction' may not always yield nonnegative values for all residuals $(u_j-\mu)$ in empirical applications, thus failing to satisfy the frontier hypothesis of efficiency. One remedy is to correct the constant term not as in COLS but by shifting it up until all the residuals have the right signs. A second remedy is to apply a 'composed error model' to be discussed later.

B.   Stochastic Frontiers

Three types of stochastic frontiers may be easily distinguished. One is the composed error model

$$y = f(x)\, e^{\varepsilon}, \quad \varepsilon = v\text{-}u, \quad u \geq 0 \tag{1.23}$$

e.g.,

$$\ln y = \alpha_0 + \sum_{i=1}^{m} \alpha_i \ln x_i + \varepsilon, \quad \varepsilon = v - u, \quad u \geq 0$$

where the error term ε is composed of two components. A symmetric component (e.g., the component v) captures the random effects of measurement error and exogenous shocks which cause the production frontier to vary across firms, while the one-sided error component u with $u \geq 0$ captures technical inefficiency relative to the stochastic frontier.

The second type of stochastic frontier assumes that both variables (x,y) are subject to error and our object is to estimate the permanent component of output response

$$Y = f(x) \, e^{-u}, \quad u \geq 0$$

rather than the transitory component, while our observations have the following noise structure due to errors v_1 and v_2:

$$y = Y + v_1, \quad x = X + v_2$$

As in the composed error model, the error components v_1, v_2 may be assumed to be symmetric, while u is one-sided. Two basically different situations now arise. One could suppose that the unobserved components $X_1, X_2, ..., X_n$ are fixed and nonrandom in the probability universe, or one could suppose that the X_j are independent random variables with the same probability distribution. It is customary in statistical literature to refer to the first case as a 'functional' relation and to the second case as a 'structural' relation. The latter case is more prevalent in empirical studies on production functions. Consider a simple example of a two-input Cobb-Douglas function expressed in COLS form:

$$\tilde{Y} = \tilde{\alpha}_0 + \alpha_1 \tilde{X}_1 + \alpha_2 \tilde{X}_2 - \omega \tag{1.24}$$

where $\tilde{Y} = \ln Y$, $\tilde{X}_i = \ln X_i$, $\tilde{\alpha}_0 = \alpha_0 - \mu$, $\omega = u - \mu$ and μ is the mean of $u \geq 0$. Now assume that $\tilde{X}_1$ and $\tilde{X}_2$ have a joint normal distribution with variance $\sigma^2(\tilde{x}_1)$, $\sigma^2(\tilde{x}_2)$ and correlation ρ and let (v_1, v_2, ω) be independent random normal variables with zero means and variances σ_1^2, σ_2^2 and σ_3^2. Then apart from the means we have eight parameters in the model (1.24), viz., α_1, α_2, $\sigma^2(\tilde{x}_1)$, $\sigma^2(\tilde{x}_2)$, ρ, σ_1^2, σ_2^2 and σ_3^2. It is clear however that $\tilde{X}_1$, $\tilde{X}_2$ and $\tilde{Y}$ have a trivariate normal distribution which has, apart from the means, six parameters namely

$$\text{var}(\tilde{X}_1) = \sigma^2(\tilde{x}_1) + \sigma_1^2; \quad \text{var}(\tilde{X}_2) = \sigma^2(\tilde{x}_2) + \sigma_2^2$$

$$\text{var}(\tilde{Y}) = \alpha_1^2 \sigma^2(\tilde{x}_1) + 2\alpha_1 \alpha_2 \sigma(\tilde{x}_1)\sigma(\tilde{x}_2) + \alpha_2^2 \sigma^2(\tilde{x}_2) + \sigma_3^2$$

$$\text{cov}(\tilde{X}_1, \tilde{X}_2) = \rho\, \sigma(\tilde{x}_1)\sigma(\tilde{x}_2) \hspace{3cm} (1.25)$$

$$\text{cov}(\tilde{X}_1, \tilde{Y}) = \alpha_1 \sigma^2(\tilde{x}_1) + \alpha_2 \rho\, \sigma(\tilde{x}_1)\sigma(\tilde{x}_2)$$

$$\text{cov}(\tilde{X}_2, \tilde{Y}) = \alpha_2 \sigma^2(\tilde{x}_2) + \alpha_1 \rho\, \sigma(\tilde{x}_1)\sigma(\tilde{x}_2)$$

Clearly two parameters viz., α_1 and α_2 are not statistically identifiable. Various conditions for identifying these two parameters may be analyzed. In particular if we know the ratio $\lambda = \sigma_1^2/\sigma_2^2$ of the two variances σ_1^2, σ_2^2 and σ_3^2 then we have the case of just identification i.e. six parameters and six estimating equations. Another important case occurs when we have prior information that one of the two inputs is dominant in the sense that $\sigma_2^2 = k_1 \sigma_1^2$ and $\sigma_3^2 = k_2 \sigma_1^2$ where the first input is dominant. In this case we can solve the maximum likelihood equations by equating the sample second-order moments to the expressions in (1.25) with σ_2^2 and σ_3^2 replaced by $k_1 \sigma_1^2$ and $k_2 \sigma_1^2$ respectively.

Clearly this type of stochastic frontier has much wider applicability than the deterministic frontier and there is great scope of simulation studies here e.g., the case of nonnormal trivariate densities tending asymptotically to normality can be easily analyzed by Monte Carlo techniques. Furthermore the set of prior information on (λ, σ_3^2) in the trivariate normal case may be utilized in a Bayesian framework.

The third case of a stochastic frontier arises through a random parameter model. Consider for example the log-linear model (1.24) where $\tilde{X}_i$' s are assumed fixed but the individual response coefficients α_i are assumed to be random around its mean value i.e.

$$\alpha_{ij} = \bar{\alpha}_i + \varepsilon_{ij}, \quad i = 1, 2; \quad j = 1, 2, \ldots, n$$

where $\bar{\alpha}_i$ is the mean response coefficient of output with respect to input $\tilde{X}_i$ and ε_{ij} is a random error term with mean zero, variance σ_{ii}^2 and covariance zero and distributed independently of the error term w. Griffiths [20] has discussed an efficient method of estimating the mean parameters $\bar{\alpha}_i$ by $\bar{\alpha}_i$ and the error term ε_{ij} by

$$\hat{\varepsilon}_{ij} = x_{ij} \cdot \hat{\theta}_{ii}\hat{\gamma}_j / (\sum_{i=1}^{2} x_{ij}^2 \hat{\theta}_{ii}) \text{ where } \hat{\gamma}_j \text{ is the estimate of } \gamma_j = \sum_{i=1}^{2} x_{ij}\varepsilon_{ij}.$$

An empirical application to agricultural productions is discussed by Vashishtha [21].

C.   Composed Error Model

There are two different ways of looking at the composed error model (1.23), which may be written as follows by taking suitable log transformations if necessary:

$$y_j = g(x_j,\alpha) + \varepsilon_j, \quad \varepsilon_j = v_j - u_j; \quad u_j \geq 0 \qquad (j=1,2,...,n) \qquad (1.26)$$

where y_j is output for observation j, x_j is a vector of inputs and $\alpha = (\alpha_0,\alpha_1,...,\alpha_m)'$ is a vector of parameters. How to decompose the estimates $\hat{\varepsilon}_j = y_j - g(x_j, \hat{\alpha})$ of the composed error terms e_j into its two separate components $\hat{v}_j, \hat{u}_j$? This decomposition is important in economic efficiency analysis, since u_j measures technical inefficiency in the sense that it measures the shortfall of output (y_j) from its maximum value. A second issue with this model (1.26) is how to derive consistent estimates of α when we have both time series and cross-section data for each of n firms. This question is important since it shows how with additional time-series information for each firm the estimates of the parameters can be improved.

For the first issue, Jondrow et al. [22] have developed an interesting method for separating the error term of the stochastic frontier model into its two components for each observation. This makes it comprable to the DEA model which computes technical inefficiency for each observation. Their method basically exploits the theorem that the conditional distribution of u given ε is that of a normal distribution $N(\mu_*, \sigma_*^2)$ where

$\sigma^2 = \sigma_u^2 + \sigma_v^2$, $u_* = -\sigma_u^2\varepsilon/\sigma^2$, $\sigma_*^2 = \sigma_u^2\sigma_v^2/\sigma^2$ and it is assumed that each v_j (i.e. the symmetric part) is normal $N(0, \sigma_v^2)$ with mean zero and variance σ_v^2 and u_j is distributed as the absolute value of a normal variable $N(0, \sigma_u^2)$ with zero mean and variance σ_u^2. By using this theorem one can obtain a point estimate of the nonsymmetric component u by using the mean $E(u|\varepsilon)$ or, the mode $M(u|\varepsilon)$ of the conditional distribution where

$$E(u \mid \varepsilon) = \mu_* + K\sigma_* \quad ; K = f(-\mu_*/\sigma_*)/\{1 - F(-\mu_*/\sigma_*)\}$$

$$M(u \mid \varepsilon) = \begin{cases} -\varepsilon(\sigma_u^2/\sigma^2) & \text{if } \varepsilon \leq 0 \\ 0 & \text{if } \varepsilon > 0 \end{cases}$$

where $f(\cdot)$ and $F(\cdot)$ denote the standard normal density and its cumulative distribution (cdf) respectively. Thus by replacing μ_*, σ_* by their sample estimates $\hat{\mu}_*$, $\hat{\sigma}_*$ one can estimate the conditional mean $\hat{E}(u \mid \varepsilon)$.

For the second issue when we have panel data i.e. time series data for each firm j we could write e.g., in the Cobb-Douglas case:

$$\ln y_{jt} = (\alpha_0 - \mu) + \sum_{i=1}^{m} \alpha_i \ln x_{ijt} + v_{jt} - (u_j - \mu)$$

$$j=1,2,...,n; \quad t=1,2,...,T$$

where $E(u_j) = \mu > 0$ and v_{jt} is the symmetric component. On treating $\varepsilon_{jt} = v_{jt} - (u_j - \mu)$ as the disturbance term, where $u_j \sim$ iid (μ, σ_u^2) and independent of v_{jt}, Schmidt and Sickles [23] have shown that we can directly apply OLS to this equation. Then clearly the OLS estimates of $\alpha_0^* = \alpha_0 - \mu$ and $\alpha = (\alpha_1,...,\alpha_m)'$ will be consistent as $n \to \infty$ thought not as $T \to \infty$ for fixed n, if the effects u_j are uncorrelated with the regressors x_{jt}. Under these circumstances one can apply the generalized least squares (GLS) as in panel data literature i.e. GLS estimates of α_0^* and α are based on the consistent estimates of σ_u^2, σ_v^2 when they are unknown, but the consistent estimation of σ_u^2 requires that $n \to \infty$. Thus the strongest (weakest) case for GLS occurs when n is large (small) but T small (large). One advantage of this GLS procedure is that one can recover the individual firm-specific intercept term $\alpha_{0j} = \alpha_0 - u_j$ from the estimated residuals

$$\hat{e}_{jt} = y_{jt} - \sum_{i=1}^{m} \hat{\alpha}_i \ln x_{ijt}, \quad \hat{\alpha}_{0j} = \frac{1}{T} \sum_{t=1}^{T} \hat{e}_{jt}$$

These estimates $\hat{\alpha}_{0j}$ are consistent as $T \to \infty$ provided $\hat{\alpha}$ is consistent and the latter requires either $n \to \infty$ or σ_u^2 known. Two comments are in order. Although the technical inefficiency of a particular firm can be estimated here consistently as $T \to \infty$, this requires adding more observations on the same firm without any change in technology. Secondly, it is true that the parameters α here are not assumed to be uncorrelated with the regressor variables x_{ijt}, yet our discussion in case of (1.25) shows very clearly that for finite samples the consistency condition may fail to hold along with the identifiability of all the parameters.

D.   Mixed Parametric Frontiers

Parametric frontiers can also be estimated if price data are available through cost and profit frontiers, just as a Cobb-Douglas (average) production function can be estimated through factor shares of value added assuming a competitive market framework. A different type of mixed approach is to combine the nonparametric specification of the production frontier as in the DEA or Johansen model with a parametric estimation procedure. For example, Forsund and Hjalmarsson [24] applied the following form of the frontier production function to milk processing in Swedish dairy plants over the years 1964-73, where Farrell's measure of technical efficiency was used:

$$x^{\alpha(t)} e^{\beta(t)x} = A(t) \prod_{j=1}^{2} v_j^{a_j(t)}$$

Here x is output, v_1 and v_2 are the two inputs, labor and capital, A(t) denotes technical progress and the scale function parameters are $\alpha(t)$ and $\beta(t)$ where t is time in years. Clearly the elasticity $\varepsilon(x,t)$ of scale function is given by

$$\varepsilon(x,t) = [\alpha(t) + \beta(t) \, x]^{-1}$$

The estimates of the parameters $A(t)$, $\alpha(t)$, $\beta(t)$ $a_j(t)$ are computed by solving the following programming problem:

$$\text{Min} \sum_{t=1964}^{1973} \sum_{i=1}^{28} [\ln A(t) + \sum_{j=1}^{2} a_j(t)\ln v_{ij}(t)$$

$$- \alpha(t) \ln x_i(t) - \beta(t) \, x_i(t)]$$

Subject to

$$\ln A(t) + \sum_{j=1}^{2} a_j(t)\ln v_{ij}(t) - \alpha(t)\ln x_i(t) + \beta(t)x_i(t) \geq 0$$

$$i = 1,2,...,28; \quad t = 1964,...,1973$$

$$\sum_{j=1}^{2} a_j(t) = 1 \text{ (linear homogeneity assumption)}$$

$\dot{A}(t), a_j(t), \alpha(t), \beta(t)$ are ≥ 0

$\dot{\alpha}(t), \dot{\beta}(t) \leq 0$

$$\sum_{j=1}^{2} \dot{a}_j(t) = 0$$

where dot over a term denotes its first difference i.e., $\dot{a}_j(t) = a_j(t+1) - a_j(t)$. If one assumes that all time-dependent parameters are additive linear functions, then the above becomes a simple LP problem. For the empirical application they found the estimated frontier production function as follows:

$$x^{0.32 - 0.0056t} e^{(1.47 - 0.0073t)} 10^{-5} x$$
$$= 0.0024 \ v_1^{0.81 + 0.0019t} \ v_2^{0.19 - 0.0019t}$$

from which the elasticity of scale function is found to be

$$\varepsilon(x,t) = [0.32 - 0.0056t + (1.47 - 0.0073t) \ 10^{-5} \ x]^{-1}$$

This shows that the optimal scale x for $\varepsilon = 1.0$ increases from 48,644 tonnes in 1964 at t = 1 to 99,325 in 1973 at t = 10.

They did not derive the standard errors of the estimated coefficients or the statistical significance of their estimated frontier but the results of Koenker [25] on the asymptotic testing methods for L_1-regression (i.e., least absolute deviations method) show that one could apply statistical tests in an asymptotic sense and set up suitable confidence intervals for the estimated coefficients.

1.4 Nonparametric Theory: Different Facets

The nonparametric theory of efficiency measurement can be approached at four different levels: A. Specification of efficiency, B. Data consistency with the efficiency hypothesis, C. Methods of aggregation or, disaggregation of efficiency measures and D. Problems of econometric estimation.

A. Specification of Efficiency

We have already discussed briefly the efficiency characterizations due to Farrell and Johansen and the efficiency ratio model in DEA framework. Another concept of efficiency is closely related to the coefficient of resource utilization which was originally developed by Debreu [26] in a competitive general equilibrium context. To develop at a partial equiilbrium framework when there exist no input and output prices, consider a cluster of N units say, each with output and input vectors $y(j)$, $x(j)$ of dimensions m and n respectively for j=1,2,...,N. Furthermore assume a linear technology set for each j e.g.,

$$R(j) = \{(y,x) \mid A(j)\ y(j) \le x(j); \quad y(j), x(j) \ge 0\} \tag{1.27}$$

Denote by R the set of finite intersections of the sets $R(j)$ and assume that each set $R(j)$ is compact so that the intersection set R is compact. If the set R is not empty, how could we define some points in R as efficient relative to others which are not? Debreu's measure used the similarity of the constraint set for the N units to define a set R_{min} to denote the minimal physical inputs required to achieve an output level y^*, where R_{min} is a subset of R and not empty. Let y be any other vector point not belonging to R_{min}. The distance from y to the set R_{min} may then provide us with a measure of inefficiency. Thus, a vector point $y^* \in R_{min}$ is efficient if there exists no other $y \in R$, such that $y \ge y^*$, with at least one component strictly greater.

The coefficient of resource utilization due to Debreu is not limited to the convex constraint set (1.27) arising in LP models. It can be applied to any nonempty convex sets R arising for example through nonlinear production relations. But we would fix our ideas on the LP formulation for illustrative purposes. We note three basic elements of this formulation. First, we have to define a set R_{min} which attains an output level y^* with a minimal input x_0 say. This implies that we replace $x(j)$ in (1.27) by x_0 for all y = 1.2,...,N and ask how many output vectors $y(j) \in R(j)$, if any, are on or below the point y^*, i.e., $y(j) \le y^*$ with strict inequailty holding for at least one component? Suppose for j=k, it holds $y(k) < y^*$. Then, the k-th unit is not efficient in the cluster. If for no j=1,2,...,N we have $y(j) \le y^*$, then the N-component cluster is efficient. Secondly, by the convexity of the output feasibility set R_{min}, there must exist a vector of prices z such that

$z'(y^* - y) \geq 0$, i.e., $z'y \leq z'y^*$

Denote by y^0 a vector collinear with y but belonging to R_{min}, i.e., $y^0 = ry$, then it follows

$$\max_{y^* \in R_{min}} \frac{z'y}{z'y^*} = \frac{1}{r} \quad \max_{y^* \in R_{min}} \frac{z'y^0}{z'y^*} \leq \frac{1}{r} = \rho$$

where $\rho = 1/r$ is the coefficient of resource utilization, since the ratio $z'y^0/z'y^*$ equals unity when $y^0 = y^*$. Note however that these prices z associated with the vector efficient point y^* are not unique and further they may not necessarily correspond with market prices. The convexity assumption here is most critical. Thirdly, the characterization of the minimum feasibility set R_{min} is not unique, since it depends on N, the number in the cluster and the associated parameters $\theta:(A(j), x(j) = x_0, 1 \leq j \leq N)$ entering into the LP system for instance. Since for any fixed x_0, the basis matrix $B(j)$ which is feasible and optimal for a particular j, need not be feasible and optimal for other j's, the concept of the minimum feasibility set R_{min} may not be very useful in an applied sense, i.e., it may be either empty, since there is no optimal basis which is common to all j's, or very restrictive, if the optimal basis for each j is identical and common. The latter case arises in Leontief's input-output model through the non-substitution theorem, whereas the former leads to the difficult problems of defining a representative firm or unit through some form of aggregation of a set of N LP models. Sengupta [27] has discussed some of these problems.

Finally, we may mention that the DEA model which is closely related to Farrell efficiency has been extended in recent times in several new directions e.g., (i) to include inputs and outputs as categorical zero-one variables or, ordinal variables, (ii) to incorporate nonlinear forms of the frontier functions and (iii) to characterize efficiency under stochastic inut output data. Some of these aspects will be discussed later.

B.   Data Consistency

There are two basic problems when a given subset of the input-output data set fails to be consistent with the efficiency hypothesis maintained by the nonparametric theory. One problem is to characterize it in a probabilistic sense and perhaps develop some methods of truncation or censoring so that it improves the overall efficiency of the estimates of the parameters. The second problem is how to avoid influence of outlier points on efficiency measures. Methods of robust estimation appear to be attractive in such situations. To illustrate the first problem consider n data points $D_j = (x_j, y_j)$, j=1,2,...,n for each firm or decision-making unit (DMU) where y is a single good produced by the vector x of m inputs. If the inputs and outputs in the data set are nonnegative, then Afriat [3] showed that there must exist a function

$$F(x) = \max[\ \sum_{j=1}^{n} y_j \lambda_j : \sum_{j=1}^{n} x_j \lambda_j \le x, \ \sum_{j=1}^{n} \lambda_j = 1, \lambda_j \ge 0\ ]$$

$$(1.28)$$

which is non-decreasing and concave and such that $y_j \le F(x_j)$. Furthermore, there exists a non-decreasing concave function f(x) satisfying $y_j = f(x_j)$ for all j, if and only if

$$\sum_{j=1}^{n} x_j \lambda_j \le x_s \text{ implies } \sum_{j=1}^{n} y_j \lambda_j \le y_s$$

$$(1.29)$$

This condition (1.29) holds if and only if $y_j = F(x_j)$. The function F(x) represents a nonparametric production frontier such that it is everywhere not greater than any other non-decreasing concave function. The observed data set $D = (D_j : j=1,2,...,n)$ is said to be consistent with the frontier function F(x) if it satisfies the conditions (1.29). The data consistency problem thus reduces to solving the linear programming problem:

$$F(x) = \max[\ \sum_{j=1}^{n} \lambda_j : \sum_{j=1}^{n} a_j \lambda_j \le x, \lambda_j \ge 0\ ]$$

$$(1.30)$$

where $a_j = x_j/y_j$ is the input coefficient vector for each j and x is any one of the n input vectors. However the observed data set D may fail this consistency test in at least two ways. One arises when the nonnegativity conditions are dropped e.g. the inputs and outputs are allowed to vary over negative and positive domains. A second situation occurs when the data set is subject to a stochastic generating mechanism. In this case, a part of the data set D may satisfy the consistency requirement with a probability p, while the remaining part may fail the consistency test i.e. may allow no feasible solution to the LP problem (1.30). If the above probability p is very low (e.g. less than 0.25), then the frontier function F(x) would have a very low probability of realization. We may thus define different cases of data consistency: e.g., the frontier production function F(x) p-rationalizes the observed data set D in a weak (strong) sense, if for all points in D the consistency requirement holds with a probability of at least p (maximum probability level). In a deterministic framework this type of data consistency problem was initiated by Varian [6] and extended by Banker and Maindiratta [10] and Sengupta [11].

C.   Aggregation Problem

Once the efficient units are characterized at the microlevel by the nonparametric approach, the question arises how to aggregate the units so as to define efficiency at the macrolevel. Three different approaches are available in the nonparametric literature. One is due to Hildenbrand [28] who assumes that the empirically given distribution of the micro units is described by a vector $\omega = (x, z)$, where $x = (x_1, x_2, ..., x_m)$ is the input requirement vector at full capacity and z is the production capacity. The distribution of micro units of type ω defines a rule of aggregation.

Let μ denote the empirical distribution of the family $(\omega_j, j=1,2,...,N)$ of production activities i.e. μ is a probability measure on A defined by

$$\mu(B) = \frac{1}{N}(\text{no. of j out of Ni } \omega_j \in B), B \subset A$$

thus $100 \cdot \mu(B)$ is the percentage of production units having their characteristics in the set B e.g., any observed vector in the support of the distribution of μ describes the input-output proportions of an existing production capacity. We define the mean production set Y_μ and its projection onto the input space by D_μ:

$$Y_\mu = \int_A [0, \omega]\, \mu(d\omega)$$

$$D_\mu = \{x | (x, z) \in Y_\mu \text{ for some } z\}$$

The short run efficient mean production function is then defined by

$$F_\mu(x) = \sup \{z | (x, z) \in Y_\mu\}$$

and the aggregate efficient production function by

$$Y = N \cdot Y_\mu, \quad D = N \cdot D_\mu, \quad F(X) = N \cdot F_\mu(\frac{X}{N})$$

where X is the aggregate input vector. It is clear that any property of the total production set or the total efficient production function F is reflected by analogous property of the mean production set Y_μ or the mean production function F_μ and vice versa.

The second approach to aggregation due to Houthakker [29] and Johansen defines the aggregation rule by adding the capacities of all microunits with the same input coefficient. Thus by using two inputs (i=1,2) and one output (y) and n production units (j=1,2,...,n), Johansen sets up the following LP model to determine the short-run industry production function $Y = F(V_1, V_2)$:

$$\text{Max } Y = \Sigma y_j$$

$$\text{subject to } \sum_{j=1}^{n} a_{ij} y_j \le V_i, \quad i = 1, 2$$

$$(1.31)$$

$$0 \le y_j \le \bar{y}_j, \quad j = 1, 2, \ldots n$$

where Y is aggregate output and V_1, V_2 are the two current inputs for the industry as a whole, where j=1,2,...,n refers to plants (or units) with a capacity of $\bar{y}_j$ assumed given. The input coefficients (a_{ij}) are associated with the full capacity levels of inputs and outputs. The necessary first order conditions are:

$$1 - \sum_i \beta_i a_{ij} = 0 \qquad \text{according as,}$$

$$y_j = \bar{y}_j$$
$$y_j \in [0, \bar{y}_j]$$
$$y_j = 0$$

The variables β_1, β_2 are the shadow prices of the two current inputs, the optimal values of which denote the marginal productivities of the inputs in the industry function. On taking the most realistic situation of the necessary conditions, we obtain the dual LP model for determining the industry production function

$$\text{Min } C = \sum_i \beta_i V_i \quad \text{subject to } \beta \in R(\beta)$$

where

$$R(\beta) = \{\beta : \sum_i \beta_i a_{ij} \ge 1, \beta_i \ge 0 \}$$

It is clear that the inputs can be increased from 2 to m, in which case the LP model is very similar to the DEA model, except for two differences. One is that the criterion of maximum industry output is used in this formulation, implying a two-stage screening process of a decentralized system. Thus each firm to be efficient must first be efficient in its own technical production function and then be efficient among all other firms in the industry as a whole. Secondly, the statistical distribution of the input coefficients (a_{ij}), which is called "capacity distribution" and their realized values determine the efficient level of the maximum industry output.

Let a_1, a_2 be the two input coefficients distributed over the n production units according to a bivariate probability density function $f(a_1, a_2)$ and let $G(a) = G(a_1,a_2) = \{(\alpha_1,\alpha_2): \beta_1 a_1 + \beta_2 a_2 \leq 1, \beta_1 \geq 0, \beta_2 \geq 0\}$ be the utilization region in the parameter space describing the pattern of exploitation of capacity with the two input coefficients a_1,a_2. Then we could define the aggregate output $(Y = \Sigma y_j)$ and the two aggregate inputs V_1, V_2 as:

$$Y = \int_G \int_{(a)} f(a_1, a_2) da_1 da_2 = g(\beta_1, \beta_2)$$

$$V_1 = \int_G \int_{(a)} a_1 f(a_1, a_2) da_1 da_2 = h_1(\beta_1, \beta_2)$$

$$(1.32)$$

$$V_2 = \int_G \int_{(a)} a_2 f(a_1, a_2) da_1 da_2 = h_2(\beta_1, \beta_2)$$

where the functions $g(\beta_1,\beta_2)$, $h_1(\beta_1,\beta_2)$ and $h_2(\beta_1,\beta_2)$ represent output and the two inputs corresponding to any given set of feasible values of β_1 and β_2 belonging to the utilization region $G(a_1,a_2)$. Assuming invertibility and other regularity conditions we may solve for β_1 and β_2 from (1.32):

$$\beta_1 = h_1^{-1}(V_1, V_2), \; \beta_2 = h_2^{-1}(V_1, V_2)$$

and substituting these values in the first equation of (1.32) we obtain the macro production function:

$$Y = g(h_1^{-1}(V_1, V_2), h_2^{-1}(V_1, V_2)) = F(V_1, V_2)$$

Two remarks may be made about this derivation. One is that there are two types of aggregation problems as pointed out by Seierstad [30], one given by the capacity distribution $f(a_1,a_2)$ within the utilization region $G(\cdot)$ as above and the other by the empirically given distribution of only those micro units which are identified by some optimal solution of LP model (1.31). The first type of aggregation implies that the capacities of all micro units with the same input coefficients can be added together for computing the total capacity of the industry. The second one constructs a core subset of efficient units from the optimal solutions of the LP models (1.32) when j belongs to a subset $\hat{D}$ of the entire set D of input-output data points. Thus the second aggregation explicitly recognizes the gap in efficiency between the two subsets D and the complement of $\hat{D}$ in D, but characterizes this gap in terms of the observed probability of the set of points belonging to the subset $\hat{D}$.

The second point to note is that the macro production function $F(V_1, V_2)$ above need not be lienar (or piecewise linear) even though the LP model (1.31) generates the macro function through suitable aggregation. Also, different distributions of the capacity distribution may generate different shapes of the aggregate production frontiers. Thus Houthakker found that if the capacity distribution follows a generalized Pareto distribution $f(a_1, a_2) = A \, a_1^{\alpha_1 - 1} \, a_2^{\alpha_2 - 1}$ where A, α_1, α_2 are constants, then the macro production function takes the Cobb-Douglas form:

$$\ln F(V_1, V_2) = \ln B + \gamma_1 \ln V_1 + \gamma_2 \ln V_2$$

where $\gamma_1 = \alpha_1/(1 + \alpha_1 + \alpha_2), \gamma_2 = \alpha_2/(1 + \alpha_1 + \alpha_2)$

B = a constant.

The third type of aggregation due to Sengupta [9,11] considers the DEA or, the Farrell model as a two-stage process; at the first stage one determines the micro units which are efficient while in the second stage different groups or clusters are formed by using or estimating the frequency at which one unit turns out to be efficient. Such aggregation rules are shown to be closely related to the dummy variable regression approach in regression theory. This method will be discussed later.

D.   Probelms of Econometric Estimation

Although parametric estimation techniques can be applied to the data satisfying the efficiency hypothesis in terms of the first stage of the DEA model, it is more appropriate to apply nonparametric techniques of estimation. Two types of nonparametric techniques have been suggested by Sengupta [9,11,12]. One is the minimax method of estimation which retains the LP structure of the DEA model, yet introducing some measure of robustness. The second approach applies a nonparametric technique of regression based on the nonparametric estimation of density of the residuals obtained from the first stage of the DEA model. These methods would be discussed in some detail in later chapters.

1.5 Implications of Nonparametric Theory

We may now add a few comments on those implications of nonparametric theory which have some importance for applied economics. First of all, the nonparametric approach is more suitable for policy applications, since it is more flexible and more data-based. Policy applications generally involve additional constraints e.g., resource constraints or technology constraints, which may be easily added to the LP formulations of the DEA and Farrell models and their shadow costs would characterize the extent of losses generated by the second-best solution. Secondly, as in the theory of optimal statistical design, the DEA efficiency model could be used to suggest resource and output reallocations which are optimizing in nature. Johansen's approach to efficiency precisely does this by replacing observed output by the optimal output, optimal from the viewpoint of the industry. A similar method can be applied to the DEA and Farrell models. Thirdly, the role of demand and capacity constraints in these models can be explicitly analyzed in terms of their shadow prices. Finally, the dynamic aspects of production frontier with multiple outputs have a great scope of application in applied production studies, since for the multiple output case the parametric specification is either nonexistent or most inadequate.

References to Chapter 1

1. Farrell, M.J. The measurement of productive efficiency. Journal of Royal Statistical Society, Series A, 120 (1957), 253-290.

2. Johansen, L. Production Functions. Amsterdam: North Holland, 1972.

3. Afriat, S.N. Efficiency estimation of production functions. International Economic Review, 13 (1972), 568-598.

4. Hanoch, G. and Rothschild. Testing the assumptions of production theory: a nonparametric approach. Journal of Political Economy, 80 (1972), 256-275.

5. Diewert, W.E. and Parkan, C. Linear programming tests of regularity conditions for production function. Quantitative Studies on Production and Prices, Vienna: Physica-Verlag, 1983.

6. Varian, H. The nonparametric approach to production analysis. Econometrica, 52 (1984), 579-597.

7. Charnes, A., Cooper, W.W. and Rhodes, E. Measuring the efficiency of decision-making units. European Journal of Operational Research, 2 (1978), 429-444.

8. Charnes, A., Cooper, W.W., Golany, B., Seiford, L and Stutz, J. Foundations of data envelopment anaysis for Pareto optimal empirical production functions. Journal of Econometrics, 30 (1985), 91-107.

9. Sengupta, J.K. Data envelopment analysis for efficiency mesurement in the stochastic case. Computers and Oeprations Research, 14 (1987), 117-129.

10. Banker, R.D. and Maindiratta, A. Nonparametric analysis of technical and allocative efficiencies. Forthcoming in Econometrica (1988).

11. Sengupta, J.K. Recent nonparametric measures of productive efficiency, in Econometrics of Planning and Efficiency, Dordrecht: Kluwer Academic Publishers, 1988.

12. Sengupta, J.K. The influence curve approach in data envelopment analysis. Paper presented at the 13th International Symposium on Mathematical Programming held in Tokyo: August 29-September 2, 1988.

13. Manning, R. Nonsubstitution over the production possibility frontier, in M.C. Kemp (ed.) Production Sets, New York: Academic Press, 1982.

14. Forsund, F.R., Lovell, C.A.K. and Schmidt, P. A survey of frontier production functions and of their relationship to efficiency measurement. Journal of Econometrics, 13 (1980), 5-25.

15. Kopp, R.J. and Diewert, W.E. The decomposition of frontier cost function deviations into measures of technical and allocative efficiency. Journal of

Econometrics, 19 (1982), 319-331.

16. Aigner, D.J. and Chu, S.F. On estimating the industry production function. American Economic Review, 58 (1968), 826-839.

17. Schmidt, P. On the statistical estimation of parametric frontier production functions. Review of Economics and Statistics, 58 (1976), 238-239.

18. Richmond, J. Estimating the efficiency of production. International Economic Review, 15 (1974), 515-521.

19. Greene, W.H. Maximum likelihood estimation of econometric frontier functions. Journal of Econometrics, 13 (1980), 27-56.

20. Griffiths, W. Estimating actual response coefficients in the Hildreth-Houck random coefficient model. Journal of American Statistical Association, 67 (1972), 633-635.

21. Vashishtha, P.S. Measurement of private efficiency under diverse technologies in Indian agriculture. Sankhya: Indian Journal of Statistics, Series C, Part 4, 39 (1978), 136-154.

22. Jondrow, J., Lovell, C.A.K., Materov, I.S. and Schmidt, P. On the estimation of technical efficiency in the stochastic frontier production function model. Journal of Econometrics, 19 (1982), 233-238.

23. Schmidt, P. and Sickles, R.C. Production frontier and panel data. Journal of Business and Economic Statistics, 2 (1984), 367-374.

24. Forsund, F.R. and Hjalmarsson, L. Generalized Farrell measures of efficiency: an application to milk processing in Swedish dairy plans. Economic Journal, 89 (1979), 294-315.

25. Koenker, R. A comparison of asymptotic testing methods for L_1-regression, in Y. Dodge (ed.) Statistical Data Analysis Based on the L_1-Norm and Related Methods, pp. 287-295, New York, Elsevier Science Publishers, 1987.

26. Debreu, G. The coefficient of resource utilization. Econometrica, 19 (1951), 273-292.

27. Sengupta, J.K. Problems in measuring frontier production functions: some theoretical results. Paper presented at the Joint National Meeting of CORS-TIMS-ORSA held in Toronto, Canada, May 3-6, 1981.

28. Hildenbrand, W. Short-run production functions based on microdata. Econometrica, 49 (1981), 1095-1126.

29. Houthakker, H.S. The Pareto distribution and the Cobb-Douglas production function in activity analysis. Review of Economic Studies, 23 (1956), 27-31.

30. Seirstad, A. Properties of production and profit functions arising from the aggregation of a capacity distribution of micro units, in Production, Multi-sectoral

<u>Growth and Planning</u>, Amsterdam: North Holland, 1985.

Chapter 2

THE NONPARAMETRIC APPROACH

The nonparametric approach to the measurement of productive efficiency can be specified either through a flexible form of the production function which satisfies the efficiency hypothesis, or a set-theoretic characterization of an efficient isoquant. In the first case the production frontier can be of any general shape satisfying some very weak conditions like quasi-concavity or monotonicity, although in most empirical and applied work piecewise linear or, log-linear functions have been frequently used. Thus both Farrell and Johansen applied linear programming models in the specification of the production frontier. Farrell's efficiency measure is based on estimating by a sequence of linear programs (LPs) a convex hull of the observed input coefficients in the input space. Two features of Farrell efficiency make it very useful in applied research. One is that it is completely data-based i.e., it uses only the observed inputs and outputs of the sample units while assuming production functions to be homogeneous of degree one. Hence it has many potential applications for the public sector units, where for most of the inputs and outputs the price data are not available. For example consider educational production functions for public schools, where outputs such as test scores in achievement tests are only proxy variables for learning; inputs such as average class size, experience of teachers or ethnic background of students do not have observed market prices. Secondly, Farrell's method uses a set of LP models to estimate the efficiency parameters, so that the production frontier appears as piecewise linear functions. Nonnegativity conditions on the parameter estimates can therefore be easily incorporated. However the Farrell model (F-model) has some disadvantages also. First of all, the case of one output for each unit (or firm) is only considered. One needs an extension to the case of multiple outputs and multiple inputs for each sample unit or firm. This is especially true for educational production functions where outputs such as cognitive and affective achievement are not completely independent. Secondly, the process of resource

39

reallocation to achieve better outputs is never explicitly used in the F-model; but the observed data set on inputs and outputs may be readily used to compute efficiency at the industry rather than the firm level as Johansen showed. Thus in case of one output and many inputs, the Johansen model (J-model) computes the aggregate level of inputs for the industry comprising different firms or units and determines the optimal allocation of such aggregatre inputs by maximizing the aggregate output.

It would be useful to examine the Farrell model in relation to other nonparameteric models of efficiency measurement e.g., data envelopment analysis (DEA) approach so that one can understand the nonparametric aspects better.

2.1   Convex Hull Method

Introduction of multiple outputs into the production function raises interesting theoretical and economic issues. One issue is the manner in which various outputs are interrelated. Are the outputs multiple products? If so are they independently or simultaneously produced? A second issue is the method by which the productivity of the various inputs is measured. Farrell used the convex hull method, since his method involved the computation of a sequence of LP models where the optimal solutions characterized efficiency. Since a production frontier includes only the most efficient units or firms, characterization of the subset of efficient units out of a given set becomes all the more important particularly when the price data are unavailable. To see the applied implictions of these two issues in modeling e.g., educational production functions let y_1 and y_2 be two output measures such as test scores in verbal and mathematical tests in public schools and x_i (i=1,2,...,m) be the m inputs such as average class size, average teacher salary, etc. If the two outputs are multiple products produced with separate inputs and are completely independent, then one specifies a separate production function for each output e.g.,

$$y_1 = f(x_1, x_2,...,x_m)$$
$$y_2 = g(x_1, x_2,...,x_m)$$

However, if the outputs are produced simultaneously, a simultaneous equation system is appropriate; in this case the system becomes

$$y_1 = f(y_2, x_1, x_2,...,x_m)$$
$$y_2 = g(y_1, x_1, x_2,...,x_m)$$

But if the outputs are joint products, a single equation production function should be estimated e.g.,

$$f(y_1, y_2, x_1, x_2,...,x_m) = 0$$

Which type of econometric model closely corresponds to the educational environment depends on the degree to which the outputs share the same inputs. Note further that the two specifications above represent only average production functions rather than the best practice functions, since the efficiency hypothesis is not explicitly incorporated there. In the single output case the Farrell efficiency may be characterized very simply by a sequence of linear programming problems. Thus let $D = (x_{ji}, y_j; j=1,2,...,n; i=1,2,...,m) = (X,y)$ be the input-output data set, where x_{ji} is the quantity of input i for the j-th decision-making unit (DMU) or firm and y_j is the single output for each j. The Farrell efficiency frontier is then specified by the optimal solution of the following linear programming (LP) model:

$$\min_{\beta} g_k = \sum_{i=1}^{m} x_{ki}\beta_i$$

subject to
$$\sum_{i=1}^{m} x_{ji}\beta_i \geq y_j, \qquad j = 1, 2, ..., n \tag{2.1}$$

$$\beta_i \geq 0; \quad i=1,2,...,m$$

where the inputs of the reference unit k is used in the objective function. For a fixed k, where k belongs to the set $I_n = \{1,2,...,n\}$ let $\beta^*(k)$ be the optimal solution of the above LP model. Then the unit k is efficient if it holds that $\sum\limits_{i=1}^{m} x_k \beta_i^*(k) = y_k$ and $s_k = y_k^* - y_k$ $= 0$ where s_k is the slack variable representing the excess of potential output

$y_k^* = \sum\limits_{i=1}^{m} x_{ki} \beta_i^*(k)$ over actual output y_k. By varying k over the set I_n we can generate the whole efficiency surface and the associated values of the production parameters: $B^* = \{\beta^*(k), k=1,2,...,n\}$.

It is clear that the Farrell efficiency surface may be viewed as a set of efficiency facets, one facet for each k where k=1,2,...,n is one of the n units. Thus an independent measure of technical efficiency can be obtained for each sample observation (i.e., each unit k is either efficient or not). This is in contrast with the parametric estimation methods which specify a particular one-sided probability distribution and define the expected value of this distribution as their measure of technical efficiency. It is clear that their measure is an average and not firm-specific.

In his empirical applications to British agricultural data Farrell used the dual of the LP model (2.1) as

$$\max_{\lambda} z_k = \sum_{j=1}^{n} \lambda_j$$

subject to $\quad \sum\limits_{j=1}^{n} \lambda_j a_{ji} \leq x_{ki}, \qquad i = 1, 2, ..., m \qquad\qquad (2.2)$

$$\lambda_j \geq 0, \quad j=1,2,...n$$

where $a_{ji} = x_{ji}/y_j$ are the input coefficients and λ_j's are the dual variables corresponding to the constraints of (2.1). The specification of the production frontier in the F-model may be compared directly with an average production function

$$y_j = \sum_{i=1}^{m} x_{ji} \beta_i + e_j \tag{2.3}$$

which is commonly fitted by least squares (LS) regression methods. Here e_j is the error term assumed to have zero mean and constant variance and the inputs x_i are assumed to be nonstochastic. The Farrell model only allows points on the frontier, hence we replace (2.3) by

$$y_j = \sum_{i=1}^{m} x_{ji} \beta_i - e_j, \qquad e_j \geq 0 \tag{2.4}$$

The regression model minimizes the sum Σe_j^2 of squared errors to obtain the estimates of $\beta = (\beta_i)$ but the F-model applies an LP method to obtain the estimates. Timmer [1] has shown that the LP method may be interpreted as a criterion of minimizing the sum of absolute value $\sum_{j=1}^{n} |e_j|$ of errors but since e_j's are nonnegative we obtain the following model:

$$\min_{\beta} \ \bar{g} = \sum_{i=1}^{m} \bar{x}_i \beta_i$$

subject to $\quad \sum_{i=1}^{m} x_{ji} \beta_i \geq y_j, \qquad j = 1, 2, \dots, n \tag{2.5}$

$$\beta_i \geq 0; \quad i=1,2,\dots,m$$

where $\bar{x}_i = (1/n) \sum_{k=1}^{m} x_{ki}$ is the mean level of input i and we have in (2.5) one LP model rather than n LPs as in (2.1). The dual of this model can be written as:

$$\max \ z = \sum_{j=1}^{n} \lambda_j$$

subject to $\quad \sum_{j=1}^{n} \lambda_j a_{ji} \leq \bar{x}_i, \qquad i = 1, 2, \ldots, m \qquad\qquad (2.6)$

$$\lambda_j \geq 0; \quad j=1,2,\ldots,n$$

Clearly this type of specification of the Farrell model has two advantages. First of all, it is based on the least absolute value (LAV) of errors as a criterion (also called the L_1-norm criterion) for obtaining the estimates and it is known [2,3] that such LAV estimates perform much better than the LS estimates if the error terms are nonnormally distributed. Secondly, the mean objective function in (2.5) represents in some sense the notion of a representative firm in the cluster of n firms, so that if the data are homogeneous and the input vectors $x_k = (x_{ki})$ tend to center around a mean or median level (e.g., $\bar{x}$) with a very low degree of dispersion, then the efficiency ranking implied by the n LP models in (2.1) would be very close to that one given by the mean LP model (2.5). An alternative interpretation is that the mean (or median) LP model provides an average measure of technical efficiency in a nonparametric form, much like the parametric theory based on one-sided probability distributions like the half normal [4]. The only difference is that the efficiency ranking by the nonparametric approach also provides an indirect estimate of inefficiency for firms not on the production frontier.

Now consider the case of multiple outputs for each firm and let y_{jh} denote output type h for the j-th firm where there are s outputs. The LP model corresponding to (2.1) now appears as:

$$\min_{\beta, \, \alpha} \ g_k = \sum_{i=1}^{m} x_{ki} \beta_i$$

subject to $\quad \sum_{i=1}^{m} x_{ji} \beta_i \geq \sum_{h=1}^{s} y_{jh} \alpha_h; \qquad j = 1, 2, \ldots, n$

$$\sum_{h=1}^{s} y_{kh}\alpha_h = 1 \qquad\qquad (2.7)$$

$$\beta_i \geq 0, \alpha_j \geq 0; \qquad \begin{array}{l} i = 1, 2, \dots, m \\ h = 1, 2, \dots, s \end{array}$$

Clearly this model would be identical with the one output case given by (2.1), if we assume the weights α_h to be given or known and $\hat{y}_j = \sum_h y_{jh}\alpha_h$ is interpreted as outputs replacing y_j in LP (2.1). A second interpretation due to the data envelopment analysis model of Charnes, Cooper and Rhodes [5] is that we minimize the weighted input-output ratio

$$\min_{\beta, \alpha} r_k = \left(\sum_{i=1}^{m} x_{ki}\beta_i\right) / \left(\sum_{h=1}^{s} y_{kh}\alpha_h\right)$$

subject to $r_j \geq 1, j=1,2,\dots,n$

$\alpha, \beta \geq 0$

where

$$r_j = \left(\sum_{i=1}^{m} x_{ji}\beta_i\right) / \left(\sum_{h=1}^{s} y_{jh}\alpha_h\right)$$

In this interpretation the second constraint (2.7) i.e., $\sum_{h=1}^{s} y_{kh}\alpha_h = 1$ is nothing but the numeraire condition of the Walrasian system. It is clear however that this numeraire condition should apply to the whole industry, rather than each firm. Hence it is more appropriate to consider the many output extension of the representative firm model (2.5) as follows:

$$\min_{\beta, \alpha} \bar{g} = \sum_{i=1}^{m} \bar{x}_i \beta_i$$

subject to $\displaystyle\sum_{i=1}^{m} x_{ji}\beta_i \geq \sum_{h=1}^{s} y_{jh}\alpha_h$ (2.8)

$\displaystyle\sum_{h=1}^{s} \bar{y}_h \alpha_h = 1; \qquad \alpha, \beta \geq 0$

Here $\bar{x} = (\bar{x}_i)$, $\bar{y} = (\bar{y}_h)$ are the mean input and output vectors and the optimal values (α^*, β^*) of $\alpha = (\alpha_h)$ and $\beta = (\beta_i)$ specify the efficiency ranking in the many output case. Some features of this extended model are to be noted. First of all, the dual of the LP model (2.8) now looks in vector-matrix terms as:

$$\max \lambda_0$$
subject to $X'\lambda \leq \bar{x}$

$Y'\lambda \geq \lambda_0 \bar{y}$ (2.9)

$\lambda \geq 0$

where $X = (x_{ji})$, $Y = (y_{jh})$ are matrices, prime denotes transpose and λ is the n-element column vector of Lagrange multipliers for the first set of constraints of (2.8) and λ_0 is the scalar Lagrange multiplier for the numeraire condition

$$\sum_{h=1}^{s} \bar{y}_h \alpha_h = 1$$

i.e.,   (2.10)

$$(1/n) \sum_{h=1}^{s} \sum_{j=1}^{n} y_{jh}\alpha_h = 1$$

Clearly this numeraire condition is based on the output of the whole industry. Since the mean input-output levels $(\bar{x}, \bar{y})$ can be replaced by the median or any other suitable location measure for specifying the representative firm, the efficiency ranking is measured relative to the representative firm in the industry. Secondly, the estimation equation for the multi-output production frontier may be written as

$$\vartheta_j = \sum_{i=1}^{m} x_{ji} \beta_i - e_j \; ; e_j \geq 0 \tag{2.11}$$

where

$$\vartheta_j = \sum_{h=1}^{s} y_{jh} \alpha_h$$

A two-stage interpretation of the estimates of β can be given in this framework as follows: Let $\alpha = (\alpha_h)$ be given so that (2.1) holds and ϑ_j's are known in (2.11); let $\hat{\beta}$ be the LAV estimate for given α and $J(\hat{\beta} | \alpha)$ be the minimum value of $\sum_{j=1}^{n} e_j$. We vary α till the minimum of $J(\hat{\beta} | \alpha)$ is found. Let $\hat{\beta}*$ be the second-stage estimate at which the minimum of $J(\hat{\beta} | \alpha)$ is achieved. Clearly this estimate $\hat{\beta}*$ is analogous to the single output case of the Farrell model in (2.5). Note that a good starting point for α's is to assume $\alpha_h = 1$ for all h i.e., to assume each output on equal footing. For educational production functions the various outputs are represented by test scores in reading, writing, spelling and mathematics, and in the absence of any prior information it is reasonable to use the same weight for computing a weighted average output. Thirdly, the extended model (2.8) with its one-sided error specification in (2.11) may be used for two main objectives: (i) to construct efficient frontiers and measure the efficiency of individual firms, or the same firm over different time periods and (ii) to screen the data set before it is used to estimate the parameters of a specific parametric functional form for the production function.

2.2 Stochastic Micro and Macro Frontier

Johansen's approach to efficiency mesurement has three basic differences from the Farrell approach. First of all, it starts from given distributions of capacity amongst a set of micro units (or firms) and solves for optimal outputs. Secondly, it uses a rule of aggregation to derive the aggregate production frontiers. Thirdly, the micro frontiers derived from the LP models need not necessarily lead to linear macro frontiers because of the probability distribution of capacity among the micro units and the domain of capacity utilization for the efficient units. For the single output case Johansen defines an aggregate (industry) input level $V_i = \sum_{j=1}^{n} x_{ji}$ for each input and then maximizes the aggregate output i.e.,

$$\max_{y} \pi = \sum_{j=1}^{n} y_j$$

$$\text{subject to} \quad \sum_{j=1}^{n} a_{ji} y_j \leq V_i ; \quad i = 1, 2, \ldots, m \tag{2.12}$$

$$y_j \geq 0, \quad j=1,2,\ldots,n$$

by optimally choosing the output vector $y = (y_j)$, where $a_{ji} = x_{ji}/y_j$, the input coefficients at the full capacity levels of inputs and outputs, are assumed to belong to the observed data set. Let $y^* = (y_j^*)$ be the otpimal output vector and π^* be the associated maximum value of the objective function of (2.12). Clearly so long as the observed outputs y_j are not equal to the optimal outputs, y_j^*, we would have $\pi^* > \Sigma y_j$. In other words, an efficient industry would comprise only those firms which produce outputs at the maximum possible levels i.e., $y_j = y_j^*$. Hence the inefficient firms (or units) in the industry are those for which y_j is less than y_j^*.

It is easy to see the equivalence of this model (2.12) with that in (2.6). However the Johansen model (J-model) and its efficiency ranking has broader implications. For one thing, it brings into sharp focus the problem of decentralization i.e., reallocation of the aggregate inputs among firms so as to increase the total industry output. Thus a firm's efficiency is linked to the efficiency at the industry level. The rationale behind aggregating inputs across firms is one of cooperation and it is clear that in many situations noncooperation and rivalry would prevail thus making the model unrealistic.

Secondly, Johansen used this model (2.12) to generate macro production frontiers by assuming the input coefficient vectors $a_j = (a_{ji})$ to be random across firms with a specified distribution. Clearly this leads to a stochastic production frontier, where the stochasticity is different from that used in the nonnegative error model (2.4). Thirdly, this model allows an evaluation of the impact of adding or deleting additional firms into the efficiency cluster. For example assume that $m < n$ and let B^* be the nonsingular optimal basis of order m:

$$B^{*\prime}y^* = V$$

or,

$$y^* = (B^{*\prime})^{-1}V = MV, \quad M = (B^{*\prime})^{-1} \tag{2.13}$$

If by adding or deleting data subsets the optimal basis B^* does not change, then the efficient output levels may be said to be robust. In empirical studies such robustness has been observed in several cases by Sengupta and Sfeir [6] in single output Farrell models. Also by noting that $M = \bar{M} + \varepsilon_M$ could be decomposed into two components, one given by the mean or median level $\bar{M}$ and the other by the error matrix ε_M of deviations, one could analyze the heterogeneity of the data structure by computing the variance of the optimal output vector y^* in (2.13) around a small neighborhood of the matrix $\bar{M}$ [7,8].

How to extend the Johansen model to the many output case? One direct way is to follow the method used in (2.11) and define a weighted output $\hat{y}_j$ as

$$\hat{y}_j = \sum_{h=1}^{s} y_{jh}\alpha_h \tag{2.14}$$

and then replace y_j by $\hat{y}_j$ in the J-model (2.12). One has to fix prior values for the non-negative weights e.g., $\alpha_h = 1$ for all h as in educational test scores. A second way is to introduce input-output specific aggregates i.e.,

$$V_{ij} = \sum_{j=1}^{n} x_{jih}, \quad Q_h = \sum_{j=1}^{n} y_{jh}$$

$$a_{jih} = x_{jih}/y_{jh} ; \quad \begin{array}{l} i = 1, 2, \ldots, m \\ h = 1, 2, \ldots, s \end{array}$$

and then set up the optimizing model with a vector objective function

$$\max_{\{y_{jh}\}} F(\pi) = \begin{pmatrix} \pi_1 \\ \pi_2 \\ \vdots \\ \pi s \end{pmatrix}$$

subject to $\quad \displaystyle\sum_{j=1}^{n} a_{jih} y_{jh} \leq V_{ih} ; \quad \begin{array}{l} i = 1, 2, \ldots, m \\ h = 1, 2, \ldots, s \end{array}$ (2.15)

$$\pi_h = \sum_{j=1}^{n} y_{jh} = Q_h, \quad h = 1, 2, \ldots, s$$

$y_{jh} \geq 0$, all j and h.

where we solve for the optimal values $\{y_{jh}^*\}$ given the data set in the form $\{a_{jhi}, V_{ih},$ $Q_h\}$. By expressing outputs y_{jh} in units of Q_h the normalization condition $\pi_h = Q_h$ can also be written as: $\displaystyle\sum_{j=1}^{n} y_{jh} = 1$

Clearly if there is an efficient vector π^* in the sense that there exists no other distinct feasible vector π with $F(\pi) \geq F(\pi^*)$, then by Kuhn-Tucker theory there must exist a nonnegative vector $w' = (w_1, w_2, \ldots, w_s)$ of weights such that the optimal values $\{y_{jh}^*\}$ associated with π^* also maximizes the scalar objective function:

$$\max \sum_{h=1}^{s} w_h \pi_h$$

(2.16)

subject to the same set of constraints as in (2.15). Note that if the two sets of weights: $\{w_h\}$ in (2.16) and $\{\alpha_h\}$ in (2.14) agree in the sense

$$\hat{y}_j = \sum_{h=1}^{s} y_{jh} \alpha_h = \sum_{h=1}^{s} y_{jh} w_h$$

then this multi-output J-model collapses to the single output case (2.12), provided y_j in (2.12) is replaced by $\hat{y}_j$ above. A two-stage interpretation can similarly be given as before.

The assumption of stochastic input coefficients of the Johansen model may be used in the context of the Farrell model (21) in a novel and interesting manner. Note that the optimal coefficient $\beta_i^*(k)$ of the F-model (2.1) would vary as k varies i.e., k=1,2,...,n. These varying response coefficients may be modeled by the assumption that the individual response coefficient is random and fluctuates around its mean value i.e.,

$$\beta_i^*(k) = \bar{\beta}_i^* + \varepsilon_i(k) \tag{2.17}$$

where $\bar{\beta}_i^*$ is the mean response coefficient and $\varepsilon_i(k)$ is a random error term distributed mutually independently with zero mean and constant variance i.e.,

$$E[\beta_i^*(k)] = \bar{\beta}_i^*$$

and

$$E\{\varepsilon_i(k)\} = 0 \text{ and var } \{\varepsilon_i(k)\} = \sigma_{ii} \text{ for all i and k}$$
$$Cov[\varepsilon_i(k), \varepsilon_{i'}(k')] = 0 \text{ for all } i \neq i', k \neq k'.$$

Let K be a subset of the n firms which are efficient by the F-model (2.1). Then for all k $\in$ K we can express the F-efficiency frontier as

$$y_j = \sum_{i=1}^{m} x_{ji} \bar{\beta}_i^* + w_j$$

where

$$w_j = \sum_{i=1}^{m} x_{ji} \varepsilon_i(k)$$

It follows that

$$E(w_j) = 0, \; Var(w_j) = \sum_{i=1}^{m} x_{ji}^2 \sigma_{ii}$$

$$Cov\,[w_{j'}, w_j] = 0 \text{ for } j \neq j'$$

Note that the sample estimates $\hat{\sigma}_{ii}$ of σ_{ii} may be computed very easily from the equation (2.17) when the observed values $\{\beta_i^*(k), \, k \in K\}$ are available from the n LP models of F-efficiency in (2.1). It is clear that in the multiple output case we can apply the same method, except that we have to replace the observed output y_j by the weighted average output $\hat{y}_j$ defined in (2.14).

Two advantages of this generalization may be noted. First, one may use efficient sample estimates of σ_{ii} if the underlying distribution of the error terms $\varepsilon_i(k)$ can be specified. This can be useful in statistically testing any null hypothesis about the sample estimate of $\bar{\beta}_i^*$. Secondly, the assumption that the individual response coefficient $\beta_i^*(k)$ deviates from the mean coefficient $\bar{\beta}_i^*$ in a random fashion may be an over simplification, especially in situations where there is reason to believe that the $\beta_i^*(k)$ coefficients vary in a systematic way with some other variables omitted in the model. If data are available, we may then capture the impact of these omitted variables by a regression approach for example. This provides an interesting interface of the non-parametric F-model with the parametric regression model.

To show the implications of the various nonparametric frontiers we illustrate two situations: one showing an empirical application to educational frontier function and the other showing a set-theoretic generalization of the efficiency concept.

A. Empirical Application and Tests

Our empirical applictions consider input-output data in logarithmic units for selected public elementary schools in California for the years 1976-77 and 1977-78, over which separate least squares estimates of educational production functions were made in earlier studies by Sengupta and Sfeir [6]. Statistics of enrollment, average teacher salary, standardized test scores in reading, writing, spelling and mathematics are all obtained from the official publications of the California State Department of Education. To compare the efficiency of public elementary school districts, three contiguous counties are selected e.g., Santa Barbara, Ventura and San Luis Obispo. From the data set of 35 school districts we eliminated those districts, which were either unified (i.e., where both secondary and elementary grades existed) or co-extensive with the high school districts. Suspecting that small schools have a larger variance in expenditure per student than large schools, we performed a Goldfeld-Quandt test [9] by dividing the data set into two equal size groups. The first group consisted of schools ranging in size from 14 to 268 students, while the second group ranged from 4214 to 9716 students. Since the Goldfeld-Quandt test rejected the null hypothesis of homoscedasticity, we had to select a subsample of 25 school districts by deleting those rural districts where the number of teachers was less than six per school. For this subsample of 25 units the null hypothesis of homoscedasticity was not rejected. As output variables (y) we took the average of students' standardized test scores in reading (y_1), writing (y_2), spelling (y_3) and mathematics (y_4). A composite output score is taken as an average of these four outputs. As input variables or their surrogates we had a choice of eight variables, of which the following four were utilized in the LP model estimates: x_1 = average instructional expenditure, x_2 = proportion of minority students, x_3 = average class size and x_4 = a proxy variable representing the parental socioeconomic background. The choice of these four inputs (and also the four outputs above) was made on the basis of their higher explanatory power observed in earlier regression studies.

Based on the subsample of 25 homogeneous units three sets of LP models are computed to obtain the estimates of the response coefficients $\beta = (\beta_i)$. The first set comprises 25 LP models in the single (composite) output case given in (2.1) and the multiple output case given in case (2.7). In the single output case, the composite output is taken as a simple average of four test scores, while in the four-output case the optimal values of the weights $\alpha = (\alpha_h)$ are determined from the LP model (2.7). The second set applies the LAV method of estimation in the single and multiple output cases of the Farrell model i.e., LP models (2.5) and (2.8). Since the data set of 25 units were found to be homogeneous by the Goldfeld-Quandt test, all the 25 observations were used in computing the mean inputs $(\bar{x}_i)$ in the objective function of (2.5) and (2.8). This resulted in two LP models for the second data set. The third set computes the Johansen-type aggregate LP models of the form (2.12) for sample sizes varying from n=9 to n=25 and estimates the response coefficients β_i from the corresponding dual models.

Table 1 specifies the proportion R_e of those units which being efficient in the one (composite) output case also turned out to be efficient in the four-output case; here efficiency means that their observed outputs equal the optimal levels. It is clear that their correspondence is very close. A simple regression estimate of the four outputs y_k, k=1,2,3,4 and the composite output $\hat{y} = \sum_{k=1}^{4} y_k/4$ on the four inputs x_i, i=1,2,3,4 also confirms the close correspondence as follows:

$y_1 = -0.80 + 0.25^{**}x_1 + 0.89^{**}x_2 + 0.88^{**}x_3 + 0.30^{**}x_4;$ $(R^2 = 0.76)$

$y_2 = -2.65^{**} + 0.38^{**}x_1 + 1.04^{**}x_2 + 1.22^{**}x_3 + 0.41^{**}x_4;$ $(R^2 = 0.74)$

$y_3 = -0.31 + 0.15^{*}x_1 + 1.03^{**}x_2 + 1.16^{**}x_3 + 0.39^{**}x_4;$ $(R^2 = 0.76)$

$y_4 = -0.35 + 0.32^{**}x_1 + 0.50^{*}x_2 + 0.64^{*}x_3 + 0.21^{*}x_4;$ $(R^2 = 0.59)$

$\hat{y} = -0.94 + 0.27^{**}x_1 + 0.86^{**}x_2 + 0.97^{**}x_3 + 0.32^{**}x_4;$ $(R^2 = 0.77)$

Table 1. Frequency of efficiency in one vs. four

output case of the Farrell model

Values of ratio R_e

LP model	0.00-0.50	0.50-0.74	0.75-0.95	0.95-1.00
Nondegenerate	0	3	3	4
Degenerate	1	3	6	5
Total	1	6	9	9

Note: R_e denotes the proposition of units efficient in one output case to that of our output

case.

Table 2. Affinity of the coefficient estimates of

the Farrell model and the LAV model

input type i	Single output			Multiple output		
	$\bar{\beta}_i$	β_i^0	s_i	$\bar{\beta}_i$	β_i^0	s_i
1	0.250	0.247	0.0088	0.052	0.066	0.0006
2	0.499	0.523	0.0889	0.129	0.114	0.0078
3	0.638	0.626	0.0665	0.181	0.132	0.0042
4	0.177	0.179	0.0073	0.053	0.041	0.0007

Note: $\bar{\beta}_i$: average of the individual response coefficients in the nondegenerate LPs

of the Farrell model

β_i^0 : the response coefficient for the mean LP or, the LAV model

s_i: standard error of the estimate $\bar{\beta}_i$

Table 3. Mean error of estimate of the

Farrell model with single and multiple outputs

LP_k	Degenerate (D)/ Nondegenerate (ND)	mean error e	
		Single output	Four output
0	ND	0.0766	0.0121
1	ND	0.1030	0.0237
2	ND	0.0810	0.0156
3	D	0.1470	3.401[a]
4	D	0.0903	0.0190
5	ND	0.0766	0.0179
6	D	0.0903	0.0170
7	ND	0.1030	0.0830
8	ND	0.0810	0.0170
9	D	0.2594[a]	0.0770
10	D	0.2277[a]	0.1560
11	D	0.1502[a]	0.0310
12	ND	0.3428[a]	0.0900
13	ND	0.0838	0.0170
14	D	0.1502	0.0560
15	D	0.3082[a]	0.0240
16	ND	0.0766	0.0420
17	D	0.2746[a]	0.1310
18	ND	0.1030	0.0170
19	D	0.6021[a]	0.1270
20	D	0.0903	0.0210
21	D	0.2942[a]	0.0570
22	D	0.1502[a]	0.0210
23	ND	0.3428[a]	0.0200
24	D	0.2746[a]	0.0400
25	ND	0.0766	0.0170

Note: The superscript "a" denotes very high values of mean error compared to
their overall average, hence the estimates may reflect "outliers".

***LP_0 denotes the mean LP model with mean inputs in the objective
function.

Table 4. Estimates of the response coefficient (bi)

in the Farrell and Johansen models

Sample	J-model (single composite output)					F-model (single composite output)				
Size										
(n)	β_1	β_2	β_3	β_4	$\bar{y}^*$	β_1	β_2	β_3	β_4	y^*
9	0.451	0.184	0	0.066	4.296	0.247	0.523	0.626	0.179	4.413
12	0.232	0.564	0.667	0.190	4.262	0.247	0.523	0.626	0.179	4.413
20	0.245	0.525	0.631	0.179	4.243	0.247	0.523	0.626	0.179	4.413
25	0.246	0.523	0.629	0.179	4.234	0.247	0.523	0.626	0.179	4.413

Note: 1. $\bar{y}^* = \sum_{j=1}^{n} y_j^*/n$ denotes the mean optimal output level.

2. J-model is Johansen's aggregate model where the single composite output is used for the four outputs.

3. F-model is Farrell's model where the single composite output is used for the four outputs.

Here the significance of | t | values at 5% and 1% levels is denoted by one and two asterisks respectively. One reason for this close correspondence is that the subsample of 25 units was homogeneous by the Goldfeld-Quandt test but the estimates of the response coefficients by the LS method above are generally lower than the average LP estimates $(\bar{\beta}_i)$ reported in Table 2, which compares the average LP estimates $\bar{\beta}_i$ obtained from the mean LP or the LAV models (2.5) and (2.8). By using the estimated standard errors s_i, a chi-square test is performed on the difference $(\bar{\beta}_i - \beta_i^0)$ and results are as follows:

	One Output Case	Four Output Case
Chi-square	0.010	1.405

Both are nonsignificant at 1% level of the chi-square test, although the composite output case is more close to the LAV estimates β^0. This suggests that the single composite output captures very well the case of multiple outputs for this data set. But this is found to be true only if we consider the nondegenerate cases of the 25 LP models. On an overall basis the four-output case performs better, as it is clearly revealed in the estimates of mean error $(\bar{e})$ reported in Table 3. For the four-output case the mean $\bar{e}$, which is comparable to mean squared error in regression models is found to be consistently less than the single (composite) output case; also the "outliers" are fewer. Hence it is clear that the four-output case is more informative and also more reliable in terms of the minimum mean error criterion.

Table 4 which compares the estimates of the response coefficients (β_i) for the Johansen model and the Farrell model shows two very striking results. One is that the two sets of estimates are very close e.g., for n=25 they are almost identical. Secondly, the estimates of the Farrell model are invariant to changes in the sample size but this is not true for the Johansen model. This dissimilarity points out one basic limitation of the F-model i.e., it does not capture the aggregate impact of the whole industry, so long as the optimal basis does not change as n increases. The J-model is more suited to analyze both the micro production frontier and the macro frontier. However since the sample set here is homogeneous the difference between the two production frontiers: the micro and the macro is not very significant.

The multiple output generationalization of the Farrell production frontier and its empirical applications reveal several interesting aspects. First of all, if the samples are homogeneous the multiple outputs could be compressed into a single composite output, provided we consider only the nondegenerate solutions of the respective LP models. Secondly, the multiple output version of the Farrell model provides more information about the numeraire concept implicit in the definition of a single composite output. The mean errors are invariably lower in a consistent fashion for the four-output case compared with the single output case. This suggests that prior screening of the data set before estimating the parameters of the Farrell production frontier may be helpful particularly in heterogeneous samples. Thirdly, one could in principle derive a macro production frontier in the J-model if the observed input coefficients are assumed to be drawn from a given probability distribution e.g., a Pareto distribution.

B. Stochastic Efficiency in Set-theoretic Context

With multiple outputs and inputs for each unit, which are subject to a stochastic generating process there is a fundamental problem of how to specify stochastic efficiency. This is not an estimation problem but a specification problem. Johansen did not address this problem since he assumed that full capacity levels of inuts and outputs are known or given, implying that the capacity distribution and the rates of utilization of capacities are part of the observed data set for a given industry. Farrell due to lack of any economic theory could not analyze the specification problem in a fully stochastic framework, although he did mention that the stochastic data variations should include perturbations in both inputs and outputs, besides the usual error components in equations (or in inequalities) as in the composed error model of parametric theory.

Methodologically speaking this raises a fundamental question: How to specify efficiency when the input and output vectors are random across firms? Clearly this raises two related issues. One, how does the production possibility set $Q = Q(x,y)$ of the Farrell model change, when the input (x) and output (y) vectors belong to sets X and Y respectively, which are subject to a random generating mechanism? Second, if we define an isoquant as a suitable boundary of the production possibility set above, then how does this isoquant get transformed when randomness is introduced through both inputs and outputs?

Two types of approaches can be suggested for this question. One is to introduce some specific distributions of the input and output vectors and some constraints (e.g., these are called capacity utilization constraints) so that the convexity of the production possibility set could be maintained along with the concept of the isoquant for the production frontier. Johansen and his associates followed this approach and introduced specific rules of aggregation by which one may pass on from the micro to the macro production frontier. A second approach purports to develop the concept of a distance from the frontier isoquant to other feasible points not on the frontier. This approach is directly related to the mesure of inefficiency first introduced by Debreu [10] in a general equilibrium framework and termed "the coefficient of resource utilization". We intend to apply this approach in Farrell's framework by first assuming that the input ($x \in X$) and output ($y \in Y$) sets are all deterministic i.e., noise free. Also we introduce specific conditions and simplifying assumptions to obtain stronger results. Hence we restrict ourselves to the sets X, Y of positive input $x = (x_j)$ and output $y = (y_j)$ vectors respectively (j=1,2,...,n) for n firms, so that the production possibility set $Q = \{(X,Y) \mid x \in X; y \in Y; x = (x_j) > 0, y = (y_j) > 0\}$ may be viewed as the input requirement set for any feasible output y which is positive. We denote the boundary of this requirement set by $I(x,y)$ which is analogous to the isoquant of the production frontier. Then we introduce the following three assumptions:

(C) Convexity: The set $Q = Q \{(X,Y) \mid x \in X, y \in Y\}$ is convex, closed and
        bounded from below for every feasible output y,

(M) Monotonicity: For any x ∈ I(x,y), if there is an output vector ◊ such that

 ◊ > y , then x ∉ I(x, ◊) , and

(D) Free Disposal: If any ◊ ∈ x and x ∈ Q(x,y), then ◊ ∈ Q(x,◊) .

Given these three assumptions (C), (M) and (D) one could easily measure the inefficiency of any feasible input output pair $(x^0,y) ∈ Q$ where $x^0 ∉ I(x,y)$ in terms of the distance from the vector point x^0 to the set I(x,y). By assumption (C) and the separating hyperplane theorem there must exist a price vector p(α) associated with each input point α ∈ I(x,y) such that

$$p(\alpha)'[x^0-\alpha] \geq 0, \text{ for all } x^0 \in Q \tag{2.18}$$

and the assumptions (M) and (D) ensure that p(α) is positive. Hence one can define the distance $d(x^0,\alpha)$ between x^0 and a point on the isoquant I(x,y) in a ratio form as

$$d(x^0,\alpha) = p(\alpha)'[x^0-\alpha]/p(\alpha)'x^0 \tag{2.19}$$

Following the convention of mesuring the distance between a point and a set as the least of the distances between the point and the elements of the set, one may finally reduce this distance measure to

$$d(x^0, y) = \inf_{\alpha \in I(X,Y)} \{d(x^0, \alpha)\} \tag{2.20}$$

where we may assume for simplicity that the infimum is always realized; then we obtain

$$d(x^0, y) = 1 - \frac{p(x^*)'x^*}{p(x^*)'x^0} \tag{2.21}$$

for some input vector x* belonging to the isoquant I*(x,y). Clearly by introducing the fraction θ in x* = θx^0, where x* $\in$ I(x,y) but $x^0 \notin$ I(x,y) it is seen that the distance function can be finally written as:

$$d(x^0,y) = 1-\theta, 0 \leq \theta \leq 1 \tag{2.22}$$

This means that the inefficiency associated with the input point x^0 is simply the largest fraction by which the actual input vector could be scaled down without rendering the actual output vector infeasible.

Some comments on this distance function are in order. First, if the input-output data are subject to a stochastic generating mechanism, the crucial assumption (C) of convexity needed for the existence of the nonnegative price vector $p(\alpha)$ in

$$d(x^0, \alpha) = p(\alpha)'[x^0 - \alpha], x^0 \notin I(x, y)$$
$$\alpha \in I(x, y)$$

may fail to hold e.g., there may exist (potential) increasing returns to scale for some points. Secondly, the distance measure $d(x^0,y)$ in (2.22) becomes stochastic as soon as the inefficient points x^0 vary across firms. One needs to derive the distribution of the distance function $d(x^0,y)$ when the domain of variation of x^0 in the set X is known. Finally, the distance function above is not very suitable for statistical testing purposes. This is because it is not related to the standard measures of distance in multivariate statistics e.g. Hotelling's T^2-statistic or, Mahalonobis's D^2-statistic. However if one can characterize the data set into two clusters, one efficient in some sense and the other nonefficient, then the distance measures of multivariate statistics can be easily applied.

2.3 Data Envelopment Analysis

Data envelopment analysis (DEA) was originally developed by Charnes, Cooper and Rhodes [5] as a new technique in operations research for measuring and comparing the relative efficiency of a set of decision-making units (DMUs). Efficiency is either technical efficiency as in Farrell model for given input-output ratios, or managerial efficiency when different clusters are compared. It applies the basic concept of Pareto optimality by stipulating that a given DMU is not relatively efficient, if it can be shown that some other DMU or, combination of DMU's can produce more of some outputs without producing less of any other and without utilizing more of any input. This technique has been found very useful in measuring efficiency for various public sector DMUs and/or quasi-market or nonmarket agencies e.g., public schools, recruitment and training programs in defense industries, hospitals, extension services and family planning programs, where price data are mostly unavailable and there are multiple goals pursued.

The DEA model has provided in recent times a most active field of research, where management science and operations research have joined econometrics and economic theory. It is expected that many new problems and exciting areas related to this model, which are yet unsolved today would be clarified in the near future. In this section we present a brief overview of the current status of the DEA approach emphasizing mainly its applied economic and econometric aspects.

A.   Robustness Aspects

Of several types of robustness issues connected with the DEA approach the following are most important in an applied context. First of all, consider the single output case of the DEA model (2.5) used by Timmer [1] in his study of the U.S. agricultural production frontier. One may ask how sensitive is the optimal basis of this LP model relative to small data perturbations? If it is not sensitive upto a certain degree, then it is relatively robust upto that degree. Since data perturbation may be either deterministic or stochastic, one could obtain two types of measures of stability. Secondly, the same method could be applied to the DEA model (2.1) to ask how close are the optimal solutions of (2.1) to the Timmer version (2.5)? Thirdly, one could apply a minimax method of minimizing the maximum error, which would replace the minimal cost criteria adopted in the DEA models (2.1) and (2.5). Finally, the probabilistic sensitivity can be analyzed through game-theoretic formulations. We may now illustrate some of these cases.

Consider first the LP model (2.5) where mean inputs $\bar{x}_i$ are used in the objective function in place of x_{ki}, k=1,2,...,n. If the DMUs refer to a more or less homogeneous cluster, the input vector $X_k = (x_{ki})$ would tend to center around a mean (or median) level with a certain degree of dispersion around the central location. The probabilistic data generating model may then take the following form

$$X_k = \bar{x} + \varepsilon_k, \quad k = 1, 2, \ldots, n$$

where $\bar{x} = (\bar{x}_i)$ is the mean input vector and ε_k is a random disturbance term. If the probability distribution of ε_k is such that it has a zero mean and a finite variance-covariance matrix V_ε, then one can easily characterize how closely the observed input vector points X_k are scattered around its mean $\bar{x}$. This may be easily done through the multivariate distance function $D^2 = D^2(x; \bar{x}, V_\varepsilon)$ defined as follows:

$$D^2 = D^2(x; \bar{x}, V_\varepsilon) = (x - \bar{x})V_\varepsilon^{-1}(x - \bar{x}) \tag{2.23}$$

where it is assumed that the variance-covariance V_ε is nonsingular and the vector x here is used to denote any vector in the set $\{X_k: k=1,2,...,n\}$. Thus if all X_k in the cluster are very close to the mean, the value of D^2 will be close to zero. The higher the value of D^2, the farther the points are scattered away from the mean level. The role of the variance-covariance matrix V_ε is more subtle however. It has two practical implications. One is that it acts as a filtering device, whereby with noisy data any difference $x_i - \bar{x}_i$ is deflated or corrected in terms of its standard errors, so that the squared distance between x and $\bar{x}$ can be more reliably computed. Secondly, if the underlying probability distribution of the errors ε can be assumed to be normal (e.g. under certain conditions by the central limit theorem), then the random quantity D^2 in (2.23) is known to follow a chi-square distribution with m degrees of freedom if the variance-covariance matrix V_ε is known. Thus one may choose a level of significance α and determine a suitable positive scalar $c = c_\alpha$ such that X defines a confidence region

$$X = \{x : D^2(x; \bar{x}, V_\varepsilon) \le c_\alpha\} \tag{2.24}$$

in the sense that for any set of points x belonging to region X we have $\text{Prob}(x \in X) = \alpha$. By varying α one can therefore vary the size of the neighborhood around $\bar{x}$. One can use the distance statistic D^2 in two different ways. First, one could choose vector points x which are very close to the mean level $\bar{x}$ with e.g., a high probbility $\alpha = 0.95$ or more and generate solutions which are very close to the mean solution vector $\bar{\beta}^*$ and hence very close together. Timmer found in his empirical production function studies such a close correspondence but was unable to explain it since he did not use any distance statistic to measure the deviation of input data points from their mean level. A second usefulness of the distance statistic D^2 arises through its connection with the central limit theorem. Denote by D_n^2 the distance statistic based on sample size n

$$D_n^2 = (\bar{x} - \mu)' V^{-1}(\bar{x} - \mu) \tag{2.25}$$

where μ is the population mean vector and V the population variance-covariance matrix for a random sample vector x. Then for all those nonnormal distributions which obey the central limit theorem, it holds that for large n, the statistic D_n^2 tends to zero with probability one, since the sample mean $\bar{x}$ tends to population mean μ of a normal distribution with probability one. Hence under large sample conditions (i.e., $n \to \infty$), the LP model (2.5) based on the sample mean vector $\bar{x}$ in the objective function may be utilized for testing sensitivity and robustness, even when the underlying distribution of the input vectors is nonnormal but has a finite mean and variance. In particular if there were two subsamples each of size s i.e., n=2s and two sample mean estimates $\bar{x}(1)$ and

$\bar{x}(2)$ are used to estimate the population mean μ in (2.25), the distance statistics

$D_s^2(\bar{x}(1))$, $D_s^2(\bar{x}(2))$ may be utilized at a given probability level α to test if they were

significantly different or not. Let $\bar{\beta}*(1)$, $\bar{\beta}*(2)$ be the two optimal solution vectors of

the LP model (2.5) for the two mean estimates $\bar{x}(1)$, $\bar{x}(2)$ in the objective function. If

the second subsample mean $\bar{x}(2)$ is not significantly different from the first mean $\bar{x}(1)$

in terms of the D_s^2 statistic at a specified level (say $\alpha=0.95$) of probability, and also

$\bar{\beta}*(2)$ is not significantly different from $\bar{\beta}*(1)$, then the first subsample is strongly ro-

bust against the second subsample.

It is clear that one can directly test if there is any significant statistical difference of

the two vector estimates $\bar{\beta}*(1)$, $\bar{\beta}*(2)$. Since the error term e_j in (2.4) is nonnegtive for

every observation j=1,2,....,n minimizing the absolute sum $\sum\limits_{i=1}^{m} |e_j|$ is equivalent to

minimizing $\bar{g} = \sum\limits_{i=1}^{m} \beta_i \bar{x}_i$ which is the objective function of the LP model (2.5).

Thus the estimates $\bar{\beta}*$ obtained by minimizing $\sum\limits_{j} e_j$ are least absolute value (LAV)

estimates in linear regressions, also known as MSAE (minimum sum of absolute errors)

estimates. One of the most extensive simulation study based on 100,000 LAV

regressions were performed by Rosenberg and Carlson [11] and their two important

results reported by Dielman and Pfaffenberger [12] and more recently by Koenker [13]

were as follows:

(a)   The LAV estimator had a significantly smaller standard error than the LS

        (least squares) estimator for nonnormal disturbances with high kurtosis, and

(b)   The error $(\hat{\bar{\beta}}* - \bar{\beta}*)$ in the LAV estimator $\hat{\bar{\beta}}*$ was approximately normally

        distributed with mean zero and covariance matrix $\lambda^2(X'X)^{-1}$, where λ^2/n is

        the asymptotic variance of the median of a sample of size n from the distur-

        bance distribution and $(X'X)$ is the standard coefficient matrix of the normal equations in linear regression.

It is clear therefore that based on the approximate asymptotic normality, the two sample

statistics $\hat{\beta}*(1)$, $\hat{\beta}*$ can be directly compared and hence their difference evaluated.

Next we turn to the problem of redundancy in LP estimation of the DEA model

(2.1), where one computes n LP models with their optimal solutions $\hat{\beta}*(k)$, k=1,2,...,n.

For a fixed k in the objective function, the t-th constraint in the LP model (2.1) is defined

to be redundant according to Karwan et al. [14] in the theory of linear progrmming only

if the two feasible regions S and S_t coincide where:

$$S = \{\beta: \sum_{i=1}^{m} x_{ij}\beta_i \geq y_j; \beta_i \geq 0; i = 1, \ldots, m, j = 1, \ldots, n\}$$

(2.26)

$$S_t = \{\beta: \sum_{i=1}^{m} x_{ij}\beta_i \geq y_j; \beta_i \geq 0; \begin{matrix} i = 1, \ldots, m, j = 1, \ldots, n \\ j \neq t \end{matrix} \}$$

Let $s_t(\beta)$ and $s_t^*(\beta)$ be two slack variables defined as

$$s_t(\beta) = \sum_{i=1}^{m} \beta_i x_{it} - y_t; t = 1, 2, \ldots, n$$

$$s_t^*(\beta) = \min \{s_t(\beta): \beta \in S_t\}$$

Then the t-th constraint in the LP model (2.1) is said to be strongly (weakly) redundant if

and only if $s_t^*(\beta)$ is positive (zero). These two concepts of redundancy may be utilized

in two ways in the LAV estimation of β by the DEA models (2.1) and (2.5). First, one

can identify for each sample the maximum frequency of occurrence in the n LP models

(2.1) as an efficient unit with no redundancy. Then arrange each sample in a decreasing

order of the frequency of occurrence as an efficient unit and finally we choose m of these ordered samples as an "efficient subset". One could enlarge this subset by adding m+1, m+2 and other ordered samples. For each such ordered samples of sizes m, m+1, m+2,...,n one could run regressions of output on the m inputs to obtain various estimates of the production function. It is clear that as we move away from the efficient subset by adding more samples, we would diverge from a production frontier more and more till we obtain an average production function containing both efficient and inefficient units. Secondly, one could evaluate the role of the efficient subset by running a regression of the observed output (y) on the m inputs (x_i) and a zero-one dummy variable D_j, where D_j = 1 if j belongs to the 'efficient subset' and D_j = 0 if j does not so belong.

A second important method of robustness in the DEA model is to estimate the production frontier from the observed data set by minimizing the maximum error. On using the error term $e_j = \sum_{i=1}^{m} x_{ji} \beta_i - y_j$ this method consists in finding a vector point β^0 at which the minimax level $L(\beta^0)$ of loss is achieved, where

$$L = L(\beta^0) = \min_{\beta} \max_{1 \le j \le n} |e_j(\beta)|$$

So long as the errors $e_j(\beta)$ are bounded, the solution β^0 also known as the Chebyshev solution always exists, even when the inequalities $e_j(\beta) \ge 0$, j=1,2,...,n are mutually inconsistent. Clearly the minimax method leads to an LP model:

$$\text{Min } \beta_{m+1}$$

subjecto to $\qquad \sum_{i=1}^{m} \beta_i x_{ij} - y_j \le \beta_{m+1}; \ j = 1, 2, \ldots, n$ \hfill (2.27)

$$\beta_i \ge 0, \ i=1,2,\ldots,m+1$$

where β_{m+1} is a nonnegative scalar. One could also adjoin the additional constraints such as

$$e_j(\beta) = \sum_{i=1}^{m} \beta_i x_{ij} - y_j \geq 0, j = 1, 2, \ldots, n$$

It is clear that if the feasible set $R = \{\beta: e_j(\beta) \geq 0, j=1,2,\ldots,n\}$ is non-empty, then an optimal solution must exist. Let $\hat{\beta}$ be an optimal solution of (2.27). Then it has some robustness properties like the LAV estimator mentioned before. Moreover, it preserves the linearity of the DEA model unlike the LS approach which would make it quadratic. By adjoining the condition $\sum_{i=1}^{m} \beta_i = 1$ to (2.27) one could also interpret the m-tuple

vector β as mixed strategies of a suitable zero-sum two-person game.

B.   Game-theoretic Aspects

In cases when the input-output data are stochastic a somewhat direct formulation of the minimax approach is more helpful. Thus let $B = (b_{ij})$ be the matrix of the normalized input-output coefficients $b_{ij} = x_{ij}/(x_{ik}y_j)$ and $p = (p_i)$, $q = (q_j)$ be the mixed strategy vectors. Then the minimax and maximin game formulations appear as follows:

$$\min_{q} u_k \text{ s. t. } Bq \leq u_k e_m, \, q' e_n = 1 \qquad\qquad (2.28)$$
$$q \geq 0$$

and

$$\max_{p} v_k \text{ s. t. } B' p \geq v_k e_n, \, p' e_m = 1 \qquad\qquad (2.29)$$
$$p \geq 0$$

where u_k, v_k are scalar quantities and e_m, e_n are respectively the m-tuple and n-tuple column vectors with each element unity.

Let S be the set of states of nature indexed by s and B(s) be the payoff matrix for state s. It is clear that for every realized $s \in S$, the optimal mixed strategy vectors $p^* = p^*(s)$ and $q^* = q^*(s)$ would exist with the common value of the game $u^* = u^*(s) = v^* =$

$v^*(s) = p^{*'}(s)B(s)q^*(s)$. However if the states of nature are unknown, partly or completely the mixed strategy vectors $p^*(s)$, $q^*(s)$ above cannot be specified as the decision rules. Two types of solutions have been proposed by Blau [15] in case of random payoffs, where a chance-constrained interpretation is made of the inequalities: $Bq \leq ue_m$ and $B'p \geq ve_n$ following the earlier work of Charnes, Kirby and Raike [16]. In the first, called the payoff maximization model we have for player 1 the following model:

$$\max_{p} \delta \text{ s. t. } \min_{q} \text{Prob}(p' Bq \geq \delta) \geq \varepsilon$$

$$p'e_m = 1, p, q \geq 0 \qquad (2.30)$$

$$\varepsilon \text{ preassigned } (0 < \varepsilon < 1)$$

where he seeks a strategy p that gives him the largest payoff, while at the same time guaranteeing at any round that the probability of his conditional expected payoff exceeding the payoff level δ is at least ε, $0 < \varepsilon < 1$. Likewise for second player who controls the strategy vector q. In the second case, called the probability maximization model, player 1 specifies the value of δ and solves for the optimal value of p and ε as follows:

$$\max_{p} \varepsilon \quad \text{s. t. } \min_{q} \text{Prob}(p' Bq \geq \delta) \geq \varepsilon$$

$$p'e_m = 1, p, q \geq 0$$

Note two features of these solutions for the DEA model. First, the optimal vectors p^*, q^* which can be used for efficiency ranking and measurement are now dependent either on the level ε of the chance-constraints or on the level δ of payoff acceptable to the players. Second, by using suitable probability distributions for the random variable $\phi = \phi(s) = p'(s)B(s)q(s)$, $s \in S$ one could explicitly compute the nonlinear programming models resulting from the above game-theoretic formulations.

One advantage of these game-theoretic formulations is that the consequence of merger or coalition of some of the n DMUs may be easily evaluated in terms of the concept of a core. Thus assume that the n DMUs form a set $N = \{1, 2, ..., n\}$ of n players who can form coalitions (or mergers) of different sizes. Let S be a coalition of less than n players and N is the grand coalition of all the n players. For the LP problem

$$\text{Max } z = \sum_{j \in S} y_j \lambda_j$$

$$\text{s. t. } \sum_{j \in S} x_{ij} \lambda_j \leq \ell_i, \, i = 1, 2, \ldots, m \qquad (2.31)$$

$$\lambda_j \geq 0 \quad j \in S$$

We may form the characteristic function $v(S)$ for the coalition $S \subset N$ as

$$v(S) = \max \sum_{j \in S} y_j \lambda_j$$

$$\text{s. t. } \sum_{j \in S} x_{ij} \lambda_j \leq \ell_i(S), \, i = 1, 2, \ldots, m \qquad (2.32)$$

$$\lambda_j \geq 0, \, j \in S$$

where $\ell_i(S)$ is a particular allocation of input i from the total amount $\sum_{j \in S} x_{ij}$ the coalition has. It is easy to show that this input-allocation game has a nonempty core and hence a nonempty set of allocations. Thus in practical terms one could analyze the various optimal solutions resulting from the merger of n DMUs which form coalitions. Thus let S_1 and S_2 be two mutually disjoint coalitions of the grand coalition N, then so long as $v(S_1) > v(S_2) > 0$, one can improve the total payoff by a reallocation process. If the payoffs for the grand coalition N and any other coalition S are $v(N)$ and $v(S)$ respectively, the associated optimal vectors $(\lambda^*(N), \beta^*(N))$ and $(\lambda^*(S), \beta^*(S))$ may be used to characterize the efficiency ranking and measurement. The concept of a Pareto solution in case of grand coalition arises very naturally in this framework. Thus one may discuss the efficiency in the core by considering the primal form (2.1) of the DEA model as a game where the n DMUs are viewed as n players. They can form coalitions of different sizes, where the grand coalition of all n players is denoted by a set N = {1,2,...,n} and any proper subset of N is denoted by S. Several incentives exist in practical situations when, e.g., the DMUs in (2.1) refer to competing firms supplying a given output. One incentive is that by agreeing to cooperate in a coalition S, a player can reduce his cost and improve his performance. Thus min $g_k = x'_k \beta$ in (2.1) can be lowered for some $k \in S$. A second advantage is that the input-allocation game defined in (2.32) can be used to characterize a nonempty core and hence a nonempty set of allocations for a fixed set of the data matrix (X,y) which would of course be dependent on the coalition S. Thirdly, if the data matrix is subject to a probability generating mechanism and $\hat{x}_i(s)$ in (2.32) viewed as a particular allocation from the total amount $\sum_{j \in S} x_{ij}$, then the objective function of (2.1) representing k-th DMU would be

$$\min_{\beta} \ g_k = \hat{x}_k(S)' \beta, \ \hat{x}_k(S) = \hat{x}_{ik}(S) \tag{2.33}$$

and it would have stochastic variations conditional on a given allocation process defined by a matrix U where $U(\sum_{j \in S} x_{ij}) = \hat{x}_i(S)$. For a fixed S, an equal allocation would imply $U(\bullet) = (1/n) \sum_j x_{ij} = \bar{x}_i(S)$, i.e., mean inputs.

On the basis of this formulation of the allocation game we could define three types of coalitions as follows:

(a)   One-player coalitions: Here the n players do not cooperate and the minimax definition of optimality can be used to specify an equilibrium. Thus player k assumes all the other players to be playing against him and choosing their strategies to maximize his cost of g_k in (2.33). Let $\beta(N-I)$ denote the (n-1)-tuple vector with elements

$(\beta(1),\beta(2),...,\beta(k-1),...,\beta(k+1),...,\beta(n))$ and B_{N-I} would be feasible set of solutions specifying the admissible strategies. Then $\beta^*(k)$ is a minimax control for player k if and only if for all $\beta(k) \in B_K$ we have

$$\max_{\beta(N-I)} g_k(\beta^*(k), \beta(N-I)) \le \max_{\beta(N-I)} g_k(\beta(k), \beta(N-I))$$

where $\beta(N-I) \in B_{N-I}$ and it is assumed that the objective function $g_k(\cdot)$ is finite for all the cases considered. It is clear that if a pure strategy saddle point solution exists for the two-player zero-sum game with cost $g_k(\beta(k), \beta(N-I))$, then the minimax strategy $\beta^*(k)$ for player k must exist for player k.

(b)   n-player coalitions: Here each of n players may agree to cooperate and hence each may be able to achieve a lower cost than he would if all the players played their minimax strategies. Here the concept of Pareto optimality is most useful. We define a feasible n-tuple vector β^* to be Pareto-optimal, if and only if for every feasible n-tuple vector β we have,

either, $g_k(\beta) = g_k(\beta^*)$, all $k \in \{1,2,...,n\}$

or, at least for one k, $g_k(\beta) > g_k(\beta^*)$

(c)   r-player coalitions $(1 < r < n)$: Here we have a coalition formed by less than n players. Let players $1,2,...,r$ form a coalition and their strategies be denoted by an r-tuple vector $\beta(R)$ belonging to a feasible set $B(R)$. The strategies of other players are denoted by the (n-r)-tuple vector $\beta(N-R)$ belonging to a feasible set $B(N-R)$. Then the r-tuple vector $\beta^*(R) = (\beta^*(1), \beta^*(2),...,\beta^*(r))$ is Pareto-optimal up to coalition size r, if and only if we have,

either $\Delta g_k = \max_{\beta(N-R)} g_k(\beta(R), \beta(N-R)) - \max_{\beta(N-R)} g_k(\beta^*(R), \beta(N-R))$

$= 0$ for all $k \in \{1,2,...,r\}$ (2.34) or, at least for one k, $k \in \{1,2,...,r\}$, $\Delta g_k > 0$.

Now let P be the set of all possible coalitions S, where S may have different sizes from 1,2,.... up to n. Let $\bar{\beta}*$ be optimal for every such coalition in P, i.e., (2.34) holds for every $S \in P$ (i.e., collective optimality), then the vector $(g_1(\bar{\beta}*), g_2(\bar{\beta}*), \ldots, g_r(\bar{\beta}*))$ belongs to the core.

Theorem 1

Let $\bar{\beta}*$ be the Pareto-optimal solution belonging to the core for a given data matrix $D = (X,y)$. Then there exists an n-tuple vector $w = (w_1,w_2,...,w_n)$ of nonnegative weights w_k not all zero, such that $\bar{\beta}*$ minimizes the scalar objective function,

$\sum\limits_{k=1}^{n} w_k g_k(\beta)$. Conversely, if there exists a positive vector $w > 0$ of weights such that $\sum\limits_{k} w_k g_k(\beta) \geq \sum\limits_{k} w_k g_k(\bar{\beta}*)$ for all feasible vectors β, then $\bar{\beta}*$ is Pareto-optimal.

Proof: This follows immediately by applying Kuhn-Tucker theory to the vector minimum problem.

Remark 1.1

Let the data matrix change to $D_t = (X_t, y_t)$ where $x_{ij} = \bar{x}_i + e_{ij}/t$, $y_j = \bar{y} + e_j/t$, bar denotes mean values (either weighted or unweighted) and e_{ij}, e_j are disturbance terms. If for every t, the Pareto optimal solution now denoted by $\bar{\beta}_t^*$ exists, then the limiting solution $\bar{\beta}* = \lim\limits_{t \to \infty} \bar{\beta}_t$ also exists if e_{ij}/t and e_j/t tends to zero for $t \to \infty$. One could thus construct replicated games to interpret $\bar{\beta}*$ as the steady-state solution.

Remark 1.2

If the optimality of the Pareto-solution $\bar{\beta}*$ is unaffected by a certain type of enlargement of the data matrix, then it may be said to be robust for this type of enlargement. For example consider three DMUs producing one unit of a single output using the following two inputs (x_1, x_2):

	1	2	3
x_1	2	3	4
x_2	2	2	1

Clearly the second DMU is not Pareto-efficient, since it is dominated by the first DMU requring less of input x_1. Now consider data enlargement in the form of the second column replaced by $(3+\varepsilon, 2+\varepsilon)'$ where ε is a nonnegative random variable. Clearly, the optimality of the Pareto-solution $\bar{\beta}^*$ would be unaffected.

Some implications of the core concept may now be briefly outlined. First of all, consider two coalitions S and N-S, where N is the grand coalition. The values of the two coalitions are v(S) and v(N-S) defined before, where the complementary coalition (N-S) can obtain v(N-S) without any cooperation from coalition S. If the coalition S knows that the value of the grand coalition is v(N), then there may be a positive surplus defined by [v(N) - v(S) - v(N-S)]. Following Johansen [17] one may utilize here the notion of the degree of aggressiveness of coalition S as the share γ_S which the coalition will aspire to get in the surplus. Thus the claim of coalition S will be

$$R(S) = v(S) + \gamma_S [v(N) - v(S) - v(N-S)]$$

If γ_S is zero for all coalitions, then we have the ordinary core; but with $\gamma_S = 1$ for all coalitions we have the maximally aggressive core. The case where $0 < \gamma_S < 1$ for all coalitions, we have the intermediate degree of aggressiveness in the core. Note that this claim R(S) of coalition S in the surplus becomes probabilistic, when the data set (X,y) is subject to a stochastic generating mechanism. Let $F_S = F_S(x(S))$ denote the probability

Prob[R(S) ≤ t], then $[1 - F_S(x(S))]$ measures the probability that the claim of the coalition S is at least t or higher. So long as the data variations are such that the excess $[v(N) - v(S) - v(N-S)]$ is positive, it is clear that this probability $(1 - F_S(x(s))$ is finite and positive. Hence we have the result:

Theorem 2

The minimax problem

$$\min \delta$$
$$\text{s.t.} \quad 1 - F_S(x(s)) \leq \delta, S \subseteq N \qquad\qquad (2.35)$$
$$0 \leq \delta \leq 1$$

has an optimal solution, provided data variations are such that

$$v(N) - v(S) - v(N-S) \geq 0$$

Proof

Under the given conditions on the data set the excess $E(S) = v(N) - v(S) - v(N-S)$ is nonnegative for all $S \subseteq N$ and since the LP model defining $v(S)$ has a nontrivial optimal solution for every set of nonnegative inputs and outputs, the probabilities F_s and $1 - F_S$ are well defined; furthermore the feasibility set of (2.35) is compact. Hence an optimal solution exists.

Remark 2.1

The minimax solution above indirectly serves to determine a value γ_S^* of the degree of aggressiveness in the core. Like all minimax solutions it also has some robustness properties.

Remark 2.2

The minimax problem (2.35) is generally nonlinear, since the distribution F_S of the value of the claim R(S) involves the allocations x(S) nonlinearly.

An interesting implication of the core concept in the standard DEA model (2.1) is as follows. Assume that we solve n LP models from (2.1) and a small subset n* (n* < n) of DMU's turns out to be efficient in every LP model. Then this subset n* may be said to be strongly efficient. In some empirical applications [6-8] we found that such strongly efficient subsets and their sizes have significant impact on the overall efficiency.

C.   Types of DEA Frontiers

While the DEA frontiers in (2.1) and (2.7) are linear, several nonlinear forms have been proposed e.g., (1) piecewise loglinear forms [18], (2) multiplicative models for efficiency analysis [19], and (3) quadratic forms of the frontier [20]. These generalized formulations are able to locate inefficiencies better than their parametric equivlents. Also some numerical comparisons [21] show that these generalized efficiency measures perform better than the average production functions estimated by ordinary least squares. Another line of extension is due to Banker [22] who generalized the LAV regression model by replacing the restrictive parametric specification with a flexible nonparametric formulation for estimating monotonic and functional corrspondences. For the single output case he uses four postulates for estimating the frontier correspondence $y = f(x)$ relating the single output y to the input vector x:

Postulate 1 (monotonicity): If $y = f(x)$, $\hat{y} = f(\hat{x})$

and $x \geq \hat{x}$, then $y \geq \hat{y}$

Postulate 2 (concavity: If $y = f(x)$, $\hat{y} = f(\hat{x})$

and $0 \leq \lambda \leq 1$, then $(1 - \lambda)y + \lambda\hat{y} \leq f((1 - \lambda)x + \lambda\hat{x})$

Postulate 3 (envelopment): For each observation j=1,2,...,n we have $y_j \leq f(x_j)$.

Postulate 4 (minimum extrapolation): If there exists any function g(x) satisfying the three postulates above, then $g(x) \geq f(x)$ for all $x \in X$, where X is the convex hull of all input vectors x_j.

The above production frontier correspondence $f(x)$, $x \in X$ can be computed from the following LP model:

$$f(x) = \max \sum_{k=1}^{n} \lambda_k y_k$$

$$\text{s. t.} \sum_{k=1}^{n} \lambda_k x_k \leq x; \quad \sum_{k=1}^{n} \lambda_k = 1; \lambda_k \geq 0 \qquad (2.36)$$

The efficiency of any DMU j is then measured as $h_j = y_j/f(x_j)$, where x_j is an m-tuple input vector for each observation j. Note that the monotonicity and concavity posulates above specify the desirable conditions which we require in the economic theory of production, although they can be relaxed e.g., quasi-concavity. The other two properties guarantee that actual or observed output values is on or below the frontier value thus implying the asymmetric one-sided error. Note further that the dual of the LP model (2.36) can be written as:

$$f(x) = \min (w_0 + w'x)$$
$$\text{s.t.} \quad w_0 + w'x_k \geq y_k; \; k=1,2,...,n$$
$$w \geq 0, w_0 \text{ is unconstrained in sign}$$

If w^*_{oj} and w^*_j define an optimal solution to this dual LP model, then it has been shown by Banker, Charnes and Cooper [23] that the hyperplane $y = w^*_{oj} + w^*_j{}'x$ is tangential to the production frontier at the point (x_j, y_j) where $y_j = f(x_j)$. It is this property which is very useful for characterizing a monotonic and concave production frontier. Thus if a function $y = f(x)$ is monotonic increasing and concave over $x \in X$, $x_0 \in X$ and $y_0 = f(x_0)$ then there must exist some vector $w \geq 0$ and a scalar w_0 such that

$y_0 = w_0 + w'x_0$ and, $f(x) \leq w_0 + w'x$ for all $x \in X$

The above two conditions jointly yield the result

$f(x_0) - f(x) \geq w'(x - x_0)$ for all $x \in X$

Note two points. The existence of (w, w_0) need not be unique and therefore more than one characterization is possible when the postulates are relaxed suitably. Secondly, an analogous result could be derived for the case of multiple outputs.

2.4   Consistency Approach Through Data Adjustment

For any observed set of input-output data two major questions arise when we set up the efficiency hypothesis characterized by a production frontier or, an efficient production set. One is the consistency problem i.e., is the data consistent with the efficiency hypothesis? If price data are also observed then one may ask: is the data consistent with the profit maximization or cost minimization hypothesis? This type of question was first posed by Afriat [24] and later analyzed by Varian [25], Diewert and Parkan [26], Banker and Maindiratta [27] and Sengupta [28]. A second question is: How can we estimate the production frontier when the observed data have the contamination that they contain points not satisfying the efficiency hypothesis? This question has also implications for recovering the information about efficiency and for extrapolation in environments which are different from those observed.

Consider n data points $D_j = (x_j, y_j)$, $j=1,2,...,n$ for each firm or decision-making unit where y is a single good produced by the vector x of m inputs. If the inputs and outputs in the data set are nonnegative, then Afriat showed that there must exist a function

$$f(x) = \max[\sum_{j=1}^{n} y_j \lambda_j : \sum_{j=1}^{n} x_j \lambda_j \leq x, \sum_{j=1}^{n} \lambda_j = 1, \lambda_j \geq 0] \qquad (2.37)$$

which is non-decreasing concave and such that $y_j \leq f(x_j)$. Furthermore, there exists a non-decreasing concave function $f(x)$ satisfying $y_j = f(x_j)$ for all j, if and only if

$$\sum_{j=1}^{n} x_j \lambda_j \leq x_s \text{ implies } \sum_{j=1}^{n} y_j \lambda_j \leq y_s \qquad (2.38)$$

The condition (2.38) holds if and only if $y_j = f(x_j)$. The function $f(x)$ represents a nonparametric production frontier such that it is everywhere not greater than any other non-decreasing concave function. The observed data set $D = (D_j: j=1,2,...,n)$ is said to be consistent with the frontier function $f(x)$ if it satisfies the conditions (2.38). The data consistency problem thus reduces to solving the linear programming problem:

$$f(x) = \max [\sum_{j=1}^{n} \lambda_j : \sum_{j=1}^{n} a_j \lambda_j \leq x, \lambda_j \geq 0] \qquad (2.39)$$

where $a_j = x_j/y_j$ is the input coefficient vector for each j and x is any of the n input vectors. If the input price vector w is also available i.e., the observed data is now $D_j = (x_j, w_j; y_j)$ where y_j is a scalar, then the family of input requirement sets (y), is defiend by Varian to c-rationalize the oberved data if x_j solves the LP problem:

Min w'x   s.t. $x \in V(y_j)$

i.e. $w'_j x_j \leq w'_j x$ for all $x \in V(y_j)$

The "c" in c-rationalizes stands for "cost". He proved that a production function c-rationalizes the observed behavior if the two conditions $f(x_j) = y_j$ and $f(x) \geq f(x_j)$ imply

$w'_j x \geq w'_j x_j$ for j=1,2,...,n. This means that the vector x_j minimizes costs over all bundles that can produce at least the output level y_j. If the price p of output is also available, then a production possibility set T may be defined to "strongly rationalize" the set of observed data $D = (D_j, j=1,...,n)$ if for each $j \in D$, (y_j,x_j) belongs to T and

$p_j y_j - w'_j x_j \geq p_j y - w'_j x$ for all $(y,x) \in T$. However due to technical and allocative

inefficiencies in the operations of the firms, the set of observations in many cases may

not be strongly rationalizable. Hence Banker and Maindiratta introduced the concept of

subset rationalization. Thus a production possibility set T is defined to "subset

rationalize" the set $H \subseteq D$ if for each $j \in D$ belonging to the set T and for each $j \in H$ we

have $p_j y_j - w'_j x_j \geq p_j y - w'_j x$ for all $(y,x) \in T$. Furthermore such a set of

observations H is said to be "subset rationalizable" if there exists some production

possibility set T that can subset rationalize H. By using this subset rationalization

criterion they have developed technical, allocative and aggregate efficiency measures,

which are associated with Farrell's approach.

Another way to interpret the data consistency problem is in terms of the existence of

suitable Lagrange multipliers. This is the approach by Diewert and Parkan. Clearly the

primal LP problem (2.39) has a feasible soution (and hence the optimal solution) if and

only if the dual variables (i.e., the Lagrange multipliers) are feasible for the dual problem:

Min u'x   s.t. $u'a_j \geq 1$, $u \geq 0$

Note however that the above conditions for testing data consistency are all deterministic,

hence it does not apply when the data set is subject to a stochastic generating mechanism.

In this case, a part of the data set D may satisfy the consistency requirement with a

probability p, while the remaining part may fail the consistency test i.e., may allow no

feasible solution to the LP problem (2.39) for instance. If the above probability p is very

low (e.g., less than 0.25), then the frontier function $f(x)$ would have a very low

probability of realization. We may thus define two cases of data consistency:

(1)   The frontier production function $f(x)$ rationalizes the observed data set D in a

weak sense, if for all points in D the consistency reuirement holds with a probability of at least p $(0 \leq p \leq 1)$.

(2)   The frontier production function $f(x)$ rationalizes the observed data set D in a *strong sense*, if for all points in D the probability of satisfying the consistency requirement is at its maximum possible value p.

Note that these definitions can be applied to the dual of the LP model (2.39):

$$G(x) = \min\ [\beta'x:\ \beta'a_j \geq 1,\ j=1,2,...,n,\quad \beta > 0] \tag{2.40}$$

where β is the m-element dual vector and prime denotes its transpose. Let u_j be the marginal probability of feasibility:

$$Prob(\beta'a_j \geq 1,\ \beta \geq 0) \geq u_j \quad 0 < u_j \leq 1$$

and assume it to be positive for all j belonging to the data subset $\hat{D}$. We then define the programming model:

$$H(x,p^*) = \min_{\beta}\ \max_{p}\ [\beta'\ x:\ \beta \in S_p]$$

where

$$S_p = \{p:\ p = \min_{1 \leq j \leq n} u_j\ \text{as defined above}\} \tag{2.41}$$

$$p^* = \text{optimal value of } p,\ 0 < p \leq 1$$

Then we may characterize a third case of rationalization i.e., the frontier production function $H(x,p^*)$ rationalizes the observed data set D, if for all points in D we have the minimax solution (β^*,p^*) in (2.41), where β^* is the optimal value of vector β.

Note some consequences of these definitions. First, the consistency tests, stochastic as they are, may not always maintain the LP structure. For instance the chance-constrained model (2.41) is generally nonlinear for random variations of the input coefficient vectors a_j and various types of decision rules e.g., zero-order, first order, second order may be used as suboptimal solutions.

Second, the consistency (or efficiency) hypothesis may hold only for a proper subset $\hat{D}$ of D in the sense that for all points not belonging to $\hat{D}$, either the consistency requirement fails or holds only with a probability less than p. This implies that one may characterize the 'statistical contamination' of the subset $\hat{D}$ when it is enlarged to include more and more points of D not belonging to $\hat{D}$. The standard regression approach estimates the model $y_j = \beta'x_j + \varepsilon_j$, where the disturbance term ε is assumed to be symmetric around the mean value of zero and j belongs to D. But the nonparametric production frontier approach screens the data set D to identify a subset $\hat{D}$ such that for each $k \in \hat{D}$ we must have $\beta^{*'}x_k = y_k$, $\beta^* \geq 0$ in the LP problem (2.40) i.e., if for any j we get $\beta^{*'}x_j > y_j$, $\beta^* \geq 0$, then the unit j is not efficient, i.e., $j \notin \hat{D}$. It is thus clear that the statistical divergence of the regression model and nonparametric model can be tested in terms of the contamination of the efficiency subset $\hat{D}$. Third, the probabilistic nature of the consistency (or efficiency) hypothesis implies that the ad hoc procedure of replacing the random variables by their mean values and solving for the LP model at the mean may not have a very high probabiity of realization in many situations. This type of criticism applies equally well to the LP method of efficiency estimation by Timmer [1] who used the mean inputs in the objective function as:

$$G(\bar{x}) = \min [\beta' \bar{x} : \beta' a_j \geq 1, \beta \geq 0, j = 1, 2, \dots, n]$$

where $\bar{x} = (\bar{x}_i)$ is the mean input vector. On the basis of these definitions above one can state some theoretical results.

Theorem 3

If the elements of the data set $D = (D_j: j=1,...,n))$ are all positive, then there must exist a nonempty subset $\hat{D}$ of D and a frontier production function $f(x)$, such that $f(x)$ rationalizes the data subset $\hat{D}$ in a weak sense for some positive p $(0 < p \leq 1)$. Furthermore, there must exist another subset $\tilde{D}$ of D and a frontier function $H(x,p^*)$ such that $H(x,p^*)$ rationalizes the data subset $\tilde{D}$.

Proof

Since the input vector a_j is always positive, the LP model (2.39) is always feasible for any positive input vector x. Let D be the region of feasibility and T be the region in the data space where the objective function of (2.37) attains its maximum. We may then construct a subset $\hat{D}$ in the data space by taking the intersection of the two regions D and T. This intersection cannot be empty and since $\hat{D}$ is a subset of D, it must have a positive probability p. By a similar argument it can be shown that a subset $\tilde{D}$ exists such that it is rationalized by some frontier function $H(x,p^*)$.

Theorem 4

Let D_{m+1} be the set of subsets of order m+1 (i.e., one output and m inputs) of the data set D and $\hat{D}_{m+1}(p^*)$ be an efficiency subset of D_{m+1} that is p*-rationalized in a strong sense. Then any enlargement of the efficiency subset $\hat{D}_{m+1}$ by adding extra points from the set D cannot increase the probability p*.

Proof

Let p_k denote the relative frequency at which the unit k $(k \in D_{m+1})$ turns out to be efficient in terms of the LP model (2.40)in the sense $\{ \sum_{i=1}^{m} a_{ki}\beta_i^* - 1 = 0, \beta^* \geq 0\}$.

For any fixed set D_{m+1} we can arrange the n DMU (units) in a decreasing order as $p_{(1)} \geq$

$P_{(2)} \geq \ldots \geq P_{(n)} > 0$ which indicates a rearrangement of the n units in a decreasing scale of efficiency frequency i.e., $DMU_{(1)}$ is the most often efficient and $DMU_{(n)}$ is the least often. Let p^* be defined such that $p^* = \max u$, $u = \{\min P_{(k)}: k \in D_{m+1}\}$ and $\hat{D}_{m+1}(p^*)$ is the efficiency subset shich includes only those units which are efficient at least with a probability $p^* > 0$. Hence the result.

Two implications of this result are of some practical value. One is that it develops a method of clustering the data set into a modal efficiency subset $\hat{D}_{m+1}(p^*)$ and its explanatory vaule can be easily assessed by a simple linear regression model with dummy variables (i.e., zero-one categorical variables) as regressors explaining the output response [6]. Secondly, the divergence between the average practice production function and the best practice one can be directly analyzed in terms of truncation or enlargement of the efficiency subset $\hat{D}_{m+1}(p^*)$.

2.5   Distribution of Technical and Price Efficiency

We have seen before that in both Farrell's approach and the DEA model the efficiency surface defined e.g., by (2.1) may be viewed as a set of efficiency facets, one facet for each k where k=1,2,...,n is one of the n units. Thus an independent measure of technical efficiency can be obtained for each sample observation. In his empirical application to British agricultural production Farrell applied two methods e.g,. the grouping method and the overall method to estimate the empirical frequency distribution of the efficiency ratios $E_j = y_j/y_j^*$ where y_j^* is the optimal output (i.e., maximum output technically feasible). The grouping method based on homogeneous sets of subsamples yielded a J-shaped empirical distribution, which was considered to be more plausible by Farrell than the bimodal distribution which was found by the overall method.

The Johansen model utilizes the capacity distribution to define technical efficiency. Thus the efficiency in this model is specified by the LP model:

$$\text{Max } Y = \sum_{j=1}^{n} y_j$$

subject to $\quad \sum_{j=1}^{n} y_j \tilde{a}_{ji} \leq V_i, \, i = 1, 2, \ldots, m$

$$0 \leq y_j \leq y_j^0, \, j = 1, 2, \ldots, \ldots, n$$

where Y is the aggregate (industry) output, $V_i = \sum_{j=1}^{n} x_{ji}$ the aggregate input of type i

and the index set $I_n = \{1,2,\ldots,m\}$ refers to n firms (or units) each with capacity output

y_j^0 assumed given. Given the data set of inputs (x_{ji}) and capacity outputs (y_j^0), the

input coefficients $\tilde{a}_{ji} = x_{ji}/y_j^0$ characterizing the production frontier can be computed

and hence the optimal output levels y_j^* determined.

Johansen considers the stochastic situation when the input coefficient vector $\tilde{a}_j$ is

distributed across firms in a certain way i.e., the capacity distribution. Unlike the Farrell

approach he computes the optimal output vector $y^* = (y_j^*)$, which can be directly com-

pared with the observed output. Some empirical estimates of this capacity distribution in

Swedish dairy industry have been reported by Muysken [28] under the simplifying

assumption that the industry has only one variable input, labor and each production unit

has a fixed amount of capacity output y in the short run and a fixed labor productivity α.

The labor productivity has a maximum value α^0. The capacity distribution of the

production units in the industry is then specified by the distribution δ of capacity output

of the industry in terms of the labor productivity of the units ie.,

$$\delta(\alpha; \alpha^0, \theta) > 0 \text{ for } 0 < \alpha < \alpha^0$$

where α^0 and θ denote its set of parameters. Thus the capacity distribution is defined

such that the sum $\int_{L}^{H} \delta(\alpha; \alpha^0, \theta) d\alpha$ specifies the aggregate capacity output of all units

whose productivities lie in the interval $L < \alpha < H$. Assuming profit maximization at

given prices the aggregate short-run production function for the industry can be derived

as we have seen before. It takes the following generic form:

$$Y/C = F(\frac{\alpha^0 V}{C}; \theta)$$

where C is the aggregate capacity output of the industry having Y as its aggregate output

and V for its aggregate employment.

Maximum likelihood methods of estimating the parameters (α^0, θ) are discussed by

Muysken assuming that the capacity distribution $\delta = \delta(\alpha; \alpha^0, \theta)$ follows a beta density.

Note that the Johansen model could be interpreted as an optimal process of

allocating the aggregate inputs V_i between the different firms or units. Thus if some

inputs are not transferable across firms, one may consider additional restrictions leading

to second best solutions.

The method of computing optimal output levels (y_j^*) in this model can be directly

applied to the data envelopment approach of the Farrell model as follows. Given the data

set (x_{ji}, y_j) and the input levels x_{0i} of the reference unit, we may seek an optimal level of

output (y_o^*) for the reference unit, if it exists by solving the following LP model with

respect to y_o and $\beta = (\beta_i)$:

$$y_0^* = \max_{\beta} \{ \sum_{i=1}^{m} \beta_i x_{0i} - y_0 \geq \sum_{i=1}^{m} \beta_i x_{ji} - y_j, \qquad j = 1, \dots, n\}$$

Let $X = \{x_{ji}, j \in I_n; i \in I_m\}$ be the set of feasible inputs and $Y^* = \{y_0^*$ for every feasible

$x \in X$} be the set of optimal outputs. Then Y^* specifying the *undominated convex hull* may be interpreted as the competitive output frontier. It should be noted that the value of the undominated hull at the input-mix of the reference unit (x_{0i}) is here computed from the inputs and outputs of all other units except the reference unit. For this reason, units with outputs *below* the undominated hull (i.e., undominated or indomitable units) can be found as well as outputs *above* the undominated hull (i.e., dominated units). This may be seen very clearly if an average representative unit with mean inputs $\bar{x}_i$ is taken as the reference unit; then we would obtain

$$\bar{y}^* = \max_{\beta} \; \{ \bar{y} \mid \sum_{i=1}^{m} \beta_i \bar{x}_i - \bar{y} \geq \sum_{i=1}^{m} \beta_i x_{ji} - y_j, \quad j \in I_n \}$$

This can also be obtained as the solution to the dual minimization problem:

$$\bar{y}^* = \min_{\lambda} \; \{ \sum_{j=1}^{n} \lambda_j y_j \mid \sum_{j=1}^{n} \lambda_j x_{ji} \geq \bar{x}_i, \; \Sigma \lambda_j = 1 \}$$

Again the distribution of $\bar{y}^*$ for every feasible $x \in X$ in the input space can be plotted in a frequency diagram and the scatter-plot of the residuals from the undominated convex hull $(\bar{y}^* - y)$ may be analyzed to test either the explanatory usefulness of the representative unit, or to locate possible sources of heteroscedasticity due possibly to exogeneous inputs not already incorporated. It is clear that this method provides a mechanism through which the points which are close to the production frontier are allowed to play their explanatory roles. The J-model in its simpler version

$$Y^* = \max_{y} \; \{ \sum_{j=1}^{n} y_j \mid \sum_{j=1}^{n} y_j \tilde{a}_j \leq V, \quad y \geq 0 \} \tag{2.42}$$

has some interesting economic implications of a competitive equilibrium, if we impose the market clearing conditions for aggregate output $Y = Y_s = Y_D$, where $Y_s = \Sigma y_j$ and $Y_D = g_1 - h_1 p$, p being the price of output common to al the n firms, which are assumed to be price-takers. Hence we obtain the inverse demand function:

$$p = g - h \Sigma y_j, \ g = g_1/h_1, \ h = 1/h_1 \qquad (2.43)$$

on using which the J-model can be viewed as:

$$\max_{y} \ \sum_{j=1}^{n} p y_j = gY - hY^2$$

$$\text{s. t.} \ \sum_{j=1}^{n} \tilde{a}_{ji} y_j \leq V_i, \ i \in I_m; \ y_j \geq 0; \ j \in I_n \qquad (2.44)$$

Note that this is a quadratic programming model, hence it does not have the dimensionality restriction of an optimal basis of an LP model. Also if the shadow price (b_i^*) of V_i and the optimal output level y_j^* are positive, then we obtain for a given set of the input coefficients $\tilde{a}_j$, the following Kuhn-Tucker conditions

$$Y^* = \Sigma \ y_j^* = (2h)^{-1} \{g - \sum_i \tilde{a}_{ji} b_i^*\}$$

$$V_i = \sum_j \tilde{a}_{ji} y_j^*, \ i \in I_m$$

It is clear that for all positive levels of aggregate output $Y = \Sigma y_j$ the price variable p is defined by (2.43). Given this p we solve the LP model (2.42) to obtain $y^* = (y_j^*)$ and hence $Y^* = \Sigma \ y_j^*$. The mapping $F(y): y \to p \to y^*$ can easily be shown to be an upper semi-continuous and convex function from the compact feasible set S of (2.44) into itself such that for all p in S, the set F(p) is nonempty and convex. Hence by Brouwer-Kakutani fixed point theorem there must exist a p* in S such that $p^* \in F(p^*)$.

Thus for every set of optimal vectors y* of the J-model (2.42), one could generate a set of prices p* of a suitable model of competitive equilibrium.

The advantage of this formulation is two-fold. One is that the implications of noncooperative game-theoretic equilibria e.g., Cournot-Nash equilibria can be easily analyzed in this framework. Secondly, one could introduce an additive error component to the inverse demand function (2.43) above and then compute its impact on the optimal solutions of the Johansen model.

The distribution of price efficiency can also be analyzed by imposing demand constraints in the Johansen or Farrell model (i.e., outputs produced must satisfy a set of demand constraints) and computing the scatter of shadow prices [29,30]. This is particularly useful in analyzing unemployment and underemployment of labor inputs under conditions of demand uncertainty.

References

1. Timmer, C.P. Using a probabilistic frontier production to measure technical efficiency. Journal of Political Economy, 79 (1971), 776-794.

2. Bloomfield, P. and Steiger, W.L. Absolute Deviations: Theory, Applictaions and Algorithms, Boston: Birkhauser Publishing, 1983.

3. Dodge, Y. (ed.) Statistical Data Analysis Based on the L_1-Norm and Related Methods, New York: Elsevier Science Pubishers, 1987.

4. Schmidt, P. and Sickles, R.C. Production frontier and panel data, Journal of Business and Economic Statistics, 2 (1984), 367-374.

5. Charnes, A., Cooper, W.W. and Rhodes, E. Measuring the efficiency of decision-making units, European Journal of Operational Research, 2 (1978), 429-444.

6. Sengupta, J.K. and Sfeir, R.E. Efficiency measurement by data envelopment analysis with econometric applications, Appiled Economics, 20 (1988), 285-294.

7. Sengupta, J.K. The measurement of productive efficiency: a robust minimax approach, Managerial and Decision Economics, 9 (1988), 153-161.

8. Sengupta, J.K. A robust approach to the measurement of Farrell efficiency, Applied Economics, 20 (1988), 273-283.

9. Goldfeld, S.M. and Quandt, R.E. Some tests for homoscedasticity, Journal of American Statistical Association, 60 (1965), 539-547.

10. Debreu, G. The coefficient of resource utilization, Econometrica, 19 (1951), 273-292.

11. Rosenberg, B. and Carlson, D. The sampling distribution of least absolute residuals in regression estimates, Mimeographed paper, University of California, Berkeley.

12. Dielman, T. and Pfaffenberger, R. Least absolute value estimation in linear regression: a review, in S.H. Zianakis and J.S. Rustagi (eds.) Optimization in Statistics, Amsterdam: North Holland, 1982.

13. Koenker, R. A comparison of asymptotic testing methods for L_1-regression, in V. Dodge (ed), Statistical Data Analysis Based on the L_1-norm and Related Methods, New York: Elsevier Science Publishers, 1987.

14. Karwan, M.H., Lotfi, V., Telgen, J. and Zionts, S. Redundancy in Mathematical Programming, Berlin: Springer-Verlag, 1983.

15. Blau, R.A. Random-payoff two-person zero-sum games, Operations Research, 22 (1974), 1243-1251.

16. Charnes, A., Kirby, M. and Raike, W. Chance-constrained games with partially controllable strategies, Operations Research, 16 (1968), 142-149.

17. Johansen, L. Cores, aggressiveness and the breakdown of cooperation in economic games, Journal of Economic Behavior and Organization, 3 (1982), 1-37.

18. Banker, R.D. and Maindiratta, A. Piecewise loglinear estimation of efficient production surfaces, Management Science, 32 (1986), 126-135.

19. Charnes, A., Cooper, W.W., Seiford, L. and Stutz, J. A multipicative model for efficiency analysis, Journal of Socio-Economic Planning Science, 16 (1982), 223-224.

20. Sengupta, J.K. Nonlienar measures of technical efficiency, Forthcoming in Computers and Operations Research (1988).

21. Bowlin, W.F., Charnes, A., Cooper, W.W. and Sherman, H.D. Data envelopment analysis and regression approaches to efficiency estimation and evaluation, in R.G. Thompson and R.M. Thrall (eds.) Normative Analysis in Policy Decisions: Public and Private, Basel: Baltzer, A.G. Pubishers, 1985.

22. Banker, R.D. Stochastic data envelopment analysis, mimeo report December 1, 1986, Carnegie-Mellon University.

23. Banker, R.D., Charnes, A. and Cooper, W.W. Models for the estimation of technical and scale inefficiencies in data envelopment analysis, Management Science, 30 (1984), 1078-1092.

24. Afriat, S.N. Efficiency estimation of production functions, International Economic Review, 13 (1972), 568-598.

25. Varian, H.R. The nonparametric approach to production analysis, Econometrica, 52 (1984), 579-598.

26. Diewert, W.E. and Parkan, C. Tests for the consistency of consumer data, Journal of Econometrics, 30 (1985), 127-147.

27. Banker, R.D. and Maindiratta, A. Nonparametric analysis of technical and allocative efficiencies, forthcoming in Econometrica (1988).

28. Muysken, J. Estimation of the capacity distribution of an industry: the Swedish dairy industry 1964-1973, in F.R. Forsund, M. Hoel and S. Longva (eds.) Production, Multi-sectoral Growth and Planning, New York: Elsevier Science Publishers, 1985.

29. Fraser, R. Demand uncertainty and unemployment, Oxford Economic Papers 36 (1984), 27-36.

30. Sengupta, J.K. Data envelopment analysis for efficiency measurement in the stochastic case, Computers and Operations Research, 14 (1987), 117-129.

Chapter 3

INTERFACE WITH PARAMETRIC THEORY

The nonparametric approach to efficiency measurement has several levels of interaction with the parametric theory e.g., specification, aggregation and econometric estimation. Although the linear programming (LP) specification was used by both Farrell, Johansen and the founders of the DEA model, one could certainly use nonlinear and parametric specifications for the frontier functions. For example one could reformulate Johansen's model as

$$\text{Max} \sum_{j=1}^{n} y_j \quad \text{s. t.} \sum_{j=1}^{n} f_{ji}(x, \theta) y_j \leq V_i, \quad i \in I_m$$

$$0 \leq y_j \leq y_j^0, \qquad j \in I_n$$

where $f_{ji}(x,\theta)$ is a nonlinear convex function of the inputs per unit of capacity outputs containing the parameters θ, of which the linear approximation is $\tilde{a}_j = (\tilde{a}_{ji})$ as defined in (2.42). These parametric and nonlinear specifications have to be defended of course either in terms of predictive power or, technical features of production. At the level of aggregation the problem is one of combining the unit-specific efficiency measures proposed by the DEA and Farrell models e.g., (2.1). Timmer added the individual objective functions to define the mean objective function of (2.5) e.g.,

$$\min \bar{g} = \sum_{i=1}^{m} \bar{x}_i \beta_i$$

whereas Johansen aggregated the micro units through the capacity distribution and its domains of utilization. Different types of clustering methods [1,2] utilize different rules of aggregation different from the above, and in particular, the nonparametric clustering techniques based on suitable distance functions are also applicable. For the estimation of the frontier one could again apply a parametric method based on the assumption of a specific distribution of the error term, or of the inputs and outputs, or a nonparametric method which is more or less distribution free.

3.1   Average vs. Optimal Production Function

One major interface with the parametric theory is provided by the comparison of an average production function based on all data points with a production frontier which uses only those data points which satisfy the efficiency hypothesis. Three types of issues have been posed here. One is the comparison of the ordinary regression models with the DEA model [3], where the latter has shown several aspects of superiority in empirical studies in terms of goodness of fit and other criteria. Second, the piecewise linear and loglinear forms of the frontier used in the DEA model [4,5] have been more successful in locating the relative inefficiencies of micro units than the average regression approach. Third, the models of efficiency of Farrell and DEA have been used to generate subsets of data points or clusters such that some clusters are closer to the average regression approach and some are not. Since this latter aspect has wider scope of potential applications, it is worth discussing further.

We must note at the outset that when suitably interpreted, the method of convex closure of the efficient points specified by the programming framework of the Farrell and DEA models may be utilized to stratify the heterogeneous data structure into two subsets, one more efficient than the other and then separate regressions may be run over the two subsets. Such comparisons of the DEA model with the regression approach of econometrics would clearly show the extent to which the production frontier differs from the average production function estimate. This difference can also be assessed by analyzing the role of dummy variables in frontier production function studies. A dummy variable e.g., one for efficient units and zero for others, provides here a nonparametric procedure for econometrically testing the hypothesis that the observed input-output data are consistent with a production frontier. This procedure is more general than that of

Hanoch and Rothschild [6] who considered only nonstatistical tests to see if the observed input-output data are consistent with a production frontier hypothesis.

Our objective in this section is twofold: to present a brief overview of the DEA model and its linkages with the average production function estimated by the standard regression method, and to show the usefulness of the Farrell and DEA models by relating their optimal solutions to generate one or more dummy variables which can be used as regressors with high explanatory power. These two objectives provide an indirect test of the sensitivity and robustness of the parameter estimates obtained by a constrained linear programming (LP) method of estimation following from the DEA model. This LP method of estimation is appiled empirically to measure and evaluate the relative efficiency of selected public schools in an urban school district in California with 25 DMUs, where the single output variable (y) is in terms of achievement scores of sixth grade pupils and the four inputs selected are average teacher salary (x_1), proportion of Anglo-American students in class (x_2), average class size (x_3) and a proxy variable (x_4) denoting parental background. The sample set of 25 units was selected from a larger set (as referred to in earlier chapters) for the academic year 1977-78 in order to retain more homogeneity e.g., very small rural schools with less than six teachers per school were deleted.

Consider the programming framework of a DEA model, where we assume that each of n DMUs has input output vectors (x_j, y_j) of dimensions m and r respectively and we define the efficiency ratio by h_j:

$$h_j = (\sum_{i=1}^{r} u_i y_{ij})/(\sum_{s=1}^{m} v_s x_{sj}) \tag{3.1}$$

$$s=1,2,...,m; \quad i=1,2,...,r; \quad j=1,2,...,n$$

Let k be the reference DMU which is to be compared in efficiency relative to other DMUs in the cluster. Then we solve for the optimal values of vectors u and v:

$$\underset{u,\, v\, \geq\, 0}{\text{Max}} \; \{h_k = h_k(u, v) : h_j \leq 1; u, v \geq 0; j = 1, 2,. \ldots, n\} \tag{3.2}$$

For any fixed k, where k may be parametrically varied as k=1,2,...,n this involves solving mathematical programs which are known as linear functional fractional programs, which by suitable transformations can be reduced to LP models. Let $u^* = u^*(k)$ and $v^* = v^*(k)$ be the optimal solution vectors for the k-th DMU belonging to the cluster of n units and h_k^* be the maximal value of the objective function. It can be shown that if the observed input and output vectors are all positive and known constants i.e., they imply optimal behavior in the given environment, then the optimal set $\{u^*(k), v^*(k), h_k^*\}$ would exist.

If for any k, $1 \leq k \leq n$ we have $0 < h_k^* < 1$, then the k-th DMU is not efficient relative to others in the cluster and hence the entire set of input-output data is not consistent with the efficiency hypothesis. Thus $\delta_k^* = 1 - h_k^*$ may be used as a measure of inefficiency i.e., a measure of violation of the efficiency hypothesis for the k-th unit. Two implications of this measure are useful in economic terms. One is that h_k^* is associated with the optimal vectors $u^*(k)$, $v^*(k)$ which may be interpreted either as optimal weights or optimal shadow prices. Thus if h_k^* cannot attain the value 1.0, which characterizes the efficient DMUs, it cannot be efficient for any other optimal vectors $u^*(q)$, $v^*(q)$ where $q \neq k$ and $1 \leq q \leq n$. One could thus use this efficiency measure to rank the set of n DMUs in an efficiency scale from the lowest to the highest, provided the reference DMU is representative. Secondly, the DEA model (3.2) clearly defines a nonparametric procedure through its specification of the convex closure of the efficient points. This can then be directly compared with the production frontier approach or the statistical approach of an average production function.

Now consider for simplicity the framework where each DMU has one output but m inputs and the DEA method seeks to determine a vector of optimal weights in terms of which any reference unit can be compared in efficiency.

Let x_{ij} denote the quantity of input i=1,2,...,m and y_j be the single output for j-th DMU (j=1,2,...,n). Then the DEA model as we saw before, may be reduced to the following LP model:

$$\min_{\beta} \ g_k = \sum_{i=1}^{m} \beta_i x_{ik}$$

subject to
$$\sum_{i=1}^{m} \beta_i x_{ij} \geq y_j; \qquad j = 1, 2, \ldots, n \tag{3.3}$$

$$\beta_i \geq 0; \quad i=1,2,\ldots,m$$

By letting the reference DMU index k vary over 1,2,...,n one may determine n optimal weights $\beta^*(k)$, k=1,2,...,n for the inputs. In empirical applications the observed input and output quantities are generally positive and hence there always exist a feasible solution and therefore a feasible optimal vector $\beta^* = \beta^*(k)$, for k=1,2,...,n. Two interpretations of the optimal vector β are useful in economic terms. The first and perhaps the most important is that they are statistical estimates of the parameters defining a production frontier. Define $\hat{y}_j = \sum_{i=1}^{m} \beta_i x_{ij}$ as the points on the production frontier and express any output level y_j as

$$y_j = \hat{y}_j - e_j$$

with
$$\tag{3.4}$$

$$e_j \geq 0 \quad j=1,2,\ldots,n$$

where e_j is the random disturbance term.

It is clear that

$$\hat{y}_j = \sum_{i=1}^{m} \beta_i x_{ij} \geq y_j \qquad j = 1, 2, \ldots, n \tag{3.5}$$

and it is only the efficient units which will satisfy the relationship (3.3) with an equality. In order to estimate the parameters β_i in (3.3) one has to note that the errors (e_j) are constrained to be nonnegative. Although one could minimize the sum of squared errors,

$\sum_{j=1} e_j^2$ in order to obtain the estimates of β_i i.e., adopt the ordinary least squares (OLS) principle but this would have two undesirable consequences. One is that it would accentuate the extreme observations and therefore distort the estimate of the efficiency frontier. Secondly, the errors under the nonnegativity constraint are no longer symmetric around the mean and hence the LS principle usually based on the normality of distribution of errors is no longer appropriate. One attractive alternative is to adopt the criterion of minimum sum of absolute errors, which in this case leads to minimizing the sum

$\sum_{j=1} e_j$ subject to (3.5). This leads to the mean LP model for estimating β_i, which was first used by Timmer [7]:

$$\min_{\beta} \ \bar{g} = \sum_{i=1}^{m} \beta_i \bar{x}_i$$

subject to $\quad \sum_{i=1}^{m} \beta_i x_{ij} \geq y_j; \qquad j = 1, 2, \ldots, n$ (3.6)

$$\beta_i \geq 0; \quad i = 1, 2, \ldots, n$$

A second interpretation considers the β^* coefficients as the parameters of a suitable production function, which can thus be easily related to the econometric theory of a stochastic production frontier. Recently Banker, Charnes, Cooper and Schinnar [4] have attempted to incorporate the problem of statistical estimation of a production frontier in the DEA model. The data variation problem they consider arises in those situations where one has reason to assume that the concept of a parametric production function (e.g., a Cobb-Douglas type function) is reasonable for the n DMUs and the object is to estimate the parameters of the frontier production function by a DEA model. Such attempts at combining ordinary regression approach to estimate a parametric production function with the DEA model have generally produced better results in estimating the frontier function through more systematic screening of relatively inefficient units from the data set.

One important aspect of the Farrell and DEA models is the manner in which the stochastic components e_j in (3.3) affect the parameter estimates of β. This has two econometric implications. One is the issue of robustness for the estimates $\hat{\beta}$ of the parameter vector, since one needs to compute n LP models of the type (3.3) to generate n optimal vectors $\hat{\beta}^*(k)$, k=1,2,...,n. Second, these LP estimates of the frontier production function fail to utilize any information from the sample units which are very close to the efficient units e.g., 95 to 99% close. This is so because by the optimal basis theorem of an LP model, at most m of the n units (m<n) can be efficient. Thus for n DMUs and 4 inputs, at most 4 DMUs can be efficient in the sense $\sum_{i=1}^{4} \beta_i x_{ij} = y_j$, j=1,...,4. In degenerate cases even less than 4 DMUs may turn out to be efficient. The (n-4) other sample DMUs turn out to be redundant in this method of efficiency estimation. It is clear that any increase in sample size is of no consequence, so long as the original DMUs remain efficient as defined.

From an applied viewpoint the robustness of constrained estimates obtained from LP models (3.3) may be analyzed in several ways as follows. First, we obtain on the basis of this LP model n estimates of the m-element vector $\beta^* = \beta^*(k)$, k=1,2,...,n where the condition n > m is assumed for identification. For each k we determine which m DMUs are 100% efficient in the sense $\sum_{i=1}^{m} \beta_i x_{ij} = y_j$, j=1,2,...,m. Denote this set by M = $\{m_k: k=1,...,n\}$. We select m units out of M by the rule of highest frequency of occurrence. For example if m = 4, we select the first unit if it occurs most often in the set M i.e., the mode, then the second unit if it occurs next most often and so on up to the fourth unit. We thus define a modal subset of m DMUs out of n and then construct the mean inputs $\tilde{x}_i$ by averaging over the units in this modal subset. This yields the objective function $\widetilde{g} = \sum\limits_{i=1}^{m} \beta_i \widetilde{x}_i$. The final LP model then becomes

$$\min_{\beta} \widetilde{g} = \sum_{i=1}^{m} \beta_i \widetilde{x}_i$$

subject to $\quad \sum\limits_{i=1}^{m} \beta_i x_{ij} \geq y_j; \qquad\qquad j = 1, 2, \ldots, n \quad (3.7)$

$$\beta_i \geq 0, \quad i=1,2,\ldots,m$$

Note that this formulation is identical with that of (3.6), if the two averages $\{\overline{x}_i\}$ and $\{\widetilde{x}_i\}$ lead to an identical optimal basis i.e., $\quad \overline{\beta}^* = \widetilde{\beta}^*$ where $\overline{\beta}^*, \widetilde{\beta}^*$ are the optimal solution vectors of (3.6) and (3.7) respectively. Those estimates of $\beta^*(k)$, k=1,2,...,n which are very close to either $\overline{\beta}^*$ or $\widetilde{\beta}^*$ may then be characterized as robust.

A second way of evaluating robustness is by the outlier principle of multivariate statistics using a distance statistic. To fix ideas consider the LP model (3.6) where mean inputs $\overline{x}_i$ are used in the objective function in place of x_{ik}, k=1,2,...,n. If the DMUs refer to a more or less homogeneous cluster, the input vector $X_k = (x_{ik})$ would tend to center around a mean (or median) level with a certain degree of dispersion around the central location. The probabilistic data generating model may then take the following form

$$X_k = \overline{x} + \varepsilon_k, \qquad k = 1, 2, \ldots, n$$

where $\overline{x} = (\overline{x}_i)$ is the mean input vector and ε_k is a random disturbance term. If the probability distribution of ε_k is such that it has a zero mean and a finite variance-covariance matrix V_ε, then one can easily characterize how closely the observed input vector points X_k are scattered around its mean $\overline{x}$. This may be easily done through the multivariate distance function $D^2 = D^2(x; \overline{x}, V_\varepsilon)$ defined as follows:

$$D^2 = D^2(x; \bar{x}, V_\varepsilon) = (x - \bar{x})V_\varepsilon^{-1}(x - \bar{x})$$

where it is assumed that the variance-covariance matrix V_ε is nonsingular and the notation x has been used to denote any vector in the set $\{X_k: k=1,2,...,n\}$. Thus if all X_k in the cluster are very close to the mean, the value of D^2 will be close to zero. The higher the value of D^2, the farther the points are scattered away from the mean level. The role of the variance-covariance matrix V_ε is more subtle however. It has two practical implications. One is that it acts as a filtering device, whereby with noisy data any difference $x_i - \bar{x}_i$ is deflated or corrected in terms of its standard errors, so that the squared distance between x and $\bar{x}$ can be ore realiably computed. Secondly, if the underlying probability distribution of the errors ε can be assumed to be normal (e.g., under certain conditions by the central limit theorem), then the random quantity D^2 above is known to follow a chi-square distribution with m degrees of freedom if the variance-covariance matrix V_ε is known. Thus one may choose a level of significance α and determine a suitable positive scalar $c = c_\alpha$ such that X defines a confidence region

$$X = \{x: D^2(x; \bar{x}, V_\varepsilon) \leq c_\alpha\}$$

in the sense that for any set of points x belonging to region X we have $Prob(x \in X) = \alpha$. By varying α one can therefore vary the size of the neighborhood around $\bar{x}$. We have already discussed in Chapter 2 the various uses of the distance statistic D^2.

Even when normality does not hold for the input vector, the asymptotic distribution of the LAV estimators $\bar{\beta}*$ can be utiilzed [8,9] for comparing two sample groups.

There is an alternative way of analyzing the n LP models (3.3) of the DEA system. First, one can identify for each sample the maximum frequency of occurrence as an efficient unit with no redundancy in the n LP models (3.3). Then arrange each sample in a decreasing order of the frequency of occurrence as an efficient unit and finally we choose m of these ordered samples as an "efficient subset". One could enlarge this subset by adding m+1, m+2 and other ordered samples. For each such ordered samples of sizes m, m+1, m+2,...,n one could run regressions of output on the m inputs to obtain various estimates of the production function. It is clear that as we move away from the efficient subset by adding more samples, we would diverge from a production frontier more and more till we obtain an average production function containing both efficient and inefficient units. Secondly, one could evaluate the role of the efficient subset by running a regression of the observed output (y) on the m inputs (x_i) and a zero-one dummy variable D_j

$$y_j = \sum_{i=1}^{m} x_{ij} \beta_i + \alpha D_j + c$$

where   (3.8)

$$D_j = \begin{cases} 1, \text{ if } j \text{ belongs to the "efficient subset"} \\ 0, \text{ otherwise} \end{cases}$$

c = intercept term

As the sample size increases by incuding less and less efficient units (i.e., units having very low frequency of occurrence as efficient units and/or having high redundancy in strong or weak form), the value R^2 of squared multiple correlation coefficient should decline more and more till it reaches an average level that is consistent with an average production function.

The dummy variable method can be applied in a much simpler way if we restrict ourselves to the DEA model (3.6), where the objective function may be interpreted as a representative firm which represents the cluster of n units or firms so to say. In this case we have one LP model and hence one vector $\bar{\beta}^*$ of parameters. Assuming nondegeneracy of the optimal basic solution, the first m units of the ordered samples comprise the "efficient subset" now. Thus the dummy variable D_j would now act as a sample stratifying index, according as the sample belongs to the efficient subset or not. By dividing the entire sample into several strata and then running separate production regressions over each stratum, one could evaluate the extent of discrepancy between the production frontier and the average production function. The potential sources of such discrepancy may of course be several e.g., nonnormal output disturbances with high skewness and kurtosis, implicit stochastic constraints introduced by the linear restrictions and above all the fact that the dummy variable is not directly observed but imputed through a specific LP model formulation. Empirically however it is possible to analyze the frequency distribution of this discrepancy, just as the residual errors are tested for a fitted regression model.

In order to illustrate the above we consider now an empirical application which utilizes input output data in logarithmic units for the selected public elementary schools in California for the year 1977-78, over which separate estimates were reported in earlier chapters. On the basis of this data set, we compute 25 LP models of the form (3.3) and one LP model of the form (3.6) and also several sets of OLS (ordinary least squares) estimates of the average production function which are then compared with LAV estimates obtained from the LP models. Four sets of tests are performed as follows:

(1) Test 1 considers all DMUs with serial numbers 1 through 25 and selects four DMUs which have the highest frequency of occurrence as an efficient unit in the cluster. For this test, nondegenerate LPs are separated from the degenerate ones i.e., the former has four positive elements in the solution vector, the latter having three or less. It is clear that in the nondegenerate cases, the units not selected in the optimal solution satisfy the strong form of redundancy defined before.

(2) For Test 2 we use the optimal outputs from the LP models (3.6) to rank the 25 units in a decreasing order of efficiency where efficiency is defined by the ratio y_j/y_j^* of observed to optimal output. The sample set is then divided into 6 groups with 4 units each in first five groups and 5 units in the sixth group. Thus the first group contained the 100% efficient units, the second group next four efficient (but less than 100%) units and so on till the sixth group contained the least efficient units. Six LP models from $LP_{(1)}$

through $LP_{(6)}$ are computed with these mean input vectors $\bar{x}_{(1)}$ through $\bar{x}_{(6)}$ in the objective function of the LP model (3.6). This test is designed to analyze the sensitivity of the optimal β^* coefficients for the different mean input vectors in the objective function; also we allow truncation in the sample space, where 4 units from the top are successively deleted (these deletions are done up to sample size n =13) from both the constraints and the objective function thus generating four LP models with n = 25, 21, 17 and 13. These four LP models are designed to evaluate the effect of truncation in the sample space on the optimal coefficients β^* which characterize the production frontier.

(3)   Test 3 constructs an efficient subset of DMUs or, units out of the total 25 units by incuding only four or five which have the highest frequency of occurrence as an efficient unit as judged by Test 1. Contamination of this efficient subset by including more units which are less frequently efficient (or more frequently inefficient) is then tested by two methods. One is the OLS method where the output score is regressed on the four inputs. The second is the dummy variable method, where an efficiency dummy D is used along with the four inputs as explanatory variables. Here D takes the value one if the sample is from the efficient subset, otherwise it takes a value zero. This test is designed to evaluate in terms of the R^2 value the extent to which reduced contamination helps improve the explanatory power of the OLS model.

(4)   For Test 4 we compute the efficiency ratio y_j/y_j^* from the optimal solutions of the LP models (3.6) and analyze its distribution over the 25 sample observations. This was the method followed by Farrell and Fieldhouse [10] in their analysis of efficiency of British agricultural farms. But unlike their approach we compare the two approaches of LP and OLS for estimating the parameters of the production response function.

Now we return to analyze the resul of Test 1 applied to generate 25 LP models of the form (3.3). In terms of the highest relative frequency of occurrence as efficient units, the DMUs with serial numbers 23, 3, 16 and 25 belong to the efficient subset, as is apparent from Table 1 below:

Table 1: Highest frequency (f) of occurrence as efficient units

Units (serial no.)	value of f(%) in LPs		
	nondegenerate	degenerate	combined
DMU_{23}	100	78	88
DMU_3	54	50	52
DMU_{16}	82	21	48
DMU_{25}	54	28	40
DMU_7	27	21	24
DMU_{12}	18	21	20
DMU_9	27	7	16

Table 2. Estimates of Production Response by

OLS Method for Selected Samples

Sample	c	β_1	β_2	β_3	β_4	R^2	DW
S_1	-11.48** (9.07)	-0.11* (2.54)	4.98** (10.17)	5.33** (10.16)	1.58** (10.28)	0.99	0.0
S_2	-1.21 (0.76)	0.24* (2.94)	1.04 (1.85)	1.042 (1.77)	0.34 (1.95)	0.96	0.62
S_3	-0.41 (0.32)	0.25* (2.81)	0.65 (1.48)	0.75 (1.67)	0.22 (1.63)	0.90	1.98
S_{10}	-0.94 (1.04)	0.27** (4.18)	0.97** (4.23)	0.86** (3.75)	0.32** (4.55)	0.77	1.81

Note: 1. Absolute values of t-statistics are in parentheses; significance at 5% and 1%

levels is denoted by one and two asterisks respectively.

2. All inputs (x_i) and output (y) are measured in natural logarithmic units.

Table 3. Sensitivity of Parameter Estimates (LP model)

A. LP estimates for six groups

	$LP_{(1)}$	$LP_{(2)}$	$LP_{(3)}$	$LP_{(4)}$	$LP_{(5)}$	$LP_{(6)}$
β_1	0.247	0.247	0.247	0.451	0.0	0.359
β_2	0.523	0.523	0.523	0.206	1.169	0.146
β_3	0.626	0.626	0.626	0.0	1.503	0.350
β_4	0.179	0.179	0.179	0.074	0.417	0.079

B. LP estimates for truncated samples

Sample Size n	β_1	β_2	β_3	β_4	
25	0.247	0.523	0.626	0.179	
21	0.151	0.804	0.935	0.276	
17	0.100	0.682	1.087	0.241	
13	<u>0.175</u>	<u>0.701</u>	<u>0.692</u>	<u>0.189</u>	
Average	0.168	0.677	0.835	0.221	
Regression Sample S_{10}	0.270	0.971	0.861	0.320	$R^2 = 0.77$

Table 4. Parameter Estimates of the Production Frontier (LP Method: Five subgroups)

Subgroup	β_1	β_2	β_3	β_4	% frequency out of nondegenerate LPs	all LPs
SS_1	0.247	0.523	0.626	0.179	27	12
SS_2	0.359	0.146	0.349	0.049	27	12
SS_3	0.452	0.206	0.0	0.074	-	12
SS_4	0.443	1.988	0.0	0.599	-	12
SS_5	0.157	0.790	0.899	0.262	18	8

Table 5. Parameter Estimates for Samples in Groups II and III (OLS method)

Sample	c	β_1	β_2	β_3	β_4	R^2	DW
S_4 (top 6)	1.298 (.067)	0.271* (3.96)	0.067 (0.09)	0.142 (0.18)	0.035 (0.15)	0.997	0.0
S_5 (top 8)	0.151 (0.28)	0.234** (6.86)	0.529* (2.45)	0.614* (2.92)	0.18* (2.65)	0.987	0.0
S_6 (top 10)	0.201 (0.26)	0.248** (5.36)	0.475 (1.73)	0.552* (2.11)	0.162 (1.88)	0.963	1.22
S_7	-1.700 (0.34)	0.602 (1.41)	0.647 (0.53)	0.073 (0.09)	0.209 (0.57)	0.96	0.0
S_8	0.282 (0.12)	0.232 (1.63)	.664 (0.83)	0.582 (0.72)	0.227 (0.92)	0.87	0.0
S_9	-0.181 (0.11)	0.218 (1.91)	0.724 (1.30)	0.773 (1.38)	0.247 (1.44)	0.84	1.27
S_{10}	-0.94 (1.04)	0.27** (4.18)	0.97** (4.23)	0.86** (3.75)	0.32** (4.55)	0.77	1.81

Table 6. Parameter Estimates by the Dummy Variable Method (equation (3.8))

Sample	c	β_1	β_2	β_3	β_4	α	R^2	DW
S_2 (n=9)	0.602 (0.43)	0.317 (4.63)	0.178 (0.32)	0.214 (0.38)	0.073 (0.41)	0.054* (2.19)	0.99	0.29
S_3 (n=15)	-0.489 (0.52)	0.291** (4.33)	0.501 (1.51)	0.644* (1.91)	0.177 (1.71)	0.055* (3.02)	0.95	1.30
S_{10} (n=25)	0.486 (0.35)	0.246* (2.67)	0.336 (0.82)	0.483 (1.21)	0.132 (1.04)	0.072* (2.27)	0.83	1.32
S_3 (n=15)	-0.413 (0.32)	0.249* (2.81)	0.651 (1.48)	0.753 (1.67)	0.224 (1.63)	-	0.90	1.98
S_{10}(LP) (n-25)	-	0.247	0.523	0.626	0.179	-	-	-

Based on these efficiency ranking we construct thre groups of samples, the first one including mainly the units mentioned in Table 1, the second including proportions of efficient units when efficiency is measured by the ratio y_j/y_j^* as in Test 2, while the third group has sample units chosen randomly.

Group I: (efficiency subsets)

S_1 includes DMUs: 3,7,9,16,23,25; (n=6)

S_2 includes S_1 and 12,13,17; (n=9)

S_3 includes S_2 and 1,2,4,5,6,8; (n=15)

Group II: (proportional selections)

S_4 includes DMUs: 3,8,9,16,23,25 (i.e., top 6)

S_5 includes S_4 and 6,13 (i.e., top 8)

S_6 includes S_5 and 4,5 (i.e., top 10)

Group III: (random selections)

S_7 includes DMUs: 3,7,10,13,23,25

S_8 includes S_7 and 16,17,19

S_9 includes S_8 and 1,2,4,5,6,8

S_{10} includes all 25 observations

The OLS estimates of the production response $y = \sum\limits_{i=1}^{4} \beta_i x_i + c$ where c is the inter-cept term and β_i is the elasticity of output with respect to the input x_i are in Table 2 for the Samples of Group I (efficiency subsets) and the overall sample S_{10} in Group III (random selections). The OLS estimates of S_1 and S_2 are not directly comparable to those of S_{10} due to very low degrees of freedom. But one can compare S_3 and S_{10} and the average of the LAV estimates for the efficient subset comprising DMU_3, DMU_{16}, DMU_{23} and DMU_{25}, which may be termed sample S_0. The results are as follows:

Sample	Estimation method	β_1	β_2	β_3	β_4	R^2
S_3	OLS	0.25	0.65	0.75	0.22	0.90
S_{10}	OLS	0.27	0.97	0.86	0.32	0.77
S_0	LAV	0.25	0.52	0.63	0.18	-

A comparison of Chi-squared values i.e., $\chi^2 = \sum\limits_{i=1}^{4} [(\beta_i^L - \beta_i^0)^2/\beta_i^0]$ where β_i^0 is the OLS estimate and β_i^L the LAV estimate shows that the two samples S_3 and S_{10} are not different from S_0 in a statistically significant sense, although S_3 is closer to S_0 than S_{10} (i.e., $\chi^2(S_3,S_0) = 0.052$ and $\chi^2(S_{10},S_0) = 0.332$).

Two points may be noted from the OLS estimates of Table 2. First, the R^2 value declines as more and more DMUs are added to the efficient subset S_1, which are less frequently efficient. Secondly, the intercept term c is always negative implying that on the average we have y < y* i.e., observed output is lower than the efficient output.

The estimated results of Test 2 reported in Table 3 show a number of results about the sensitivity of the parameter estimates. First of all, the β estimates are unaltered for the first three LP models $LP_{(1)}$ through $LP_{(3)}$, although these three groups had substantial differences in the proportion of 100% efficient units. By the chi-square test applied at 5% level, these differences proved to be nonsignificant in a statistical sense. For the last three of the six LP estimates the conclusion is reversed however. Secondly, the mean input levels in the three LP models $LP_{(1)}$ through $LP_{(3)}$ were not significantly different in a statistical sense at 5% level from the overall mean input levels of the single objective function of the LP model (3.6). This is an important result showing that this LP model may serve appropriately as a representative DMU. Note that if we exclude the degenerate cases, 3 out of 4 i.e., 75 percent turn out to have optimal β^* identical with that of the mean LP model. Thirdly, some LP estimates of β_i^* are more sensitive to truncation in the sample space than others. Truncation has the general tendency to lower the parameter estimate in the LP models compared to the OLS estimate, although for very small sample sizes this may not hold for each individual coefficient. This finding is much more stable in our case than the econometric results of Timmer [7] which were very uneven. Fourthly, it is clear from the five subgroups in the 25 LP estimates of the LP model (3.3), that the first two subgroups SS_1 and SS_2 have the highest frequency (27%) among nondegenerate cases but SS_1 is closer to the regression estimate of sample S_{10} than S_2, when closeness is measured at 5% level of the chi-square test referred to before. In this sense the LP estimate of SS_1 which is identical with the estimate of $LP_{(1)}$ in Table 3 is robust.

Between the different subgroups we reach another conclusion, when a chi-square test is made on the basis of the T^2 statistic

$$T^2_{(i),\,4} = (\beta(i) - \bar{\beta})'\, V^{-1}_{\beta(i)}(\beta(i) - \bar{\beta})$$

where $\bar{\beta}$ is the estimate for subgroup SS_1 in Table 4 and $\beta(i)$ for the three other subgroups SS_2, SS_3 and SS_4. The numerical values of $T^2_{(i)}$ with four degrees of freedom are as follows:

	SS_2	SS_3	SS_4
$T^2_{(i)}$	3.513	8.342	45.301

It is clear that SS_2 is the closest to the subgroup SS_1.

The results of Test 3 reported in Tables 5-6 show very remarkably the impact of contamination i.e., enlarging the efficient subset by including the less efficient (or less frequently efficient) units, on the individual coefficients β^*_i and their statistical significance. First of all, the OLS results (in Table 5) show very uniformly a decline in explanatory power measured by R^2 with more contamination. Secondly, as the sample size is increased from S_4 to S_6 the LP coefficients tend to stabilize along with a high R^2 value. This result is strongly reinforced by the dummy variable regression in Table 6. The regression coefficient (α) of the dummy variable D turns out to be consistently significant at 5% level of t-test clearly implying that in terms of efficiency the data set represents two subclusters, one efficient and the other less so.

Test 4 is designed to look at the overall distribution of the efficiency measures, when the mean LP model (3.6) is applied. Denote by $\bar{e}_j = 1 - e_j$ the inefficiency ratio, $e_j = y_j / y^*_j$ ($y_j \leq y^*_j$) where j=1,2,...,25 then the overall distribution of $\bar{e}_j$ appears as follows:

domain of of $\bar{e}_j$	0.03	.04-.07	.08-.11	.12-.15	.16-.19	.20 & above
frequency (%):	36	20	28	4	8	4

Clearly the distribution of inefficiency ($\bar{e}$) is asymmetrical and a Kolmogorov-Smirnov nonparametric test rejected the null hypothesis at 5% that this distribution is normal [11].

Two implications of the asymmetrical distribution above may be noted. First, the usual regression model based on the normal additive disturbances would not be very appropriate here, especially for statistical testing of any null hypothesis about the β coefficients. Second, the exponential distribution is one of the forms empirically found by Farrell and Fieldhouse in their studies on agricultural production frontier.

One way to evaluate the impact of heterogeneity of input output data is to decompose the output variable into four component scores in reading (R), writing (W), spelling (S) and Mathematics (M) and use the same four independent variables in a regression model. The empirical results are as follows:

	c	β_1	β_2	β_3	β_4	R^2
R	-0.77	0.25*	0.85*	0.86*	0.29*	0.76
	(.75)	(3.46)	(3.08)	(3.19)	(3.43)	
W	-0.30	0.15*	1.15**	1.02*	0.38**	0.76
	(.30)	(2.11)	(4.33)	(3.90)	(4.65)	
S	-0.48	0.32**	0.80*	0.62*	0.27*	0.61
	(.49)	(4.55)	(2.94)	(2.36)	(3.08)	
M	-2.58*	0.38**	1.14**	0.96*	0.38**	0.74
	(2.11)	(4.35)	(3.49)	(3.01)	(3.76)	
Average	-1.032	0.275	0.985	0.865	0.330	____
Overall regression (S_{10})	-0.94	0.27**	0.97**	0.86**	0.32**	0.77
	(1.04)	(4.18)	(4.23)	(3.75)	(4.55)	

It is clear that the average regression estimate based on the four component scores is very close to the overall regression estimate based on sample S_{10} and the sample S_{10} is very close to the LP estimates $LP_{(1)}$ through $LP_{(3)}$ in Table 3. In general however the estimates of β_i coefficients by the LP model are lower than the regression estimates.

If we regress the efficiency ratio ($e_j = y_j/y_j^*$ where $y_j^* = \sum\limits_{i=1}^{4} \beta_i \bar{x}_i$) on the four inputs $\bar{x}_1$ through $\bar{x}_4$, the squared multiple correlation coefficient R^2 never exceeds the value 0.42, if the samples are randomly selected out of n=25. However if the efficient units are selected either by the LP model (3.3) or (3.6) or, by the dummy variable method, the value of R^2 jumps to at least 0.80 or more. This shows that the DEA model of efficiency ranking and measurement could prove valuable in improving regression estimates by suitable clustering of data sets into groups, efficient and not so efficient.

3.2 Estimation of Production Frontier

Since the production frontier can be specified either as parametric (P) or non-parametric (N) functional forms and the econometric estimation can be based on either a specified error distribution in a parametric form (P) or, a nonparametric class of distributions (N), we have four cases: P/P, P/N, N/P and N/N. Thus the case N/P arises when e.g., we have n LP models in the DEA system (3.3) and we compute parametric regression models in the form (3.8). Likewise the case N/N arises when e.g., we apply the DEA model (3.3) in the specification stage and then from the set of optimal solutions of the r (r $\leq$ n) LP models we may apply the nonparametric regression method by nonparametrically estimating the density of the error term e_j defined in (3.3). Empirical estimation of the frontier production function has however faced two major problems. One is the lack of any a priori knowledge as to which units are efficient and which are not, thus the ordinary least squares method of regression becomes inapplicable. Secondly, the maximum level of output is only a hypothetical concept much like the potential output, which is not as observable as the actual realized output. Thus for the inefficient units the maximum output level may appear sometimes to be a distant goal. One shortcoming of the DEA model, first emphasized by Farrell [12] is that the LP method of convex hull estimation of the production frontier involves a great waste of information, since only a handful of the so-called "efficient" units or observations contribute directly to the estimate of the parameters, the rest being ignored. Increasing the sample size may thus be of very little consequence, if the optimal basis associated with the efficient subset remains unaltered. Secondly, the standard statistical criteria of estimating efficiency through the standard error of the estimator are usually not available here when the LP method of estimation is followed. Hence one cannot effectively perform any statistical comparison of alternative estimates of efficiency.

We propose here three operational criteria for efficiency comparisons in the DEA framework. Our first criterion of comparison is derived from the fact that in (3.3) we have n LP models where the constraint set is the same but the objective function is different i.e., one for each of n DMUs. Thus we have r ($r \leq n$) sets of optimal vectors $\beta^*(k)$, k=1,2,...,r for each of which we can associate an optimal basis $B^*(k)$. Let us write the objective function (3.3) for the reference unit as

$$\min \ g_k = \sum_{i=1}^{m} (\bar{x}_i + u_k)\beta_i$$

where $x_{ki} = \bar{x}_i + u_k$ is viewed as the sum of the mean input level $\bar{x}_i = (1/n)$ $\sum_{k=1}^{n} x_{ki}$ and the deviation or error component u_k. Clearly if the scatter x_{ki} of points are closely centered around the mean level $\bar{x}_i$, then the set of optimal basic matrices $B^*(k)$ would be identical with the optimal basis $\bar{B}^*$ associated with the mean inputs $\bar{x}_i$ say. In other words we may rank the set of optimal bases $B^*(k)$ in terms of their frequency of occurrence. Let $B^*_{(0)}$ denote the *modal* optimal basis where $\beta^*_{(0)}$ has the highest frequency of occurrence. Clearly the lowest frequency is 1/n, when all the n optimal bases are distinct and the highest possible frequency is unity, when $x_{ki} = \bar{x}_i$ for all k and we have the identical optimal basis denoted by $\bar{B}^*$ above. For the next highest frequency of occurrence the optimal basis may be denoted by $B^*_{(1)}$ and the associated vector by $\beta^*_{(1)}$. Thus if $p_0, p_1, p_2, ...$ are the consecutive relative frequencies of occurrence or probabilities with $p_0 \geq p_1 \geq p_2 \geq \ldots$ we have the optimal basis $B^*(k)$ ordered as

$B^*_{(0)}, B^*_{(1)}, B^*_{(2)} \ldots$ with their corresponding vectors $\beta^*_{(0)}, \beta^*_{(1)}, \beta^*_{(2)}$ and so on. Our first criterion is based on the *modal* optimal basis $B^*_{(0)}$ and its associated efficiency

vector $\beta^*_{(0)}$. To evaluate the role of $\beta^*_{(0)}$ in efficiency comparison we use a dummy variable method of stratification of the entire data set before we perform an OLS method of linear regression e.g., we regress the observed output (y) on the m inputs (x_i) and a zero-one dummy variable D_j as indicated in (3.8) before. Note further that the effect of "contamination" could now be analyzed by extending the coverage of the dummy variable D_j as follows

$$D_j = \begin{cases} 1, & \text{if j belongs to } B^*_{(0)}, \text{ or } B^*_{(1)}, \text{ or } B^*_{(2)} \\ 0, & \text{otherwise} \end{cases}$$

In other words we could observe the effect of including less frequently efficient units in our sample i.e., the optimal production function would tend towards an average-practice production function.

Our second criterion views the set of optimal basic matrices $B^*(k)$ as alternative designs in the statistical theory of experimental design and chooses that design to be the best which minimizes the generalized variance of the estimates $\beta^*(k)$ by interpreting the optimal basis equations as normal equations of a regression model.

Our third criterion analyzes the distribution of the efficiency ratio $e_j = y_j/y_j^*$ in terms of a logit model, where y_j^* is the maximal output and y_j the observed. Clearly if j

includes only the efficient units then $y_j = y_j^* = \sum_{i=1}^{m} x_i \beta_i^*$ and hence $e_j = 1.0$. We ask which of the m inputs is most important in determining the probability that the efficiency ratio e_j is very high? If any such critical input can be found, then the difference in efficiency of the various units can be related to the unequal ownership of this critical input. Thus the relative inefficiency can be attributed to the lack of adequate supply of this critical input, which is sometimes identified with managerial experience, talent or technical knowledge.

We may now briefly consider the three criteria.

A.   Modal efficiency

The concept of modal efficiency has two important applications. The first characterized by the dummy variable equatin (3.8) shows the effect of "contamination" of the modal efficiency set by including units which are less often efficient. Thus the greater the extent of contamination, the lower the value of the multiple correlation coefficient R^2 and the higher the estimated value of α which is seen to be the efficiency gap in terms of the ratio y_j/y_j^*. The second type of application compares the mean efficiency levels of the two sets, the modal efficiency set (S_1) and the remaining set S_2 and accounts for their difference in terms of one or more important inputs (x_i). The self-selectivity model [13] may then be easily applied as follows. Let x_1 be the single most important input whose regression coefficient β_1 in (3.8) appears more important or, more significant in case the dummy variable D_j includes only the units in the modal efficiency set S_1. As the samples from the other set S_2 are added on, the resulting regression estimate of β_1 should either decline or, appear less significant statistically.

To illustrate these applications consider our earlier example of 25 public elementary school districts in California, where the output variable (y) is in terms of achievement scores of sixth grade pupils and the four inputs selected as regressors are average teacher salary (x_1), proportion of Anglo-American students in class (x_2), average class size (x_3) and a proxy variable (x_4) denoting parental background of pupils. On using this data set we compute 25 LP models of the form (3.3), where we obtain only 11 nondegenerate optimal solutions with each coefficient β_i^* positive. Three optimal vectors

$$\beta^*_{(0)} = \begin{pmatrix} 0.\ 247 \\ 0.\ 523 \\ 0.\ 626 \\ 0.\ 179 \end{pmatrix}, \quad \beta^*_{(1)} = \begin{pmatrix} 0.\ 157 \\ 0.\ 790 \\ 0.\ 898 \\ 0.\ 262 \end{pmatrix}, \quad \beta^*_{(2)} = \begin{pmatrix} 0.\ 117 \\ 0.\ 906 \\ 1.\ 022 \\ 0.\ 299 \end{pmatrix}$$

occur with the following frequencies 0.27, 0.18 and 0.09. On using the modal efficiency set S_1 we run the dummy variable regression equatin (3.8), along with an alternative estimate based on the complete sample $S = S_1 + S_2$ with 25 observations. The results are as follows:

Sample	c	β_1	β_2	β_3	β_4	α	R^2
S_1	0.602	0.317*	0.178	0.214	.073	0.054*	0.99
		(4.63)	(0.32)	(0.38)	(0.41)	(2.19)	
$S=S_1+S_2$	0.486	0.246*	0.336	0.483	0.132	0.072*	0.83
		(2.67)	(0.82)	(1.21)	(1.04)	(2.27)	

with t-values in parentheses. It is clear that enlarging the modal efficiency set by contamination increases the efficiency gap (a) from 0.054 to 0.072 and reduces the value and statistical significance of the most important coefficient β_1 (i.e., it changes from 0.317 to 0.246 with t-values most halved). Also it is clear that the teacher salary (input x_1) representing the quality of instruction turns out to be the most important variable which explains the difference in efficiency levels of schools.

B. Selectivity Criterion

For the second application let $\bar{y}_1, \bar{y}_2$ be the mean output levels for the two groups of samples S_1, S_2 where S_1 is the modal efficiency set. When the input-output data set contains errors of observation we can write

$$\bar{y}_i = \mu_i + u_i \qquad i = 1, 2 \tag{3.9}$$

where μ_i is the population mean for sample S_i and u_i is the error of observation. As a large sample approximation we may assume u_1, u_2 to have a bivariate normal distribution with means zero, variances σ_1^2, σ_2^2 and the covariance σ_{12}. Now we redefine the dummy variable D as

$$D = \begin{cases} 1, & \text{if } \mu_1 > \mu_2 \\ 0 & \text{othe rwise} \end{cases} \tag{3.10}$$

Clearly if we add the further assumption that $\bar{y}_1 > \bar{y}_2$ if and only if $\mu_1 > \mu_2$, then this definition of dummy variable would be equivalent to the first one in (3.8). However the stochastic interpretation (3.9) permits a more satisfactory measure of the efficiency gap between the two sample sets. The basic question is: we observe the sample difference $\bar{y}_1 > \bar{y}_2$, what does it imply in terms of the difference in their permanent components: $(\mu_1 - \mu_2)$?

Put in another way, does the observed difference in teacher salary lead to real (or permanent) differences in student performance? Let λ be the probability

$$\lambda = \text{Prob } (\bar{y}_2 < \bar{y}_1) = \text{Prob } (u_2 - u_1 < \mu_1 - \mu_2)$$

$$\tag{3.11}$$

$$= \text{Prob } (u < z) = \int_{-\infty}^{z} (\sqrt{2\pi})^{-1} \exp(-t^2/2) dt$$

where

$$u = \frac{u_2 - u_1}{\sigma}, \sigma^2 = \sigma_1^2 + \sigma_2^2 - 2\sigma_{12}$$

$$z = \frac{\mu_1 - \mu_2}{\sigma}$$

then looking at the proportion of units which belong to the modal efficiency set we can estimate λ. In our example we have a direct estimate of λ as 0.27 and an estimate of σ as 0.12. Hence we obtain from (3.11) above the difference $\mu_1 - \mu_2 = 0.059$. But if instead of 25 LP models we run one LP model with mean inputs in the objective function:

$$\min \ \bar{g} = \sum_{i=1}^{4} \beta_i \bar{x}_i ,$$ we would obtain 4 out of 25 units in the optimal basis, i.e., $\lambda =$

$4/25 = 0.16$ provides an alternative estimate. But with this estimate the efficiency gap would be $\mu_1 - \mu_2 = 0.109$. Thus the effect of increasing the LP models from one to n=25 is to allow randomization in the input-output space so that a more precise estimate of the efficiency difference could be made between the two sample groups: the modal efficiency set S_1 and the other set S_2. The larger the positive difference $(\mu_1 - \mu_2)$, the greater the role of the inefficient units in causing a divergence between the production frontier and the average production function.

C.   A Logit Model Criterion

The third approach for efficiency comparison is a logit model criterion based on the empirical scatter (i.e. distribution) of the efficiency ratios $e_j = y_j / y_j^*$ obtained from the n LP models in (3.3). Here we do not restrict ourselves to the optimal basic solutions but consider each DMU separately and ask how often it turns out to be efficient.

Now the probability of becoming efficient must depend on some characteristics of the inputs used and output produced by the units. If we use a dummy variable D defined in (3.8) to screen the efficient units, then we can perform a linear regression

$$D = \alpha + \beta z + \text{error}$$

on some measurable factor z (e.g., the output levels or any of the inputs) to explain how efficiency rises with the level of the regressor z. However D is only a binary variable taking values either zero or one; hence it cannot explain the probability of becoming efficient in a random sample of n units. Hence we introduce the probability f in place of D, where f is the relative frequency of becoming efficient. To fix ideas let z be the output level as a regressor. We try to explain how f changes as the output level increases. A logit model assumes a logistic function representation for this behavior as follows:

$$f = 1/[1 + \exp(-(\alpha + \beta z))] \qquad (3.11)$$

For the production frontier case, this logistic representation (3.11) is appealing for two reasons. One is that it allows a continuous representation of the dummy variable measure D defined above, so that it can explain for example if the units with higher (lower) outputs have a higher (lower) probability of becoming efficient. Secondly, the frequency or probabiilty f may be estimated from sample observations when data are available for proportions turning out to be efficient. Taking natural logarithms the logistic equation (3.11) may be further reduced to an OLS form:

$$\log \left(\frac{f}{1-f}\right) = \alpha + \beta z + u$$

where u is the error term with mean zero and fixed variance.

In our educational example we use efficiency ratios $e_j = y_j / y_j^*$ as the sample estimates of the relative frequency $f = f_j$, when we arrange the n units in an increasing order of efficiency and for z we use the three inputs (in log units) x_1 through x_3 and a fourth factor $\hat{x}_4$ which measures managerial ability or the quality of instruction. But since $\hat{x}_4$ is not observable we use the proxy variable of performance scores computed from the four component scores in reading, writing, spelling and mathematics. The regression results are as follows:

α	x_1	x_2	β x_3	x_4	R^2
4.65 (0.26)	-1.83 (1.00)				0.0
4.88 (8.51)	-	-0.67 (3.67)			0.37
13.4 (2.6)	-	-	-3.23 (2.00)		0.15
-28.8 (5.3)	-	-	-	7.64 (5.87)	0.61

where t-values are in parentheses. If we exclude four units from the sample set of n=25 which have the lowest levels of efficiency, our last regression equation turns out to be

$$\log \left(\frac{f}{1-f}\right) = -25.9 + 6.87\,\ell_4 \qquad R^2 = 0.75 \qquad (3.12)$$
$$\quad\;\; (6.8) \quad (7.48)$$

It is clear that the fourth factor measuring the quality of instruction offers the best explanation of the efficiency frequencies. As Maddala [13] has shown the value of the multiple correlation coefficient (R^2) is not a very good measure of fit in case of logit models, but a pseudo-R^2 mesure based on the likelihood ratio statistic may be more appropriate. The highest value of R^2 by this alternative method turns out to be 0.80 in this example. Hence the value $R^2 = 0.75$ is statistically very significant.

It is clear that we can estimate from (3.12) the efficiency proportion for any level of ℓ_4 chosen i.e.,

$$f = \frac{1}{1 + \exp\,(25.9 - 6.87\,\ell_4)}$$

To the extent that experience adds to the quality of instruction and the latter affects the other three inputs (i.e. factor augmenting properties), the logit model captures the cumulative role of experience-related factors which have been sometimes called as 'learning by doing'.

3.3   Robust Methods of Estimation

Robustness in estimation of production frontier can be approached in an applied sense in two ways: either in a regression framework or, in a nonparametric sense through nonparametric estimation of the error density. In a regression framework the robustness of an estimator has two important features. One emphasizes the relative insensitivity of the estimator to the outlying observations and the other, to the departure from the assumption of normality of the error distribution underlying the frontier. Timmer emphasized the first aspect as the main reason for his preferring the linear programming method of estimation over that of ordinary least squares. The second aspect, commonly termed 'contaminations' tends to inflate the standard error of the sample mean (median) as an estimator of the population mean (median) and hence reduces its estimation efficiency. See e.g., Barnett and Lewis [14].

The minimax method of estimation is known to possess both of these robustness properties. It minimizes the maximum absolute error and retains the LP model structure. Thus if the additional data points are within the maximum absoulte error, the estimates do not change; also the LP method of Farrell and DEA models is maintained.

In the general case this minimax estimator is obtained by minimizing the maximum absolute deviation between the observed y_j and predicted y_j i.e.,

$$\min \beta_0$$

$$\text{s.t.} \quad \beta_0 \geq y_j - \sum_{i=1}^{m} x_{ji} \beta_i, \qquad j = 1, 2, \ldots, n \tag{3.13}$$

$$\beta_0 \geq -y_j + \sum_{i=1}^{m} x_{ji} \beta_i, \qquad j = 1, 2, \ldots, n$$

$$\beta_0 \geq 0$$

But in the production frontier case we have only two subsets of data points, one lying on

the frontier which is efficient and the other not on the frontier, which is not efficient (or

less efficient). But since the second subset lies below the frontier we always have

$$y_j - \sum_{i=1}^{m} x_{ji} \beta_i \geq 0, \text{ all } j$$

where the data set (X,y) have all positive elements. Hence the second constraint of

(3.13) may be dropped and the estimates of $\beta = (\beta_i)$ are required to be nonnegative for

economic realism. Now suppose the data set is such that it maintains a probabilistic

feasibility for each constraint j at least at a level α $(0 < \alpha < 1)$, then the following LP

model provides a minimax method of obtaining the estimates of β, when each of the

chance constraints $X\beta \geq y$ has the 100α percent probability of feasibility:

$$\min \beta_0 \quad \text{s.t.} \quad X\beta - y \leq \beta_0 u; \quad X\beta \geq y$$
$$u = \text{vector with each element unity} \qquad\qquad (3.14)$$
$$\beta \geq 0; \quad \beta_0 \geq 0$$

From an applied viewpoint we may mention several important implications of the

minimax method viewed in the context of Farrell and DEA efficient frontier. First of all,

one notes that the minimax solution of (3.14) would be statistically the closest to one or

more of the n solutions of the n LP models (3.3), when closeness is measured in terms of

the statistical distance of the optimal β vectors in the two cases. This is because the

mean LP model (3.6) would be the closest to one or more of the n solutions (3.3) and the

minimax model (3.14) would select for very small values of β_0^* those units as efficient,

which are previously found to be so in (3.6). Secondly, the minimax method being

relatively insensitive to data variations can handle robustness much better than the convex

hull method of Farrell efficiency. Thus, if an enlargement of the data set $D = (X,y)$

maintains the efficiency of a subset of m units, called "the core subset" in r percent of the times, the same enlargement for the minimax model would preserve efficiency in more than r percent of the times. Thirdly, the minimax solution is likely to be more diversified than the Farrell measure because it is a mixed strategy solution and hence it is more likely to have a nondegenerate optimal basis. In our empirical application to educational production in California discussed before, this was found to be consistently true. Lastly, the minimax estimates $(\beta*, \beta_0^*)$ of the approximate LP model (3.14) can be given a novel economic interpretation by treating β_0^* as measuring the nondiscretionary component of the production function as is done by Banker and Morey [15]. Following their approach we formulate the traditional production function as

$$y_j = g(x_j, w_j) \tag{3.15}$$

where the m-element vector x_j represents the inputs controlled by each firm j and w_j denotes the nondiscretionary inputs serving as external objective conditions affecting output. The nondiscretionary inputs w_j are like human capital, managerial ability or disembodied form of technical change. One of the simplest ways to model the production function (3.15) is to write it as

$$y_j = h(w_j) \cdot y_j^* \tag{3.16}$$

where $y_j^* = f(x_{j1}, x_{j2}, \ldots, x_{jm}) = \sum_{i=1}^{m} x_{ji} \beta_i$ for example and $0 < h(w_j) \le 1$ for all j. In this case $h(w_j)$ acts like Hicks-neutral technical change, i.e., $y_j = y_j^*$ if $h(w_j) = 1$ for any efficient subset to which j belongs and $y_j < y_j^*$, for $h(w_j) < 1$ when j does not belong to the efficient production function. The efficiency gap between y_j and y_j^* is expressed in (3.16) as a ratio but if one writes it as a difference we would get

$$y_j = y_j^* - \beta_0(w_j) \tag{3.17}$$

where the nonnegative variable $\beta_0(w_j)$ now represents the efficiency gap between the two sets, the efficient set of points (y_j^*, x_j) and the rest which are not efficient. An optimal estimate β_0^* of $\beta_0(w_j)$ is obtained from the linearized version of the minimax model:

$$\min \beta_0$$

s.t.
$$\sum_{i=1}^{m} x_{ji}\beta_i - y_j \leq \beta_0 \qquad\qquad j=1,2,...,n \qquad\qquad (3.18)$$

$$\beta_i \geq 0, \quad \beta_0 \geq 0, \qquad\qquad i=1,2,...,m$$

It is clear that this efficiency gap β_0^* would be the lowest when the sample includes only those units which are most often efficient with a high frequency. But as more and more units are randomly added to the sample bringing in less efficient units, this gap would increase. Out empirical estimates for the educational data referred to before cloearly confirm this tendency, as Table 7 shows as follows:

Table 7. Minimax Estimates of Linear Production Frontier (Model 3.18) with and without normalization)

		β^*_0	β^*_1	β^*_2	β^*_3	β^*_4
A. Normalization Condition $\sum_1^4 \beta_i = 1$ imposed						
Sample groups	S_3	0.211	0.391	0.242	0266	0.101
	S_2	0.116	0.378	0.281	0.238	0.103
	S_1	0.054	0.348	0.249	0.316	0.087
B. Normalization Condition not imposed						
Sample groups	S_3	0.201	0.351	0.148	0.129	0.051
	S_2	0.115	0.419	0.159	0.130	0.070
	S_1	0.027	0.276	0.477	0.535	0.163

Here the sample group S_1 includes 7 units having the efficiency frequency of 15 or
higher, S_2 contains 6 more units having efficiency frequency of at least 8 and the sample
group S_3 comprises all the 25 units.

In nonparametric estimation we consider the DEA model in two ways; either as a
method of deriving envelopes out of a set of data points, or as a technique of estimating
efficiency in the input-output space. In both cases we have to assess the influence of
indivdual data points. Two types of robustness techniques have been recently applied in

DEA models. One is the influence curve approach [2] which may be both parametric and nonparametric. This approach utilizes the residuals from the DEA and Farrell models just like the estimated residuals from a fitted regression curve and utilizes them for various diagnostic searches and sensitivity tests. A second approach is based on a nonparametric method of estimating the distribution of the efficiency specified by the DEA model (3.3), which can also be utilized in Afriat and Johansen models.

For the DEA model denote its solutions by the set $B^* = \{\beta^*(k), k \in I_n\}$. For any reference unit k we denote the efficiency ratio $e_j(k) = y_j/y_j^*(k)$, where $y_j^*(k) = \sum_i \beta_i^*(k)x_{ij}$ is the optimal output for the selection k in the objective function. The samples $\{e(1),e(2),...,e(n)\}$ of efficiency ratio may be viewed as random drawings from a parent population, which we assume for simplicity to have an unknown absolutely continuous probability density with a poisitive domain [a,b]. If the unknown density, say g(e) has infinite range, we only consider estimating the truncated density

$$f(e) = g(e) / \int_a^b g(t)\,dt, \qquad a \le e < b$$

due to practical considerations. We partition the closed interval [a,b] by $a = t_0 < t_1 < ... < t_k = b$ and consider the histogram estimators $f_H(t)$ of the form:

$$f_H(t) = \begin{cases} c_r & \text{for } t_r \le t < t_{r+1}, r = 0, 1, ..., k-1 \\ c_{r-1} & \text{for } t_k = b \\ 0 & \text{othe rwise} \end{cases} \tag{3.19}$$

where $f_H(t) \ge 0$ and $\int_a^b f_H(t)\,dt = 1$. To estimate the population historgram of the form (3.19), we consider the entire sample space $\{e_j(k), j \in I_n, k \in I_n)$ and count the number of observations falling in the r-th interval. Let n_r be this number; then the population parameter c_r above can be estimated by

$$\hat{c}_r = \frac{n_r}{n(t_{r+1} - t_r)} \text{ for } r = 0, 1, \ldots, k-1$$

and hence

$$\hat{f}_H(t) = \begin{cases} \hat{c}_r & \text{for } t_r \leq t < t_{r+1}, \ r=0,1,\ldots,k-1 \\ \hat{c}_{r-1} & \text{for } t_k = b \\ 0 & \text{otherwise} \end{cases} \qquad (3.20)$$

The intuitive appeal of the sample estimate $\hat{f}_H(t)$ of the population density $f_H(t)$ is clear. The number of observtions falling into each of the intervals is a multinomial variate and hence the sample proportion n_r/n estimates $\int_{t_r}^{t_{r+1}} f_H(t)dr$ which for small $\Delta t = t_{r+1}$ - t_r equals $f_H(t)\Delta t$ and hence $n_r/(n\Delta t)$ estimates the population density $f_H(t)$. Rosenblatt (1956) has proved that the sample estimator $\hat{f}_H(t)$ is a consistent estimator of the population density $f_H(t) = f_H(e)$ under three regulatiry conditions: f(t) has continuous derivatives up to order three except at the endpoints of [a,b], it is bounded on [a,b] and the spacing number h_n defined by $2h_n = t_{r+1,n}$ - $t_{r,n}$ is such that if $n \rightarrow \infty$ and $h_n \rightarrow 0$, then $nh_n \rightarrow \infty$. For most applied situations these regularity conditions would hold and hence the sample histogram estimate $\hat{f}_H$ of the population density f(t) in its histogram form $f_H(t)$ can be easily applied. Also by using the multinomial distribution the likelihood function $L(n_0,n_1,\ldots,n_{r-1} \mid c_0,c_1,\ldots,c_{r-1}) = L$ can be written as

$$L = \prod_{r=0}^{k-1} (c_r)$$

where c_r has to be positive for each r for a nondegenerate likelihood function. It is clear

that by maximizing the log-likelihood function $\ln L = \sum_{r=0}^{k-1} n_r \ln c_r$ subject to

$\sum_{r=0}^{k-1} c_r(t_{r+1} - t_r) = 1$ we obtain the sample estimate $\hat{f}_H(t)$ of the population density

function $f_H(t)$ given in (3.20). Thus the estimate $\hat{f}_H(t)$ of the efficiency distribution is

both nonparametric and maximum likelihood and the latter has the consistency property

under suitable large sample conditions.

Two important uses of this nonparametric characterization of the efficiency

distribution may now be indicated. The first shows that a modal efficiency subset can be

defined by using the efficiency density $\hat{f}_H(t)$ to cluster the observed units into groups in

a scale of efficiency frequency. The difference between the production frontier (i.e.,

best-practice production function) and the average-practice production function can then

be explained in terms of contamination of the modal efficiency subset introduced by

including units which are either inefficient most frequently or efficient rarely. The second

type of use looks at the divergence between the two distributions, one given by

$\hat{f}_H(t) = \hat{f}_H(e)$ as above and the other associated with the criterion of minimum absolute

deviations i.e., $\min \sum_j |e_j| = \min \sum_j |(\sum_i \beta_i x_{ij} - y_j)|$. If the latter density is de-

noted by $\bar{f}_H(e)$, then one appied measure of divergence of the two distributions is given

by

$$d_{12} = \sum_{r=0}^{k} (\hat{c}_r - \bar{c}_r)^{1/2}$$

where $\bar{c}_r$ is the sample estimate corresponding to $\bar{f}_H(t)$. If the two densities are close

(not close) to each other, d_{12} tends to be small (large). Thus the statistic d_{12} can be used

as measure of affinity of the two distributions.

The bootstrapping technique [16,17] which are recently developing in the framework of nonparametric regression models have immense scope of application here. The technique of the bootstrap is to replace the unknown population distribution (i.e. cdf) F by the empirical distribution function F_n say of either the efficiency ratios $e_j(k)$ defined above or, the residuals of the DEA model (3.3). Since the residuals are unlikely to have mean zero, the bootstrap techniques first recenter the residuals through some weight functions called windows and then allow suitable adaptive smoothing methods. Since these techniques are very heavily databased and empirical, they have great scope of appliction in the DEA models of efficiency.

3.4 Data Screening and Cluster Analysis

We have already mentioned two methods of clustering in Farrell and DEA models. One is the ad hoc method of Timmer who proposed a method of truncating the observation set until a specified level of probabilistic feasibility is attained. The second method estimates the population probability that a subset of the microunits would turn out to be efficient and on using this estimated probability the sample data points can be arranged into subsets or sub-clusters from low to high probability.

One could also use nonparametric techniques of classification. To illustrate consider the problem of classifying on the basis of the distribution of the efficiency ratio e $= (e_j(k),\ e_j(k) = y_j/y_j^*(k))$ defined before. Let $N(z)$ be the number of sample e's in the interval $[z-h,\ z+h]$ then $N(z)/n$ is an estimate of the probability $\mathrm{Prob}\{z-h \le e \le z+h\}$. If we divide this by the length of the interval $2h$, we obtain an estimate

$\hat{f}(z) = N(z)/(2hn)$, which can also be written as

$$\hat{f}(z) = (hn)^{-1} \sum_{j=1}^{n} K\left(\frac{z - e_j(k)}{h}\right) \tag{3.21}$$

where

$$N(z) = 2 \sum_{j=1}^{n} K\left(\frac{z - e_j(k)}{h}\right), K(u) = \begin{cases} \frac{1}{2}, & |u| \leq 1 \\ 0, & \text{otherwise} \end{cases}$$

this is known as a kernel estimate, which of course will appear as a step function. To obtain a smooth version the above function may be replaced by a smooth kernel such as

$$K(u) = \left(\sqrt{2\pi}\right)^{-1} \exp\left(-u^2/2\right)$$

It is known [18] that although the kernel $K(u)$ can be a quite general function and may be chosen without knowledge of the form of the population density $f(z)$, the above estimate $\hat{f}(z)$ is still consistent. Hence if we have two groups of samples e.g., two groups of schools in our educational example we may first obtain the above nonparametric consistent estimates $\hat{f}_1(z)$ and $\hat{f}_2(z)$ then the classification of z points may be based on the ratio $\hat{f}_1(z)/\hat{f}_2(z)$ e.g., if the ratio is above $e_0 = 0.95$ say we may classify in one group, the rest belonging to the other group. Such classification techniques have well known properties such as nonparametric consistency and robustness in some sense.

A second type of approach in optimal clustering is suitable for the aggregation method adopted in Johansen's model. Instead of assuming the capacity distribution as he does, one could apply a nonparametric method of estimating the distribution and then consider a method of mixtures for combining the different subclusters. Thus suppose we have k subclusters (or intervals), then we may define an aggregation procedure to be "convex admissible" if the convex hulls of the k clusters produced are pairwise disjoint. The data requirements for this method may however be quite significant and hence simulation data may have to be used. Of course, one could apply here a parametric theory of optimal statistical design. For instance, write the optimal basis of the DEA model (3.3) as

$$X^*(k)\hat{\beta}^*(k) = y(k)$$

where $B^*(k)$ is denoted by the square matrix $X^*(k)$ of order m. Assuming nondegeneracy of the optimal basis we obtain $\hat{\beta}^*(k) = X^{*-1} y(k)$, where the vector $\hat{\beta}^*(k)$ has nonnegative elements. We now assume that the output vector $y(k)$ is random as follows:

$$y(k) = \mu(k) + u(k)$$

where $u(k)$ is the error vector assumed to be normally distributed with zero mean and a variance-covariance matrix V fixed for all $k=1,2,...,n$. Thus we obtain the pseudo-regression equation

$$y(k) = X^*(k)\beta^*(k) + u(k)$$

where we assume that the conditional expectation $E(y(k)|X^*(k))$ of $y(k)$ equals $X^*(k)\beta^*(k)$, since $E(u(k)|X(k))$ is assumed to be zero. In OLS (ordinary least squares) models this assumption is necessarily fulfilled but in this case it may not be, hence we term it the pseudo-normal equations of the pseudo-regression model where the population mean vector $\mu(k)$ equals $X^*(k)\beta^*(k)$. Note that the errors $u(k)$ above are disturbances constrained under the optimal basis $X^*(k)$.

Since our LP estimate $\hat{\beta}^*(k)$ is obtainable in the nondegenerate case as:

$$\hat{\beta}^*(k) = X^{*-1}(k)y(k) = X^{*-1}(k)[X^*(k)\beta^*(k) + u(k)]$$

therefore its variance-covariance matrix is

$$E[(\hat{\beta}^*(k) - \beta^*(k))(\hat{\beta}^*(k) - \beta^*(k))'] = X^{*-1}(k)VX^*(k)'^{-1}$$

where prime denotes transpose. Which of the n LP estimators $\hat{\beta}(k)$ would we now accept as the best? By the optimal design criterion we minimize the generalized variance:

$$\min_{k} \ d = \left| X^{*-1}(k) V X^{*}(k)^{'-1} \right|$$

$$= |(X^{*}(k)'X^{*}(k))^{-1}| \bullet |V|$$

to obtain the best estimator $\hat{\beta}(0)$ say. But since V is not estimable due to lack of degrees

of freedom, this estimator $\hat{\beta}(0)$ is obtained by maximizing the determinant of

$[X^{*}(k)'X^{*}(k)]$. As Chernoff [19] has shown the design associated with $\hat{\beta}(0)$, also

called the D-optimal design is equivalent under certain regularity and continuity

conditions to the so-called A-optimal design based on the Chebyshev criterion which

minimizes the maximum variance of prediction among the linear unbiased estimators of

$\beta^{*}(k)$.

3.5   Problems in Parametric Theory

The nonparametric approach may be used as a stepping stone to a suitable

parametric model, as more and more input-output data become available. When frontier

function is either a cost or a profit frontier this procedure of combining the nonparametric

with the parametric model may be particularly helpful for two reasons. First of all,

several functional forms such as the translog and CES functions have been widely

applied as average production functions in empirical economic literature and one may like

to compare the frontier estimates with these. This may indicate in suitable cases the scope

for resource reallocation and/or output reallocation so as to increase the overall scale,

technical and price efficiency. Secondly, the parameters of the translog and CES

functions for instance may be easily related to the underlying conditions of a competitive

market in some cases and hence one could analyze the source of inefficiency due to

various forms of market distortions due to several unknown factors such as risk

sensitivity of the agents and their rivalrous behavior. Much more theoretical and

empirical work is needed here to clarify the interface with parametric theory and

modeling.

References

1.   Sengupta, J.K.   Recent nonparametric measures of productive efficiency, in Econometrics of Planning and Efficiency, Dordrecht: Kluwer Academic Publishers, 1988.

2.   Sengupta, J.K.   The influence curve approach in data envelopment analysis, paper presented at the 13th International symposium on Mathematical Programming held in Tokyo, August, 1988.

3.   Bowlin, W.F., Charnes, A., Cooper, W.W. and Sherman, H.D.   Data envelopment analysis and regression approaches to efficiency estimation and evaluation, in Normative Analysis in Policy Decisions: Pubic and Private, Basel: Baltzer, A.G. Publishers, 1985.

4.   Banker, R.D., Charnes, A., Cooper, W.W. and Schinnar, A.P.   A bi-extremal principle for frontier estimation and efficiency evaluation, Management Science, 27 (1981), 1370-1382.

5.   Sengupta, J.K.   Nonlinear measures of technical efficiency, forthcoming in Computers and Operations Reserach (1988).

6.   Hanoch, G. and Rothschild, M.   Testing the assumptions of production theory: a nonparametric approach, Journal of Political Economy, 80 (1972), 256-275.

7.   Timmer, C.P.   Using a probabilistic frontier production function to measure technical efficiency, Journal of Political Economy, 5 (1971), 383-394.

8.   Dielman, T. and Pfaffenberger, R.   Least absolute value estimation in linear regression: a review, Optimization in Statistics, Amsterdam: North Holland, 1982.

9.   Koenker, R.   A comparison of asymptotic testing methods for L_1-regression, in Y. Dodge (ed.), Statistical Data Analysis Based on the L_1-norm and Related Methods, New York: Elsevier Science Publishers, 1987.

10.   Farrell, M.J. and Fieldhouse, M.   Estimating efficiency in production functions under increasing returns to scale, Journal of Royal Statistical Society, Series A, 125 (1962), 252-267.

11.   Sengupta, J.K.   Data envelopment analysis for efficiency measurement in the stochastic case, Computers and Operations Research, 14 (1987), 117-129.

12.   Farrell, M.J.   The measurement of productive efficiency, Journal of Royal Statistical Society, Series A, 120 (1957), 253-290.

13.   Maddala, G.S.   Limited Dependent and Qualitative Variables in Econometrics, Cambridge: Cambridge University Press, 1983.

14.   Barnett, V. and Lewis, T.   Outliers in Statistical Data, New York: John Wiley, 1978.

15.   Banker, R.D. and Morey, R.C. Efficiency analysis for exogeneously fixed inputs and outputs, Operations Research, 34 (1986), 45-57.

16.   Efron, B. and Tibshirani, R. Bootstrap methods for standard errors, confidence intervals and other measures of statistical accuracy, Statistical Science, 1 (1986), 54-77.

17.   Hardle, W. and Bowman, A.W. Bootstrapping in nonparametric regression: local adaptive smoothing and confidence bands, Journal of American Statistical Association, 83 (1988), 123-127.

18.   Broffitt, J.D. Nonparametric classification, in Krishnaiah, P.R. and Kanal, L.N. (eds.), Handbook of Statistics, Vol. 2, Amsterdam: North Holland.

19.   Chernoff, H. Sequential Analysis and Optimal Design, Philadephia: Society for Industrial and Applied Mathematics, 1972.

Chapter 4

IMPLICATIONS OF NONPARAMETRIC THEORY

The nonparametric approach to the measurement of productive efficiency has several implications for different disciplines. As a method of data screening, the DEA model through its envelopment of data provides an optimal method of clustering or aggregation. The DEA model has been generalized in recent times to include the categorical (i.e., zero-one) variable as inputs and outputs and also ordinal relations among the multipliers. The latter is closely related to the problems of isotonic regression, where the parameters are subject to an ordering relation. As a stepping stone to a parametric model, the DEA and Farrell models could be used to locate relative inefficiencies which are otherwise missed by the average regression model. Two other lines where this method can be applied has not yet been fully explsored. One is the situation when the microunits face conflicting objective functions as in game theory; sometimes this may be due to their subjective reactions to a given uncertainty of the environment. The second aspect is concerned with its interface with information theory. Since the latter is basically an empirical databased approach it is quite natural that it would have some important implications. Some aspects of these issues would be discussed in later chapters.

4.1 Economic Implications

Two types of economic implications are very important in the nonparametric approach. One is the role of information and data requirement and the second is the extension of the static framework of short run production frontiers to long run environments, where there may be different vintages of capital equipment.

A.   Information Economics

One type of information structure (IS) arises very naturally when one associates the

136

Pareto-Koopmans type of efficiency with the optimization models in DEA. In case of industry-level efficiency one could characterize two sets of parameters, one set for the center and the other for the units (agents) and suppose these parameters are regarded as random drawings from a given probability distribution e.g., the concept of capacity distribution in Johansen's model. If the input coefficient matrix $A = (a_{ij})$ is given by the realized values of the capacity distribution, then the Johansen model solves for the optimal output vector y* from the aggregate LP model

$$\max z = e'y, \, y \in R = \{y: \, Ay \leq V, \, y \geq 0\} \tag{4.1}$$

where e is an n-element column vector with each element unity and $V = (v_i)$ is the aggregate input vector. If all information were available to all agents, then the optimal allocation of the aggregate inputs to any agent would be determined by his parameters and by the realized empirical distribution of others' parameters. To illustrate from the industry model (4.1) let x_k replace the aggregate input vector V by an allocation mechanism U, i.e., $x_k = U(V)$. Taking the dual one would obtain the usual DEA model for one output. But the optimal allocation would depend on the industry optimum, i.e., maximum of aggregate output and hence on the levels of exchange of information e.g., one could distinguish between (a) no exchange of information, (b) limited exchange of information, (c) full exchange of information and (d) exchange of agents' information with the center.

   A second type of IS analysis arises when we have production functions, e.g., for agricultural production and the input coefficients reflect alternative technology IS. Questions of information sharing about the best-practice technology then naturally arise and the distance of average practice technology from the best practice ones may be evaluated in terms of potential gains or losses. Following this line of research the expected payoffs may be compared for different communication structures, e.g., (a) full vs. limited exchange of information and (b) complete or limited transfer of inputs across units.

If instead of the realized values of the capacity distribution we use the observed input coefficient $a_{ij} = x_{ij}/y_j$ from the DEA model

$$\text{Min } g_k = \sum_{i=1}^{m} \beta_i x_{ik}$$

$$\text{s. t. } \sum_{i=1}^{m} \beta_i x_{ij} \geq y_j \tag{4.2}$$

$$\beta_i \geq 0; \ i \in I_m; \ j \in I_n; \ I_s = \{1,2,...,s\}$$

we obtain a data-based mesure of efficiency, which can be used to define an aggregate LP model as:

$$\text{Max } z = \sum_{j=1}^{n} \lambda_j$$

$$\text{s. t. } \sum_{j=1}^{n} a_{ij} \lambda_j \leq V_i, \ i \in I_m \tag{4.3}$$

$$\lambda_j \geq 0, \ j \in I_n$$

where $V_i = \sum_{j=1}^{n} x_{ij}$ is the aggregate of input $i=1,2,...,m$. Let $A = (a_{ij})$ be the input co-efficient matrix and $A(s)$ be its realization when the random state of nature $s \in S$ is observed. The LP model then becomes:

$$\text{Max } z = e'\lambda(s)$$

$$\text{s.t. } A(s) \ \lambda(s) \leq V, \ \lambda(s) \geq 0 \tag{4.4}$$

where e is an n-element column vector with each element unity, prime denotes transpose and it is assumed that the aggregate input vector $V = (V_i)$ is fixed at some positive level for each input. In case the state of nature is random, the constraints of (3.4) become stochastic and hence the objective function and the optimal solutions have to be redefined.

Consider a given state of nature and two clusters of DMUs each with the input matrix A^r and the aggregate input vector V^r (r=1,2) such that the aggregate output $z = e'\lambda^r$ is maximized as in (4.4). Let (λ^{*r}, z_r^*) be the optimal solution for each r=1,2 when each cluster operates independently, i.e.,

$$z_r^* = \text{Max} \{ z_r = e' \lambda^r : A^r \lambda^r \leq V^r, \lambda^r \geq 0 \} \qquad (4.5)$$

Here there is no information sharing between the two clusters. Several cases of information sharing through communication and availability of transmission channels may now be analyzed.

<u>Case A</u>   (Information sharing in technology)

Here the technology set $\{A^1, A^2\}$ is available to each cluster, so that the cluster r solves the LP model:

$$\text{Max } z(A,V^r) = e'\lambda^1 + e'\lambda^2$$
$$\text{s.t. } A^1\lambda^1 + A^2\lambda^2 \leq V^r, \ \lambda^1, \lambda^2 \geq 0 \qquad (4.6)$$

Let $z^*(A,V^r)$ be the optimal output. Clearly if for each r=1,2 we have $z^*(A,V^r) > z_r^*$, then there is positive incentive for such information sharing, assuming of course there is enough organizational flexibility to adopt any technology matrix. The relative gain (G_r^*) in such information sharing may thus be measured by

$$G_r^* = z^*(A, V^r) - z_r^* \geq 0 \qquad (r=1,2) \qquad (4.7)$$

<u>Case B</u>   (Resource sharing)

Let $V_a = V^1 + V^2$ be the pooled vector of inputs of the two custers. Define

$$z_r^*(A^r, V_a) = \text{Max}\{z_r = e'\lambda^r : A^r\lambda^r \le V_a, \lambda^r \ge 0\}$$

If $z_2^*(A^2, V_a) > z_1^*(A^1, V_a)$ then the second technology matrix (A^2) would be preferred and there would be a positive incentive for merger of the two clusters if $z_2^*(A^2, V_a) > z_1^*(A^1, V^1) + z_2^*(A^2, V^2)$.

Case C   (Complete merger)

Here resources and technology are both shared, i.e.,

$$z^*(A, V_a) = \text{Max}\{z(A, V_a) = e'(\lambda^1 + \lambda^2) : A^1\lambda^1 + A^2\lambda^2 \le V_a, \lambda^1, \lambda^2 \ge 0\} \quad (4.8)$$

Clearly the case of complete merger represents the best possible situation and hence it would ordinarily hold that

$$z^*(A, V_a) \ge \text{Max}\{z^*(A, V^r), z_r^*(A^r, V_a)\}$$

Case D   (Limited sharing in technology information)

This is closely related to Case A, except that only a subset of the elements of the matrix $A = (A^1, A^2)$ is shared through *public* information channels, but the others are kept *private* (and not shared). Clearly the optimal output level attainable here would be equal to or less than that of Case A.

From an applied viewpoint the most interesting cases of information sharing are those in Cases A and D, since it allows private ownership of the resources by each cluster of DMUs. For example if the cluster represents schools, it allows them to avoid complete merger which forces the inefficient units to merge and or close.

Consider next the situation where we have for every fixed r (r=1,2) a set of N values of the sample realizations $s \in I_N$ where $I_N = \{1,2,...,N\}$ from the set S and let

$z_r^*(s)$ be the optimand of the LP model (3.4). Denote the cumulative distribution of $\{z_r^*(s)\}$ by $F_r(t) = \text{Prob}(z_r^*(s) \leq t; s \in I_N)$ and the associated density function by $f_r(t)$. The affinity of the two distributions $F_1(t)$ and $F_2(t)$ and their moment characteristics may then be analyzed to compare the efficiency of the two clusters. Some examples may illustrate the point more clearly.

Example 1

Let $I(f_1, f_2) = -\int [f_1 \log (f_1/f_2)]dt$ be the Kullback-Leibler information measure [1] of closeness (or distance) of the two distributions $F_1(t)$, $F_2(t)$ above and assume that these distributions are normal with means μ_1, μ_2 and a common variance σ^2 then

$$I(f_1, f_2) = \frac{1}{2}(\mu_1 - \mu_2)^2/\sigma^2 \tag{4.9}$$

and if $\mu_1 > \mu_2$ we have the first custer more efficient on the average than the second.

Example 2

If the distribution functions are such that $F_1(t) < F_2(t)$ for all t, then $\mu_1 > \mu_2$. Moreover if $\lambda^{(r)}$ is the vector associated with the mean level μ_r (r=1,2), then $\lambda^{(1)}$ may be defined to be more efficient than the vector $\lambda^{(2)}$, since it genreates a higher level of mean output. In case the two distribution functions $F_1(t)$, $F_2(t)$ intersect once at t_0, such that $F_2(t) > F_1(t)$ for all $t > t_0$, then in the right domain $t > t_0$, the first cluster may enjoy stochastic dominance. Also, concepts of higher order stochastic dominance can be easily applied.

The information set S used to compute the distributions $F_r(t)$ of optimal output z_r^* may provide other useful insights into the problem of efficiency characterization. First of all, one may partition the set S into two mutually disjoint subset S_0 and S_1, where S_0 is the reference set such that $z^*(s_0)$ is optimal for the LP model (4.4), i.e., $z^*(s_0) =$

$$\max_{s \in S_0} z = e' \lambda(s) \text{ in } (4.4).$$ If the optimality of $z^*(s_0)$ is maintained for any proper sub-

set of S_1, then the sample realization s_0 may be said to be *relatively* robust. If this holds for all subsets of S_1, then s_0 may be *absolutely* robust. Thus the enlargement of the reference set S_0 by adding subsets of S_1 may be analyzed to see the extent to which the robustness property is preserved.

Secondly, the data set S may be partitioned into subsets S_0, S_1 such that $z^*(s_0) \geq z^*(s_1)$ where $s_0 \in S_0$ and $s_1 \in S_1$. Let p_0 and p_1 be the probability measures associated with S_0 and S_1 respectively. Then the ordered pairs $\{z^*(s_0), p_0; s_0 \in S_0\}, \{z^*(s_1), p_1; s_1 \in S_1\}$ may specify alternative designs. Thus the efficiency of the realization s_0 in S_0 may not be acceptable to the decision-maker if the associated probability p_0 is very low, i.e., $p_0 \ll p_1$. This leads to the concept of the probability of the efficient design, i.e., how often the selections s_0 turn out to be the highest or the best. The best design of course is one which maintains the isotonic property $z^*(s_0) \geq z^*(s_1)$ with a very high probability $p_0 \gg p_1$. In default the decision-maker has to settle for some compromises e.g., minimax designs.

Thirdly, one may compress or enlarge the data set in terms of the model (4.4). For instance one may consider the mean vlaue $\overline{A}$ of the coefficient matrix $A(s)$ in (4.4) and solve for the optimal vector $\overline{\lambda}^*$. Let B^* be the associated optimal basis satisfying the basis equations

$$B^* \overline{\lambda}^*_{B^*} = V, \overline{\lambda}^*_B \geq 0$$

Since the optimal vector $\overline{\lambda}^*_{B^*}$ associated with B^* is a continuous function of the elements of B^*, there must exist a neighborhood $N_\delta(B^*)$ around B^* throughout which the optimality would be retained. By restricting ourselves to random perturbations within this constrained neighborhood, the mean and variance of the optimal vector $\overline{\lambda}^*_B$ and the associated optimand z^*_B may be estimated and their stability analyzed.

Several stochastic situations arise when the state of nature s in the information set S is random. Consider the particular case when the input coefficients are stochastic and we have the decision model:

$$\text{Max}_{\lambda} \ \tilde{z} \qquad \text{s. t. } \tilde{A}\lambda = V, \lambda \geq 0$$

where $\tilde{A} = \tilde{A}(s)$, $\lambda = \lambda(s)$ and $\tilde{z} = \tilde{z}(s) = e'\lambda(s)$ denotes the random pay-off points. This model may be interpreted either as a team decision problem under different forms of cooperation and information sharing, or as the industry manager's planning problem. Taking the latter case the industry manager has to optimally choose the output-mix vector λ when the input coefficient $\tilde{A}$ contain stochastic elements.

Two types of solutions can be proposed in this framework. One is to seek a pure strategy solution by defining a suitable von Neumann utility function $u(\tilde{z})$ and maximizing its expected utility: $E\{u(\tilde{z})\}$. Thus if $u(\tilde{z}) = \tilde{z}$ one may use the LP model at the mean:

$$\text{Max}\{\bar{z} \mid \lambda \in \bar{R}\} \tag{4.10}$$

where $\bar{R} = \{\lambda \mid \bar{A}\lambda \leq V, \lambda \geq 0\}$ and a bar over A and z denote their expected values over random states of nature. A second approach is to use a mixed strategy solution of the form $\{\lambda(s), \delta_s\}$ where δ_s is the probability at the vector point $\lambda(s)$ for each s, i.e, with N states of nature we would have $\sum_{s=1}^{N} \delta_s = 1, \delta_s \geq 0, s \in I_N$. The decision problem is now

$$\text{Max} \ \sum_{s=1}^{N} \tilde{z}(s)\delta_s$$

$$\text{s.t.} \sum_{s=1}^{N} \delta_s y_i(\hat{\lambda}(s)) \geq 0, \hat{\lambda} \geq 0 \qquad i = 1, 2, \ldots, m \tag{4.11}$$

where s.t. $\sum_{s=1}^{N} \delta_s y_i(\lambda(s)) \geq 0, \hat{\lambda} \geq 0 \qquad i = 1, 2, \ldots, m$ and

$\hat{\lambda} = \{\lambda(1), \lambda(2), \ldots, \lambda(N)\}$ and our object is to find an n-dimensional probability distribution $D(\hat{\lambda})$ over the set $\hat{\lambda} \geq 0$. In (4.11) we maximize the expected value of $\tilde{z}(s)$ subject to the constraints that the average or expected value of each input constraint is feasible. For simplicity we assume only discrete probability distributions and a finite value of N, though in principle N could be infinitely large.

Following Fromovitz [2] we now define an ε-optimal randomized solution of the problem (4.10) as follows:

Definition

The n-dimensional probability distribution $D^\varepsilon(\hat{\lambda})$ over the set $\hat{\lambda} \geq 0$ is ε-optimal if any other probability distribution which satisfies (4.11) cannot further increase the objective function by more than ε, where ε is a positive scalar. Fromovitz showed that an ε-optimal solution always exists under two very mild conditions: (i) there exists a nonnegative vector $\hat{\lambda}^0$ such that $y_i(\hat{\lambda}^0) \geq 0$ for each $i \in I_m$ and (ii) there exists a vector $t = (t_0, t_1, \ldots, t_m)$ of Lagrange multipliers and a positive constant M such that

$$t_0 \tilde{z} + \sum_{i=1}^{m} t_i y_i(\hat{\lambda}) \leq M, t_0 > 0$$

These conditions are nothing but the requirement that a feasible and bounded solution exists.

Theorem 1

If there is an optimal soution λ^* of the LP model (4.10) at the mean, then there must exist an ε-optimal randomized solution of the model (4.11). Furthermore there must exist a neighborhood around which this optimality is preserved.

Proof

The existence of the optimal solution λ^* of (4.10) implies that the two conditions of feasibility and boundedness are satisfied and hence by Fromovitz' theorem there must exist an n-dimensional probability distribution $D^{\varepsilon}(\hat{\lambda})$ over the set $\hat{\lambda} \geq 0$ which is ε-optimal. Let $\hat{\lambda}^*$ denote an ε-optimal solution. Then one can represent this solution as a discrete probabilty distribution over $\hat{\lambda} \geq 0$ with probabiilty δ_j^* at the vector points $\hat{\lambda}^*(j)$ or, $dD^{\varepsilon}(\hat{\lambda}^*) = \delta_j^*$ for $1 \leq j \leq N \leq m$. Furthermore the optimal solution λ^* of (4.10) is a continuous function of the elements $\bar{a}_{ij}$ of the matrix $\bar{A}$ denoted by N_α say, throughout which λ^* is optimal. For any subset of this set N_α, there must exist an ε-optimal randomized solution $\{\hat{\lambda}^*(\alpha), \alpha \in N_\alpha\}$, since the two conditions of feasibility and boundedness are satisfied in this neighborhood. Hence the result.

Two remarks may be added. First of all, a similar result can be proved when the objective function $\bar{z}$ of (4.10) and $\bar{z}(s)$ in (4.11) are replaced by $\bar{u}(z)$ and $\tilde{u}(s) = u(\bar{z}(s))$, where the utility function $u(\cdot)$ need not be linear.

Secondly, the effect of increasing the sample size N on the optimal solution may be assessed as follows: let $\bar{A}_N$ denote the mean based on N values and let $(\lambda_N^*, \bar{z}_N^*)$ denote the corresponding optimal values of λ^* and $\bar{z}^*$. If there exists a number N_1 such that for all $N \geq N_1$, the optimal values $(\lambda_N^*, \bar{z}_N^*)$ do not change by more than η, where η is a very small positive number, then the solution vector λ_N^* may be said to possess η-stability. Likewise one could characterize the η-stability of the ε-optimal randomized solution $(\hat{\lambda}^*, \delta^*)$, where $\hat{\lambda}^* = (\hat{\lambda}^*(j))$ and $\delta^* = (\delta_j^*)$ for $1 \leq j \leq N \leq m$.

Theorem 2

Let $\theta = (\theta_i)$ be a vector of tolerance measures where $\lambda = \lambda(\theta)$ satisfies

$$\text{Prob}[\sum_{j=1}^{n} \tilde{a}_{ij}\lambda_j \leq V_i] \geq \theta_i, \, i \in I_m \tag{4.12}$$

Let $\theta_0 = \min_i \theta_i$. If θ_0 is positive, then there exists an optimal value θ_0^* which solves the programming problem: Max θ_0 subject to (4.12). Furthermore if θ_0 is positive and the probability distribution of $\tilde{a}_{ij}$ is continuous, then there exists an optimal solution θ^{**} of vector θ which maximizes the system reliability measure $R(\theta) = \sum_i \log \theta_i$ subject to (4.12).

Proof

Since $\lambda(\theta)$ is feasible for (4.12) and each θ_i is positive by the condition $\theta_0 > 0$, hence $\lambda(\theta_0)$ is feasible. Let $F_i(\cdot)$ denote the cumulative (marginal) density

$\text{Prob}[\sum_j \tilde{a}_{ij}\lambda_j \leq V_i]$ and we have $F_i = F_i(\lambda) \geq \theta_0$. Since the cumulative density is continuous and increasing it has an inverse. Hence there is a compact neighborhood $N(\theta_0)$ around θ_0 throughout which $\lambda(\theta_0)$ would remain feasible. Now vary θ_0 within the compact domain $D = \{\theta_0 \mid 0 < a \leq \theta_0 \leq 1\}$ until a maximizing value θ_0^* is reached.

By the same reasoning the system reliability measure $R(\theta) = \sum_{i=1}^{m} \log \theta_i$ is a strictly concave function of vector θ in the compact domain D above. Hence there must exist a maximizing value θ^{**} and the associated vector $\lambda(\theta^{**})$.

Note that for alternative probability distributions defining the mixed strategy solution, a distance measure can be used to test their closeness or divergence. Thus if $\delta(A)$, $\delta(B)$ are the probabilities associated with two information structures on the random states of nature we could apply the Kullback-Leibler information measure as follows:

$$I(\delta(A), \delta(B)) = - \sum_j \delta_j(A) \log(\delta_j(A)/\delta_j(B))$$

to test their affinity. Alternatively, the difference in their optimal system reliability measures $R(\theta_A^{**})$, $R(\theta_B^{**})$ may be evaluated.

Two general implications of the mixed strategy solutions to characterize efficiency are important for many applied problems. One is to compare the relative costs of choosing a pure strategy against a mixed strategy under conditions of uncertain information structures. The second is to compare two clusters of DMUs, one containing units more frequently efficient than the other.

For illustrating the first implication we adapt a simple example from Vajda [3]:

Let λ be a scalar and we minimize the expected value of λ subject to $\lambda \geq 0$ and Prob$\{\lambda \geq b\} \geq \theta$ where the scalar variable b is random in the intervak $(0,1)$ with a probability density 2b such that $\int_0^1 2b \, db = 1$. The deterministic equivalent to the chance constraint is $\lambda^2 \geq q$, hence the otpimal soution is $\lambda^* = E\lambda = \sqrt{\theta}$.

Next we introduce mixed strategies and assume the probabilities $\delta(\lambda)$ of $\lambda = j/n$ $(j=0,1,2,...,n)$ to be positive. We have now the LP problem.

$$\underset{\delta}{\text{Min}} \ E\lambda = \sum_{j=0}^{n} (\frac{j}{n})\delta(\frac{j}{n})$$

$$\text{s. t.} \sum_{j=0}^{n} \delta(\frac{j}{n}) = 1, \ \sum_{j=0}^{n} \left(\frac{j}{n}\right)^2 \delta(\frac{j}{n}) = \theta$$

The unknowns are the probabilities $\delta(j/n)$. The optimal solution to this LP problem is $\delta^*(0) = 1-\theta$, $\delta^*(1) = \theta$ and $\delta^*(j/n) = 0$ for all j not equal to zero or n and the optimal objective function is $\lambda_{\delta^*} = E\lambda = \theta$. clearly λ_{δ^*} is less than the deterministic optimal solution $\lambda^* = \sqrt{\theta}$, if θ is a proper fraction. Clearly this result is more general and more widely applicable. Since mixed strategy solutions are defined even when the objective function is partly concave in some domain and partly convex in others, we may apply them to more generalized classes of decision models.

The second important area of application arises in the DEA model (4.2) where by varying k in the objective fucntion we can generate at most n clusters $S_1, S_2, ..., S_n$ according as $P_{(1)} \geq P_{(2)} \geq P_{(3)} \geq ... \geq P_{(n)}$. Then the cluster $S_{(1)}$ has the highest observed probability and $S_{(n)}$ has the lowest. Let $g^*(k)$ be the optimal value of the objective function in (4.2) for cluster k which has the probability $p_{(k)}$. How to compare two or more of these clusters? Two operational criteria may be readily suggested. One is to choose that cluster $S_{(j)}$ for which the probability $p_{(j)}$ is highest. This may be called the modal criterion, which was anlyzed in earlier chapters. One could also use the cluster arising in the mean LP model (4.10), say S_0 as the reference and compare the distance between $S_{(k)}$ and S_0. Note that similar comparative analysis may be made for the four cases A through D mentioned before.

B.   Dynamic Aspects of Technology

Johansen has considered in some detail the various unsolved problems connected with the specification of a dynamic efficiency frontier. He has acknowledged that there may be heterogeneity in different types of capital inputs along with various types of interactions between different vintages of capital equipment e.g., certain basic structures already acquired may facilitate the installment of new pieces of equipment, but to simplify the analysis he made the fundamental assumption that the dynamic decision is separable in two stages. Thus the essential technological choice between factor proportions and exploitation of new production techniques has to be made at the stage when the investment in new production equipment called capital takes place. At later stages choice is made about the extent of utilization of the capital equipment within bounds set by its capacity. Thus at the outset we start with the *exante* function at the microlevel

$$\bar{y} = \phi(\bar{v}_1, \bar{v}_2, \bar{k}) \tag{4.13}$$

where $\bar{y}$ is the capacity measured by maximum output for the new production unit, $\bar{v}_1, \bar{v}_2$ are the two input quantities when the unit is operated at full capacity, $\bar{k}$ is the amount of capital invested in the production unit and the functional form $\phi(\cdot)$ indicates the range of substitution possibilities. At the second stage we have the *expost* production function

$$y = \text{Min}\left(\frac{v_1}{a_1}, \frac{v_2}{a_2}, \bar{y}\right); \ 0 \le y \le \bar{y}$$

$$v_i = a_i y, \ a_i = \bar{v}_i / \bar{y}, \qquad i = 1, 2$$

where $(\bar{v}_1, \bar{v}_2, \bar{y}, \bar{k})$ are no longer variables but fixed i.e., embodied in the technology and the production possibility already chosen. However, not all the microunits may operate at the full capacity level, also the capacity levels may vary across the units. Hence, Johansen assumes the existence of a capacity distribution $f(a_1, a_2)$ which is the probability distribution of the full capacity coefficients a_1, a_2 in the two-input case and also an utilization function $u = u(a_1, a_2)$ such that $0 \le u \le 1$ which he calls the capacity utilization function. By using these two functions he writes in the continuous case the aggregate output Y and the two aggregate inuts V_i as:

$$Y = \iint\limits_{G(a)} f(a_1, a_2) u(a_1, a_2) da_1 da_2$$

$$(4.14)$$

$$V_i = \iint\limits_{G(a)} a_i u(a_1, a_2) f(a_1, a_2) da_1 da_2$$

where $G(a)$ is the utilization region indicating a certain pattern of capacity utilization. As indicated in equation (1.32) of Chapter one we can use the implicit relation (4.14) and the shadow price relation for the quasi-rents i.e. $G(a) = G(\beta_1, \beta_2) = \{\beta_1 a_1 + \beta_2 a_2 \le 1, \beta_1, \beta_2 \ge 0\}$ to define a macro production frontier as:

$$Y = F(V_1, V_2)$$

In case new capacity is introduced, the definitions of macro output and the macro inputs are modified as:

$$Y = g(\beta_1, \beta_2) + Y^+ g^+(\beta_1, \beta_2)$$

$$V_1 = h_1(\beta_1, \beta_2) + Y^+ h_1^+(\beta_1, \beta_2) \qquad (4.15)$$

$$V_2 = h_2(\beta_1, \beta_2) + Y^+ h_2^+(\beta_1, \beta_2)$$

where the functions $g^+(\cdot)$ and $h_i^+(\cdot)$

$$g^+(\beta_1, \beta_2) = \iint\limits_{G(\beta_1, \beta_2)} f^+(a_1 a_2) \, da_1 da_2$$

$$h_i^+(\beta_1, \beta_2) = \iint\limits_{G(\beta_1, \beta_2)} a_i f^+(a_1, a_2) \, da_1 da_2$$

specify additional output realized and additional inputs used per unit of new capacity when the zero quasi-rent line $\beta_1 a_2 + \beta_2 a_2 = 1$ is followed, thus indicating full capacity utilization. The new capacity output is denoted by Y^+ and $f^+(\cdot)$ gives its relative distribution across the micro units. Now the dynamic shifts in the production frontier can be represented either by embodied or disembodied technical progress. In the former case the frontier function implicitly reprsented by (4.15) may be used to define embodied technical progress as favorable shifts in the *exante* function while leaving the efficiency of the already established production units unaffected. In case of disembodied technical progress Johansen distinguishes between (a) the capacity-increasing progress, which increases the capacity of a production unit while leaving the input coefficients unaffected, and (b) the input-saving technical progress, which reduces the input coefficients of a micro unit without affecting its capacity. In the first case we have to distinguish between the pre- and post-progress function by writing the latter as

$$f'(a_1, a_2) = \{1 + \alpha\, k(a_1, a_2)\}\, f(a_1, a_2) \tag{4.16}$$

where $\alpha k(a_1, a_2)$ is the proportionate increase in production capacity for the units having the input coefficients (a_1, a_2). Note that the function $k(a_1, a_2)$ specifies the form of the shift and α is a parameter indicating the size of the shift. In the second case of input-saving technological progress of the disembodied type, we express the new input coefficients a_i^1 as a function of the initial position (a_i^0) as:

$$a_i^1 = \gamma_i(a_1^0, a_2^0), \qquad\qquad i=1,2 \tag{4.17}$$

Then the post-progress capacity distribution $f^1(a_1^1, a_2^1)$ can be derived from the pre-progress function $f^0 = f(a_1^0, a_2^0)$ as

$$f^1(a_1^1, a_2^1) = f^0(\gamma_1^{-1}(\cdot), \gamma_2^{-1}(\cdot)) \mid J(\gamma_1^{-1}, \gamma_2^{-1}) \mid$$

where γ_i^{-1} is obtained by inverting the system (4.17) and $\mid J(\gamma_1^{-1}, \gamma_2^{-1}) \mid$ is the absolute value of the Jacobian of $\gamma_1^{-1}, \gamma_2^{-1}$ with respect to (a_1^1, a_2^1). On using this new post-progress function, one can again define the macro variables

$$Y = \iint_{G(\beta_1, \beta_2)} f^1(a_1^1, a_2^1)\, da_1^1 da_2^1$$

$$\tag{4.18}$$

$$V_i = \iint_{G(\beta_1, \beta_2)} a_i^1 f^1(a_1^1, a_2^1)\, da_1^1 da_2^1 \qquad (i=1,2)$$

and in suitable cases a macro frontier can be defined either as a function or as a correspondence.

Two general comments may be added here about this dynamic characterization of efficiency. Certainly this provides a highly operational way of quantifying the dynamic efficiency, but there exists several probelms in the multiple output case. For one thing the objective function (4.1) is not definable in such cases if we have no observed market prices of outputs. Secondly, the concept of utilization function requires a tremendous amount of data requirement for the case of multiple outputs. Frequently such data are not available in most situations. Thirdly, the concept of a multivariate capacity distribution, although conceptually most appealing may be very hard to empirically estimate or quantify. Capacity sometimes may depend on the allocation or utilization pattern and may be more flexible in such situations. Hence much more applied work is needed in this new area of challenge.

A second approach to characterizing dynamic efficiency, which has been considered by Sengupta [4] in some detail elsewhere follows the method traditionally adopted in the open-dynamic Leontief input-output model. For example the DEA model (4.2) could be modified in the dynamic case as follows:

$$\text{Min } g_k(T) = \sum_{i=1}^{m_1} \beta_i(T) x_{ik}(T) + \sum_{t=1}^{T} (1+\delta)^{-t} \{ \sum_{i=m_1+1}^{m} \gamma_i(t) \Delta x_{ik}(t) \}$$

$$\text{s. t. } \sum_{i=1}^{m_1} \beta_i(t) x_{ij}(t) + \sum_{i=m_1+1}^{m} \gamma_i(t) \Delta x_{ij}(t) \geq y_j(t) + \Delta y_j(t)$$

$$\beta_i(t), \gamma_i(t) \geq 0; \Delta x_{ij}(t) = x_{ij}(t) - x_{ij}(t-1) \tag{4.19}$$

$$\Delta y_j(t) = y_j(t) - y_j(t-1)$$

Here it is assumed that there are two groups of inputs: current inputs (i.e., first m_1 in number) and the capital inputs (i.e., $m-m_1$ in number) and the initial estimates $\beta_i(0), \gamma_i(0)$

are known from the model (4.2) for example. The incremental inputs $\Delta x_{ij}(t)$ and ouputs $\Delta y_j(t)$ are assumed observable. The criterion function here is in terms of the discounted cost function (i.e. δ is the constant rate of discount) of the inputs. If we replace the k-th cost function $g_k(T)$ by its average over the n units i.e. $\overline{g}(T) = (1/n) \sum_{k=1}^{n} g_k(T)$ then this can be easily related to the LAV method of estimation we have discussed in earlier chapters. Although the above model considers the case of single output, its multi-output extension can be easily worked out. Several comments may be made about this formulation. First of all, we note that the optimal values of the parameters $\beta_i(t)$, $\gamma_i(t)$ are not independent here, since they depend through the allocation of inputs between current and future uses. Secondly, it is clear that one gets back the original DEA model (4.2) if $\Delta x_{ij}(t)$ were zero. Hence there may arise a dynamic problem of inconsistency i.e., a particular micro unit may be inefficient at t=0, yet be efficient at some later time points, due to its capital-augmenting allocation which improves future efficiency. Thirdly, one could easily incorporate other flexible features e.g., (a) log-linear formulation as was done by Forsund and Hjalmarsson [5] and referred to in chapter one, (b) two sets of input-output coefficients $a_{ij}(t) = x_{ij}(t)/y_j(t)$ and $b_{ij}(t) = \Delta x_{ij}(t)/\Delta y_j(t)$ corresponding to flow and stock coefficients of the input-output model and also (c) the various rates of utilization of the incremental capacity. Some of these aspects have been generalized by Sengupta [4] in the context of the DEA model e.g., by comparing the myopic policy of efficiency improvement by ignoring all future investment possibilities and the intertemporal optimal policy over the given planning horizon. This offers an interesting field for future research.

4.2   Econometrics and Minimax Frontiers

For an ordinary regression problem with additive errors

$$e_j = y_j - x_j'\beta \qquad\qquad (4.21)$$

the general L_p-norm method of estimation is to find an m-tuple vector β say, which minimizes the norm:

$$\underset{\beta}{\text{Min}} \ L_p = \sum_{j=1}^{n} \left| e_j \right|^p \tag{4.22}$$

For p=1 we have the LAV method of estimation discussed before, which minimizes the sum of absolute errors, for p=2 we obtain the ordinary least squares estimates, while for p=∞ we minimize the maximum of absolute errors. The last one is also called Chebyshev or minimax criterion. It is well known [6] that the L_1-norm provides maximum likelihood (ML) estimators of β if the errors e_j follow independent Laplace distributions (i.e., two-sided exponential distributions), L_2-norm provides the ML estimators if the errors follow independent normal distributions, while the L_∞-norm or the minimax criterion generates ML estimators of β if the errors e_j follow independent uniform distributions. Note that for the production frontier case of one output (y) and m inputs (x) we have the one-sided constraint $e_j \geq 0$, i.e.,

$$y_j = y_j^* - e_j, \ e_j \geq 0, \ y_j^* = \sum_{i=1}^{m} \beta_i x_{ij}$$

for each observation $j \in I_n$, hence the L_p-norm methods have to be applied under such nonnegativity constraints on the errors. Powell [7] has applied the LAV method of estimation to a slightly different model e.g., the censored regression model

$$y_j = \max \{0, \ x_j' \beta + e_j\}$$

where there is a nonnegativity constraint on the dependent variable y. Under certain regularity conditions he proved that the censored LAV estimator $\hat{\beta}$ which minimizes

$$s(\beta) = (1/n) \sum_{j=1}^{n} \left| y_j - \max\{0, x_j'\beta\} \right|$$

over all β in a compact set B is consistent and asymptotically normal for a wide class of error distributions and is also robust to heteroscedasticity.

As we saw before, the nonnegativity constraint on the error and the LAV criterion leads to the Timmer version of the Farrell model e.g., the objective function g_k in (4.2) is replaced by

$$\text{Min } \bar{g} = \sum_{i=1}^{m} \beta_i \bar{x}_i$$

where $\bar{x}_i$ is the sample mean of input x_i. Let $\tilde{\beta}$ be an estimator of β satisfying the optimal basis equation

$$X\tilde{\beta} = \tilde{y}$$

Since this estimator is not unique, McKean and Schrader [8] have defined a function $\lambda'\beta$ to be an estimable function of β if the value of $\lambda'\beta$ is unique for any value of β which satisfies $X\beta = c$ for a given c and proved the following theorem: the function $\lambda'\beta$ is an estimable function of β if and only if the vector λ lies in the row space of X. Furthermore, Bassett and Koenker [9] showed that the estimated function $\lambda'\tilde{\beta}$ is approximately normally distributed with mean $\lambda'\beta$ and variance $\tau^2\lambda'(X'X)^-\lambda$ where $(X'X)^-$ denotes the generalized inverse of $(X'X)$ and τ is the asymptotic standard deviation of the sample median of errors. A bootstrap method of estimating τ from the estimated residuals was suggested on the basis of some Monte Carlo studies. Since this result is similar to least squares except that σ^2 of OLS would replace τ^2, they suggested confidence intervals for $\lambda'\beta$ of the form:

$$\lambda' \, \beta \pm z_{\alpha/2} \hat{\tau} \sqrt{\lambda'(X'\,X)^{-}\lambda} \tag{4.24}$$

where $\hat{\tau}$ is an estimate of τ and z_α critical values are much like t-critical values of least squares theory.

The minimax estimator which minimizes the maximum error i.e.

$$\underset{\beta}{\text{Min}} \; \underset{1 \le j \le n}{\text{Max}} \; |e_j| = |\,e_j(\beta)\,|, \text{ s. t. } e_j \ge 0, \, j \in I_n \tag{4.25}$$

can be appreciated in an applied context in several different ways. First of all, one can apply [10] the statistical theory of optimal design whereby the so-called A-optimal design based on the Chebyshev criterion minimizes the maximum variance of prediction among the L_2-norm estimates. One need only replace the estimated variance $\hat{\sigma}^2$ by that of $\hat{\tau}^2$ as defined in (4.24). Secondly, its robustness can be seen in terms of probabilistic data sets. Thus assume that the data set is such that it maintains a probabilistic feasibility for each constraint j at a level α or higher ($0 < \alpha \le 1$) i.e.,

$$\text{Prob} \; (y_j \le \sum_{i=1}^{m} x_{ji}\beta_i; \, \beta_i \ge 0) \quad \alpha, \, j \in I_n \tag{4.26}$$

Then the following LP model provides a minimax method of obtaining the estimates of (β_0, β):

$$\text{Min } \beta_0 \quad \text{s.t. } X\beta = y \le \beta_0 u; \; X\beta \ge y$$
$$\beta \ge 0, \, \beta_0 \ge 0 \qquad \text{u: a vector of unit elements} \tag{4.27}$$

when each of the chance constraints $X\beta \ge y$ has 100α percent probability of feasibility. Clearly this problem would be transformed to one of nonlinear programming, when the distributional considerations implicit in the chance constraints (4.26) are explicitly introduced (e.g., decision rules higher than the zero order as it is known in the theory of chance-constrained LP models). It is clear that in suitable cases the estimate of β_0 in (4.27) would be related to the confidence interval (4.24) based on the mean estimate $\hat{\beta}$ of the Timmer model. Finally, the minimax principle may be viewed as a general method of finding a polynomial of best approxiamtion to a given set of input-output data. Thus let $P_n(\beta, x_j)$ be a polynomial involving the parameters $\beta = (\beta_1, \beta_2, ..., \beta_m)$ and input vectors x_j. For fixed n we set

$$\beta_0 = \underset{\beta \in B}{\text{Min}} \ \underset{j \in I_n}{\text{Max}} \ | \ y_j - P_n(\beta, x_j) \ | \tag{4.28}$$

where B is the set of variations of the parameters β and it is assumed that the minimum and maximum levels above are finite. In the linear case $P_n(\beta, x_j) = \sum_{i=1}^{m} x_{ji}\beta_i$ and by the definition of a frontier $P_n(\beta, x_j) \geq y_j$, hence we obtain the LP model (4.27). In the LP case one could explore how the sequence of optimal bases changes as n increases or, the tolerance level α in (4.26) changes. Such limit theorems analyzed by Demyanov and Malozemov [11] have considerable scope of application here.

4.3   The Regression and Index Number Problem

Since the DEA and Farrell model (4.2) can be viewed as n LP formulations with an identical set of feasibility constraints, a major question is how to summarize these results when the LP models are optimally solved. Since regression is a convenient method for data compression, it is natural to ask if this method could be applied in the above DEA framework. We have already discussed in earlier chapters two such applications. One is the dummy variable regression approach where the micro data are first classified as they belong to the production frontier or not (and this is done by the DEA model) and then ordinary regressions are computed. This may be called the data clustering-cum-regression (DCR) method). A second approach is to delete or truncate some data points which are found to be either efficient or more frequently efficient by the DEA model (4.2) and then test if the ordinary least squares (OSL) estimates come closer to the mean DEA model, where the mean inputs are used in the objective function. This may be called the contamination-cum-influence curve (CIC) test, since it analyzes the role of mixing efficient data points with inefficient ones by estimating their impact on the divergence between the mean DEA result and the OLS result. As we saw before, Timmer applied this method empirically to study U.S. agricultural production functions.

One may mention two other methods of data analysis which are applicable in particular to the case of multiple outputs and multiple inputs. One is the problem of comparing n LP models, each with its own set of coefficients in the objective function and in the constraints. The second method constructs index numbers based on the principal components of the observed outputs and inputs respectively and then regresses the composite output over the composite inputs, where the composite quantities are the index numbers.

Consider now n LP problems one for each micro unit j=1,2,...,N having output and input vectors y(j), x(j) of dimensions m and n respectively. Further we assume that there is a technology set R(j) for each unit as:

$$R(j) = [(y,x) \mid A(j) \ y(j) \leq x(j); \ y(j), \ x(j) \geq 0] \tag{4.29}$$

where A(j) is the fixed input-output coefficient matrix of dimension n by m. Denote by R the set of finite intersections of the sets R(j). It is clear that the set R will be compact i.e., closed and bounded, if each set R(j) is compact and the latter condition is usually satisfied for input-output data obtained from real life situtaions e.g., farm management survey data. The major problem is how to define some ponits in the set R as efficient relative to others, if it is not empty. Assume that we have an objective function for each unit as: Max $z(j) = c(j)'y(j)$. Then the dual problem can be written in terms of the dual vectors $\beta(j)$ as:

Min $g_j = \beta'(j) \, x(j)$

s.t. $\beta'(j) \, A(j) \geq c'(j)$ (4.30)

$\beta(j) \geq 0, \, j \in I_N = \{1,2,...,N\}$

Now assume $c(j) = u + \epsilon(j)$ to be equal to the mean value $u = (1/N) \sum_{j=1}^{N} c(j)$ and an error component $\epsilon(j)$ which has zero mean and assume the units such that the mean vector u has each component one. We then replace the constraints of (4.30) by the set of common constraints

$\beta'(j)A \geq u; \, \beta(j) \geq 0$

where A belongs to the set R defined before. Clearly we obtain the DEA model (4.2) by replacing j by k in the objective function. Alternatively, we can interpret the model (4.29) in terms of Johansen's efficiency by assuming first that each micro unit produces a single output and that A represents the input coefficient matrix at full capacity level of utilization. Thus we obtain

Max $z = u'y$ s.t. $Ay \leq V, \, y \geq 0$

where V is the aggregate input vector.

Empirically the interface between the optimal LP solutions of (4.29) and ordinary regressions was investigated by Desai [12] and later by Fox and Wang [13]. Desai considered a homogeneous cross-section sample of N=20 agricultural farms for each of which an LP model was computed. Two types of null hypothesis (H_0) were set up to compare the difference between the optimal (mean) farm income ($\bar{z}$) and the actual observed farm income (z_0):

(a) H_0: $z_0 = \bar{z}_0$;   (b) H_0: $1.20z_0 = \bar{z}$

He assumed that the optimal farm income is normally distributed so that the above hypotheses can be tested by the t-statistics. While the null hypothesis in case (a) was rejected at 1% level, it was not so in case (b). Thus he concluded that under the given assumptions the optimal mean farm income is at least 20% higher in a statistical sense than the observed average farm income. However the assumption of normality is very critical in this test. As a matter of fact we fitted an empirical distribution function [14] over the optimal farm income data of Desai and found the distribution to be of the form known as Pearsonian type IV density. However when we applied the nonparametric method of density estimation and the Kolmogorov-Smirnov test, we found Desai's general conclusion to be valid. In another study, Fox and Wand used the optimal solution data i.e., cotton yields per acre in a small homogeneous region in the Mississippi Delta over 1940-1967 from Day's recursive LP models and took as regressor variables the three land classes and four levels of fertilizer use, whereas the dependent variable was the yield. Then they showed that if the information set is enlarged bit by bit in a sequence and ordinary regressions of yield on land and fertilizer.use are computed, the value of R^2 increases till it attains the highest value of unity, when all the information has been incorporated into the regression model. Thus their study showed that regression methods can serve as good approximations for a set of optimal solutions of LP solutions. Clearly this technique is applicable ot the DEA, Farrell and Johansen models.

In contrast to the efficiency measures above, we discuss briefly in this section, some statistical measures oif efficiency as an index number problem. We follow the principal component approach in multivariate analysis, where we introduce two linear functions $X(j) = \beta'(j)\tilde{x}(j)$ and $Y(j) = \alpha'(j)\tilde{y}(j)$ for inputs and outputs, as index numbers. We assume that time series data are available for each j for determining the weight vectors $\alpha(j)$ and $\beta(j)$ and then by regressing outputs $Y(j)$ on inputs $X(j)$ for each j, we determine the input efficiency of j-th DMU. If the regression is linear, then one could write

$$Y(j) = a_j + b_j X(j) + \epsilon(j) \qquad\qquad (4.31)$$

with parameters a_j, b_j and the stochastic component $\epsilon(j)$. If for each j, the stochastic component $\epsilon(j)$ has zero mean and unit variance, then efficiency comparisons across N units may be easily made in suitable cases, e.g.,

(i)   If a_j is zero and $b_1 > b_2 > 0$, then the first DMU is on the average more efficient than the second in a marginal $\partial Y(j)/\partial X(j)$ and average $(Y(j)/X(j))$ sense,

(ii)   if $a_1 > a_2 > 0$, $b_1 > b_2$, then also the first DMU is more efficient in marginal and average sense. Cases $a_1 = a_2 > 0$, $b_1 > b_2$, or $a_1 > a_2 > 0$, $b_1 = b_2$ imply efficiency in marginal (average) but not average (marginal) terms,

(iii) if $0 < a_1 < a_2$, but $b_1 > b_2 > 0$, then there must exist an intersection point with a common input X_0 such that for all $X(j)$ to the right (left) of X_0, the first DMU is more (less) efficient than the second in both marginal and average terms.

(iv)   if the regression is logarithmically linear, as in economic applications

$$\log Y(j) = \hat{a}_j + \hat{b}_j \log X(j) + \log \hat{\epsilon}(j)$$

then, similar comparisons can be made in terms of the new parameters $\hat{a}_j$, $\hat{b}_j$ provided $\log \hat{\epsilon}(j)$ has independent distributions with zero mean and unit variance.

Since the DEA model (4.2) assumes that the input-output data are all positive and all data variations retain this positivity, the largest principal components are positive and by Frobenius theorem on positive matrices the optimal weight vectors $\alpha(j)$, $\beta(j)$ are positive. Hence the composite inputs $X(j)$ and outputs $Y(j)$ have meaningful economic interpretations as index numbers in such cases. However the first principal component may not always be sufficient if it explains e.g., less than 60% of total variance. Hence one may have to consider second and third principal components also but in that case the weight vectors need not necessarily be nonnegtive. Hence their economic meaning is less clear.

4.4 Joint Costs and Nonlinear Frontiers

The standard versions of the DEA and Farrell model use LP models to characterize the production frontier but the LP models assume that outputs and inputs are separable. Loglinear models are separable after the logarithmic transformation. But in the most general case we would have for each unit j=1,2,...,n an implicit function known as the production possibility function

$$F_j(x_{j1}, x_{j2}, ..., x_{jm}; \ y_{j1}, y_{j2}, ..., y_{js}) = 0$$

relating the m inputs and s outputs, where there may exist interdependence between the outputs (or inputs) themselves e.g., two outputs, wool and mutton can be produced in varying proportions by a single production process. Cases in which a single DMU produces two or more technically independent outputs are excluded if there are joint products for outputs. Likewise for joint costs. If the form of the production possibility function can be specified then it is not difficult to incorporate it in the DEA model e.g., in equation (2.7) of Chapter 2 one could adjoin this as a separate constraint. However the essense of the nonparametric theory is that the form of the production possibility function is not specified. Hence we have to explore other methods, till a satisfactory procedure is developed in current research. Of the other methods the nonlinear frontiers appear very promising.

By way of illustration the following two types of nonlinear forms of the input-output relation may be specified. In the first case output (y) is a nonlinear function of the parameters (β):

$$y = h(\beta_1, ..., \beta_m; \ \varepsilon) \tag{4.32}$$

For example the function h($\cdot$) may take two commonly used forms:

(a) $\quad y = \prod_{i=1}^{m} x_i^{\beta_i} \varepsilon, \, 0 < e \leq 1$ $\qquad$ (4.33)

(b) $\quad y = \sum_{i=1}^{m} \beta_i x_i - \sum_{i,s=1}^{m} x_i b_{is} x_s - \varepsilon, \, \varepsilon \geq 0$ $\qquad$ (4.34)

where the parameters β_i, b_{is} may be required to satisfy plausible conditions of economic realism such as the concavity of the production function $h(\cdot)$ in (4.32) with respect to the nonrandom input vector x.

In the second case output is assumed to be nonlinear in the input variables $(\tilde{x})$ which have a fixed probability distribution:

$$y = f(\tilde{x}_1, \tilde{x}_2, \dots, \tilde{x}_m)$$ $\qquad$ (4.35)

Here we have to assume for economic realism that $f(\tilde{x})$ is a concave scalar function of the random vector $\tilde{x} = (\tilde{x}_1, \tilde{x}_2, \dots, x_m)$ Again some examples of this function are:

(a) $\quad y = \prod_{i=1}^{m} \tilde{x}_i^{\beta_i}$ $\qquad$ (4.36)

(b) $\quad y = \sum_{i=1}^{m} \beta_i \tilde{x}_i - \sum_{i,s=1}^{m} \tilde{x}_i b_{is} \tilde{x}_s$ $\qquad$ (4.37)

Some comments about the two different forms of the nonlinear specification are in order. First of all, both specifications assume concavity of output with respect to the inputs and if the errors are assumed to be zero both lead to the same result i.e., $y = f(x_1, \dots, x_m) = h(\beta_1, \dots, \beta_m)$. Secondly, the estimation problems in the two cases are generally different, since the error elements enter into the two models very differently. For example the specification (4.33) leads to a linear estimation model in the transformed varibles $Y = \log y$, $X_i = \log x_i$ and $e = \log \varepsilon$ i.e.,

$$Y = \sum_{i=1}^{m} \beta_i X_i + e \qquad (4.38)$$

provided the disturbance term e is statistically independent of the explanatory variables x_i and the input-output data are all positive. In this case the error component e is unconstrained i.e., it can take positive or negative or zero values as in ordinary least squares theory. Following the LAV method of estimation described before, one could now set up the following nonlinear programming (NLP) model:

$$\text{Min } g_1 = (1/n) \sum_{j=1}^{n} \left(\prod_{i=1}^{m} x_{ji}^{\beta_i} \right)$$

subject to $\prod_{i=1}^{m} x_{ji}^{\beta_i} \geq y_j, \ j = 1, 2, \ldots, n \qquad (4.39)$

$$\beta_i \geq 0, \ i=1,2,\ldots,m$$

Here we have taken the arithmetic mean in the objective function, whereas the use of geometric mean would lead to a log-linear LAV model:

$$\text{Min } g_2 = \sum_{i=1}^{m} \beta_i \bar{X}_i$$

subject to

$$\sum_{i=1}^{m} X_{ji} \beta_i \geq Y_j; \quad j = 1, 2, \ldots, n \qquad (4.40)$$

$$\beta_i \geq 0, \ i=1,2,\ldots,m$$

where $\bar{X}_i = (1/n) \sum_{j=1}^{n} X_{ji}$ and $X_{ji} = \log x_{ji}$. Clearly the role of the error term would be important in choosing between the nonlinear form (4.39) and the log-linear form (4.40).

Similarly for the quadratic production response model (4.34) the LAV estimation model would be:

$$\text{Min } g_3 = \sum_{i=1}^{m} \beta_i \bar{x}_i - (1/n) \sum_{j=1}^{n} \sum_{i,s=1}^{m} x_{ji} b_{is} x_{js}$$

subject to

$$\sum_{i=1}^{m} x_{ji} \beta_i - \sum_{i,s=1}^{m} x_{ji} b_{is} x_{js} \geq y_j, \quad j = 1, 2, \ldots, n \tag{4.41}$$

$$\beta_i \geq 0, \quad i=1,2,\ldots,m$$

Note that this is an LP model in the parameters $\beta = (\beta_i)$, $B = (b_{is})$, where by the concavity requirement the matrix B must satisfy the condition of positive semi definiteness.

We have now to choose between the three specifications i.e., the lienar form and the two nonlinear cases. Here we adopt a goodness of fit criterion and develop a curvature measure of intrinsic nonlinearity. In a general notation we use θ for the parameter and $\hat{\theta}$ as the optimal soution of the programming models. Let $\eta_j(\hat{\theta})$ denote the residual error i.e.,

$$\eta_j(\hat{\theta}) = y_j(\hat{\theta}) - y_j, \quad j = 1, 2, \ldots, n \tag{4.42}$$

where

$$y_j(\hat{\theta}) = \begin{cases} \sum_{i=1}^{m} x_{ji} \beta_i & \text{for the linear case} \\ \prod_{i=1}^{m} x_{ji}^{\beta_i} & \text{for the nonlinear case} \end{cases}$$

$$\tag{4.39}$$

Since the estimated error $\eta_j(\hat{\theta})$ is nonnegative for the production frontier estimation,

we can define the explanatory power of any estimate $\hat{\theta}$ by the statistic $R(\hat{\theta})$:

$$R(\hat{\theta}) = 1 - \frac{\sum\limits_{j=1}^{m} \left| \eta_j(\hat{\theta}) \right|}{\Sigma y_j} = 1 - \frac{\Sigma \eta_j(\hat{\theta})}{\Sigma y_j} \tag{4.43}$$

For nonnegative output levels we must have

$$0 \le R(\hat{\Theta}) \le 1 \tag{4.44}$$

Clearly the best fit is given by that $\hat{\theta}*$ for which $R(\hat{\theta})$ is the highest i.e.,

$$\text{Max } R(\hat{\theta}) = R(\hat{\theta}*) \tag{4.45}$$

or, in error terms

$$\text{Min } E(\hat{\theta}) = E(\hat{\theta}*)$$

where $\quad E(\hat{\theta}) = \Sigma \eta_j(\hat{\theta})/\Sigma y_j = $ overall error

Note that this statistic $R(\hat{\theta})$ is analogous to the squared mutliple correlation coefficient i.e., R^2 which is most often used in standard regression theory as a measure of the explanatory power of the fitted model.

One can use the residual error $\eta_j(\hat{\theta})$ in (4.42) in another useful way e.g., to develop a linearized version of the nonlinear model (4.39). We expand the output vector

$y(\theta) = (y_j(\theta))$ in a Taylor series up to linear terms around a fixed parameter value θ^o with p components say:

$$y(\theta) = y(\theta^o) + \sum_{i=1}^{p} (\theta_i - \theta_i^o)\underline{v}_i$$

where $\underline{v}_i$ is the gradient vector evaluated at θ^o i.e., $\underline{v}_i = \partial y(\theta)/\partial\theta_i$. We can then test the sensitivity of the nonlinear model (4.39) to linearizing approximations by a suitable sequential iteration procedure [15].

Next we consider the random input model (4.35) illustrated by the two specific forms (4.36) and (4.37). Here the random input vector $\tilde{x}$ is assumed to have a fixed probability distribution with a finite mean and variance. In default of the knowledge of the parameters of this distribution we may minimize the upper bound of the following inequality

$$E[f(\tilde{x}_1, \tilde{x}_2, \ldots, \tilde{x}_m)] \leq f[(\bar{x}_1, \bar{x}_2, \ldots, \bar{x}_m)]$$

which holds by Jensen's inequality. Here E is expectation and $\bar{x} = (\bar{x}_1, \bar{x}_2, \ldots, \bar{x}_m)'$ is the mean input vector. The constraint set specification now needs some care due to the fact that the inputs are random. One method is to adopt a minimax approach which allows a chance-constrained interpretation of the constraints. Thus if P is the probability, and $u_0 = \min(u_j, u_j > 0)$ where u_j is the tolerance level for the constraint j=1,2,...,n:

$$P[\sum_i f(x_{ji}) \geq y_j] \geq u_0 \tag{4.46}$$

then the nonlinear minimax model may be specified as follows:

$$\underset{\theta}{\text{Min}} \; \underset{u_0}{\text{Max}} \; \bar{g} = f(\bar{x}_1, \bar{x}_2, \ldots \bar{x}_m) + u_0$$

subject to (4.46) and $u_0 \leq 1$ (4.47)

For the case of log-linear form (4.42) this will become

$$\underset{\theta}{\text{Min}} \; \underset{u_0}{\text{Max}} \; \bar{g} = \prod_{i=1}^{m} \bar{x}_i^{\beta_i} + u_0$$

subject to $P[\; \prod_{i=1}^{m} x_{ji}^{\beta_i} \geq y_j] \geq u_0$ (4.48)

$$u_0 \leq 1, \;\; j=1,2,\ldots,n_1; \;\; n_1 \leq n$$

Here it is assumed that n_1 of the total n sample points satisfy a tolerance level of at least u_0. If the observed data set D = $(x_{ji}, y_j; j=1,2,\ldots,n; i=1,2,\ldots,m)$ is such that they satisfy $u_0 = 1.0$ then the chance constraint relations may be dropped and one may specify an LP model in the transformed variables:

$$\underset{\beta}{\text{Min}} \; \bar{g} = \sum_{i=1}^{m} \beta_i \bar{X}_i$$

subject to

$$\sum_{i=1}^{m} X_{ji} \beta_i \geq Y_j, \;\; j = 1, 2, \ldots, n \qquad (4.49)$$

$$\beta_i \geq 0$$

where $X_{ji} = \log x_{ji}$, $\bar{X}_i = (1/n) \sum_{j=1}^{m} X_{ji}$, $Y_j = \log y_j$. Note that this formulation is equivalent to the LP model (4.40). In the general case however the equivalence may not hold due to two reasons. First, a subset of the observed input-output data set D may fail to satisfy the tolerance level $u_0 = 1.0$, in which case the chance constraints have to be invoked, which would introduce more nonlinearity.   Second, the data set may be screened in order to identify subsets $S_1, S_2, ..., S_k$ ranked by the optimal values of $u^*_{0k} = u^*_0(S_k)$:

$$u^*_{01} \geq u^*_{02} \geq u^*_{03} \geq ... \geq u^*_{0k} > 0 \qquad (4.50)$$

where u^*_{0k} is the optimal value of u_0 in (4.47) for the data set S_k.

To compute the optimal values u^*_0 of the tolerance level u_0 in (4.48) e.g., one needs to specify the probability distribution of the input vector; in default of this knowledge the nonlienar production frontier may be estimated by a criterion of minimizing the maximum derivation i.e., the Chebyshev criterion:

$$\text{Min } \beta_0$$

subject to

$$\prod_{i=1}^{m} x_{ji}^{\beta_i} \geq y_j, \; j = 1, 2, ..., n$$

$$\prod_{i=1}^{m} x_{ji}^{\beta_i} - y_j \leq \beta_0, \; j = 1, 2, ..., n \qquad (4.51)$$

$$\beta_0 \geq 0, \; \beta_i \geq 0, \; i = 1, 2, ..., m$$

These estimates of (β_0, β) are known to be robust against data perturbations. In the log-linear case (4.49) the Chebyshev criterion would lead to:

$$\text{Min } \beta_0$$

subject to

$$\prod_{i=1}^{m} X_{ji}^{\beta_i} \geq Y_j, \; j = 1, 2, ..., n$$

$$\prod_{i=1}^{m} X_{ji}^{\beta_i} - Y_j \le \beta_0, \quad j = 1, 2, \ldots, n \tag{4.52}$$

$$\beta_0 \ge 0, \quad \beta_i \ge 0, \quad i = 1, 2, \ldots, m$$

Again one could define the statistic $R(\hat{\theta})$ as in (4.43) for this minimax model (4.52) and determine which subset of the data set gives the best fit in the sense of $\max R(\hat{\theta})$.

It is clear that the nonlinear forms of the DEA model compared to the linear form have several practical advantages. First of all, if a linear DEA model fits the data set, then under mild regularity conditions a suitable nonlinear model can be constructed giving a better fit. The extent of better fit may be directly measured by the statistic $R(\hat{\theta})$ which is comparable to the squared multiple correlation coefficient. Secondly, the nonlinear production frontier may in suitable cases be more useful in locating the input interval at which average output attains its maximum. For example consider the quadratic production response model (4.41) and take those units only which are on the frontier. For these units denoted by asterisks on outputs and inputs we obtain the quadratic response:

$$y^* = \beta^{*'}x^* - x^{*'}B^*x^*, \quad B^* = (b^*_{is})$$

By construction B^* is positive definite (i.e. output is concave), hence there exists an input level, x^{**} say at which y^* is maximized i.e.,

$$x^{**} = (1/2)B^{*-1}\beta^*$$

Thus all units (x^*, y^*) on the frontier are efficient in the LAV sense but those in the vicinity of the input level x^{**} generate peak output on the strictly concave production frontier. Thirdly, in situations where a suitable nonlinear frontier provides a significantly better fit than the linear model as measured by the statistic $R(\hat{\theta})$ e.g., we may estimate the impact of nonlinearity through a sequence of linearized estimates and their convergence characteristics. Lastly, the LAV method of estimation for the production frontier case can be made more robust by the application of Chebyshev criterion i.e., minimizing the maximum deviation. So long as the minimum of maximum deviation is not altered by data perturbations, the frontier estimates of θ would remain unaffected. This holds both for the linear and the nonlienar versions of the DEA model.

As an empirical application we consider the education example used before, which is based on the sample of 25 homogeneous units. We compute three sets of programming models and obtain the LAV estimates of the response coefficients $\theta = (\theta_i)$ for the linear model, the log-linear model and the quadratic model. The values of $R(\hat{\theta})$ defined in (4.43) and the average error $\bar{\eta}(\hat{\theta}) = (1/n) \Sigma \eta_j(\hat{\theta})$ are as follows:

	$\bar{\eta}(\hat{\theta})$	$R(\hat{\theta})$
Linear	0.109	0.921
Quadratic	0.084	0.961
Log-linear	0.077	0.981

It is clear that the nonlinear models out-perform the linear model and the log-linear form performs better than the quadratic. Similarly for the minimax estimates the log-linear model out-performed the other two.

Some comments are in order about the various forms of the nonlinear frontier. First of all, the regression models on average production functions have used CES (constant elasticity of substitution) type functions, which for two inputs: capital (K) and labor (L) is of the form:

$$Y = B[\delta K^{-\rho} + (1 - \delta) L^{-\rho}]^{-\mu/\rho}$$

where the elasticity of scale parameter μ and the elasticity of substitution parameter $\sigma = (1 + \rho)^{-1}$ are constant but the output elasticities are variable if $\sigma \neq 1$. However the above form of the CES function cannot be transformed to a function linear in the parameters and is therefore very inconvenient to estimate. Some recent attempts [16] at estimation of the CES function by nonlinear least squares show that the mean, mode and median estimators of the elasticity of substitution are all biased towards unity, i.e., the Cobb-Douglas function, the median estimator showing the least percentage bias. By using an approximation based on the Taylor series expansion of $\ln f(\rho) = \ln [\delta + (1 - \delta)(K/L)^{-\rho}]$ around $\rho = 0$, the CES function is usually estimated from

$$\ln (Y/L) \simeq \ln B + h \ln L + \mu\delta \ln (K/L) - (1/2) \rho\mu\delta (1 - \delta)(\ln K/L)^2,$$
$$h = \mu - 1$$

where the approximation is better, the closer the elasticity of substitution is to unity. But if a competitive market for labor can be assumed, along with constant returns to scale and profit maximization, then the elasticity of substitution σ can be estimated directly from the marginal productivity relation:

$$\ln (Y/L) = a + \sigma \ln W$$

where Y and W are outputs and wages in real terms. However in many empirical cases increasing returns to scale may prevail as Griliches and Ringstad [17] found for Norwegian manufacturing data and also the observed price series may not be the most appropriate.

Another alternative form which is widely applied in production function studies is the translog function, which is a quadratic function in logarithmic transformations of output and several inputs. For our education data on the public school districts in California we applied this type of function [18] to estimate scale by both production frontiers and the average production functions and the results uniformly showed the existence of increasing returns to scale, although the frontier estimates specified lower values of the overall scale.

A more general functional form is available through the posynomial functions widely used in the theory of geometric programming. Here output (y_k) of type k is expressed as a sum of positive polynomials $P_j(x)$, each of which being a polynomial function of the m inupts (x_i) say:

$$y_k = \sum_{j=m_k}^{n_k} c_j P_j(x), \quad P_j(x) = x_1^{a_{j1}}, x_2^{a_{j2}}, \ldots, x_m^{a_{jm}}$$

where each c_j and each x_i are positive and a_{ji} can take positive, negative and zero values (e.g. negative vaues may indicate that the corresponding input is like pollution having negative marginal products). Various computer routines [19] are now available for solving this type and other generalized forms of geometric programming problems.

One problem with these general nonlinear forms is that the feasibility set of constraints may fail to be convex everywhere, thus resulting in the failure of the standard Kuhn-Tucker necessary and sufficient conditions. Arrow et al. [20] have suggested using suitable penalty functions as transformations to convexify the nonconvex regions, although these have not been explored in the DEA framework.

4.5 Efficiency Analysis in the Stochastic Case

From an applied decision viewpoint two issues are important in measuring productive efficiency, besides the econometric problem of estimation. The first is the characterization of efficiency when the input-output data are subject to a stochastic generating mechanism. The second is to interpret the DEA model as a conditional mixture of different facets of the entire efficiency surface. The first aspect has important implications for the DEA model viewed as a multi-criteria problem under stochastic constraints, while the second aspect introduces the notion of decision regions for each facet of the efficiency surface. These regions specify conditions which may be closely related to the minimax class of estimates discussed in earlier chapters.

Consider the DEA model (4.2) as a team decision problem:

$$\text{Min } C\beta \quad \text{s.t. } \beta \in R = \{\beta \mid X\beta \geq y; \, y \geq 0\} \tag{4.53}$$

where $C\beta$ denotes a vector with a typical element $g_k = x'_k\beta$, $k=1,2,...,n$ representing the objective of the k-th DMU. For a given set (C,X,y) of observed data it is well known from the theory of vector efficiency that any feasible solution β^* in R is efficient in (4.53) if and only if it is optimal for the problem $\underset{\beta \in R}{\text{Min }} \sum_{k=1}^{n} \lambda_k g_k$ with a given $\lambda = (\lambda_1, \lambda_2, ..., \lambda_n)$ where $\lambda_k > 0$ and $\sum_{k=1}^{n} \lambda_k = 1$. Hence the search for efficient points of the vector LP problem (4.53) reduces to he scalar problem:

$$\text{Min } \lambda'C\beta \quad \text{s.t. } \beta \in R \text{ and } \lambda \in L \tag{4.54}$$

where $L = \{\lambda \mid \lambda_k \geq 0, \sum_{k=1}^{n} \lambda_k = 1\}$ and the associated search for the set $G(\beta_B)$ of λ's which make the basic feasible solutions β_B optimal. The existence of a positive vector $\lambda = (\lambda_k)$ with $\lambda_k > 0$ in L associated with an efficient point may be interpreted under some regularity assumptions as the existence of a probability distribution as Sengupta et al. [21] have shown and in that case $G(\beta) = \lambda'C\beta = \sum_{k=1}^{n} \lambda_k g_k(\beta)$ would appear as a weighted average of the individual objectives. They have further shown that for any basic feasible solution β_B which is optimal, there exist open intervals of values of λ_k (k=1,2,...,n) for which $G(\beta)$ attains its largest and smallest values. On the basis of the range of these values for any given basic feasible solution of β_B (4.54), we can compute the probability that the solution β_B is also optimal. They proved the following theorem.

Theorem 3

Let $L = \{\lambda \mid \sum_{k=1}^{s} \lambda_k = 1, 0 < \lambda_k < 1\}$ be a s-dimensional Euclidean space E^s and let G_H be an arbitrarily assigned Lebesgue measurable subset of L and let β_B be an arbitrary basic feasible solution of the LP model (4.54). Then the following probabilities exist and can be explicitly computed:

(i)   Prob $[\beta_B$ is optimal $\mid \lambda \in G_H]$

(ii) Prob $[\lambda \in G_H \mid \beta_B$ is optimal$]$

This result has several practical implications. First of all, it shows that given any basic feasible solution, one could compute the probability that it would be optimal. Secondly, if one interprets the variations in values of $x_k = \bar{x} + w_k$ around the mean value $\bar{x}$ to be purely random, it would be possible to ascertain the decision region G_H say and the probability of a potential basic feasible solution such as β_B to become optimal. In this case one could analyze the stochastic LP model with one objective function

$$g(w) = \underset{\beta \in R}{\text{Min}} \; x_k'(w)\beta \qquad\qquad (4.55)$$

rather than multiple objective functions. Since this LP model has a single objective function it is more often likely to have an optimal solution than the vector minimum problem (4.53) for a given realized value of the random state of nature $w \in W$. With respect to this class (4.55) of stochastic LP problems Stancu-Minasian [22] has defined efficiency as follows:

A point $\beta^o \in R$ is said to be efficient with probability one if there exists no other feasible vector $\hat{\beta} \in R$ almost surely as good as β^o with respect to the objective function $x_k'(w)\beta$ and even better than β^o with a positive probability. Tammer [23] has generalized this result to define a point $\beta^o \in R$ to be ε-efficient (i.e. efficient with probability 1 - ε) if there exists no other point $\hat{\beta} \in R$ such that

$$\text{Prob}\{w \mid f(\hat{\beta}, w) \leq f(\beta^o, w)\} \geq 1 - \varepsilon$$

and

$$\text{Prob}\{w \mid f(\hat{\beta}, w) < f(\beta^o, w)\} > 0$$

where $f(\beta, w)$ is the objective function of (4.55).

Thus it is clear that one could characterize efficient points in this framework by following several recent techniques in the theory of stochastic linear programming [24].

The single objective stochastic LP model (4.55) can be viewed in an alternative way. Assume that we have a realized value of the state of nature $w \in W$ and we write the optimal basis equation as:

$$X^*(k)\tilde{\beta}^*(k) = y(k) \tag{4.56}$$

where $B^*(k)$ is denoted by the square matrix $X^*(k)$ of order m. Assuming nondegeneracy of the ptimal basis we obtain $\tilde{\beta}^*(k) = X^{*-1} y(k)$, where the vector $\tilde{\beta}^*(k)$ has nonnegative elements. We now assume for the case of random state of nature that the output vector $y(k)$ captures the random effect as follows:

$$y(k) = \mu(k) + u(k)$$
$$\mu(k) = X^*(k)\tilde{\beta}^*(k) \tag{4.57}$$

where $u(k)$ is the error vector assumed to be normally distributed with zero mean and a variance-covariance matrix V fixed for all k=1,2,...,n. In OLS models this assumption is necessarily fulfilled but in this case it may not be, hence we term it the pseudo-normal equations of the pseudo-regression model where the population mean vector $\mu(k)$ equals $X^*(k)\beta^*(k)$. Note that the errors $u(k)$ in (4.58) are disturbances constrained under the optimal basis $X^*(k)$. Which of the n LP estimators $\hat{\beta}(k)$ woudl we now accept as the best? As indicated in Chapter 3 we can apply an optimal design criterion, known as A-optimal design [25].

One has to note however that there are other criteria of optimality in the theory of statistical design and although they provide some insights for choosing one facet of the efficiency surface, their economic meaning is not always very clear. Secondly, the errors are constrained around each optimal basis $X^*(k)$, so that these are conditional models which may not apply in unconditional situations. Finally, the distribution of the errors around the optimal basis $X^*(k)$ may be estimated by a nonparametric method to see the implications of a departure from normality. Several research issues are quite open here.

References

1.   Kullback, S., Information Theory and Statistics, New York: John Wiley, 1959.

2.   Fromovitz, S., Nonlinear programming with randomization, Management Science, 11 (1965), 831-846.

3.   Vajda, S., Probabilistic Programming, New York: Academic Press, 1972.

4.   Sengupta, J.K., Efficiency measurement in nonmarket systems through data envelopment analysis, in Stochastic Optimization and Economic Models, Dordrecht: D. Reidel Publishing, 1986.

5.   Forsund, F.R. and Hjalmarsson, K., Generalized Farrell measures of efficiency: an application to milk processing in Swedish dairy plants, Economic Journal, 89 (1979), 294-315.

6.   Zanakis, S.H. and Rustagi, J.S., eds., Optimization in Statistics, Amsterdam: North Holland, 1982.

7.   Powell, J.L., Least absolute deviation for the censored regression model, Journal of Econometrics, 25 (1984), 303-325.

8.   Mckean, J.W. and Schrader, R.M., Least absolute error analysis of variance, in Statistical Data Analysis Based on the L_1-norm and Related Methods, Amsterdam: North Holland, 1987.

9.   Bassett, G. and Koenker, R., Asymptotic theory of least absolute error regression, Journal of American Statistical Association, 73 (1978), 618-622.

10. Sengupta, J.K., Recent nonparametric measures of productive efficiency, in Econometrics of Planning and Efficiency, Dordrecht: Kluwer Academic Publishers, 1988.

11. Demyanov, V.F. and Malozemov, V.N., Introduction to Minimax, Translated from Russian, New York: John Wiley, 1974.

12. Desai, D.K., Increasing income and production on Indian farms: possibilities with existing resource supplies on individual farms, in Selected Readings from Indian Journal of Agricultural Economics, Bombay, 1965.

13. Fox, K.A. and Wang, T., Estimating the effects of institutional and technological changes upon agricultural development: a comparison of multiple regression and programming approaches, in Economic Models, Estimation and Risk Programming, Berlin: Springer-Verlag, 1969.

14. Sengupta, J.K., Decision Models in Stochastic Programming, Amsterdam: North Holland, 1982.

15. Sengupta, J.K., Nonlienar measures of technical efficiency, forthcoming in Computers and Operations Research (1988).

16. Gapinski, J.H. and Kumar, T.K., On estimating the elasticity of factor substitution by nonlinear least squares, in Econometrics of Planning and Efficiency, Dordrecht: Kluwer Academic Publishers. 1988

17. Griliches, Z. and Ringstad, V., Economies of Scale and the Form of the Production Function, Amsterdam: North Holland, 1971.

18. Sengupta, J.K. and Sfeir, R.E., Production frontier estimates of scale in public schools in California, Economics of Education Review, 5 (1986), 297-307.

19. Avriel, M. ed., Advances in Geometric Programming, New York: Plenum Press, 1980.

20. Arrow, K.J., Gould, F.J. and Howe, S.M., A general saddle point result for constrained optimization, in K.J. Arrow and L. Hurwicz eds., Resource Allocation Processes, New York: Cambridge University Press, 1977.

21. Sengupta, S.S., Podrebarac, M.L. and Fernando, T.D.H., Probabilities of optima in multi-objective linear programs, in J.L. Cochrane and M. Zeleny eds., Multiple Criteria Decision Making, Coumbia: University of South Carolina Press, 1973.

22. Stancu-Minasian, I.M., Stochastic Programming with Multiple Objective Functions, Dordrecht: D. Reidel Publishing, 1984.

23. Tammer, K., Relations between stocahstic and parametric programming for decision problems with a random objective function, Math. Operationsforsch. Statist. Ser. Optim., 9 (1978), 523-535.

24. Sengupta, J.K., Optimal Decisions Under Uncertainty: Methods Models and Management, New York: Springer-Verlag, 1985.

25. Chernoff, H., Sequential Analysis and Optimal Design, Philadelphia: Society for Industrial and Applied Mathematics, 1972.

Chapter 5

EXTENSIONS OF NONPARAMETRIC APPROACH

Nonparametric efficiency analysis is one of the most active fields of current research on measuring productivity of public sector enterprises. Since this involves several disciplines such as economics, management science, statistics and operations research, it is quite natural that future generalizations would be forthcoming in all these disciplines. Although Farrell developed his efficiency concept in the context of a production frontier, his interest was mainly statistical. The DEA model on the other hand generalized the input-output ratio measure to multiple inputs and outputs, which is basically a technical measure for evaluating engineering components and plants, although this tool was widely applied in school systems, hospitals and other quasi-market organizations. The DEA model was basically designed to compare managerial efficiency of a set of relatively homogeneous DMUs. The economic theory of efficiency has sought to characterize efficiency in terms of certain implicit prices associated with certain subsets of the feasible production set. In case of single output and multiple inputs the inefficiency of a set of micro units may simply be measured as a deviation from the full capacity level of utilization. Such deviations or distortions are not so simple to measure in case of multiple outputs, since the detailed data on allocation of every input to all possible outputs are not at all available. Problems also remain in the dynamic framework, when efficiency variations over time have to be related to changes in inputs, in capacity and in the technology. Finally, there is the econometric problem of estimating the production frontier but in a nonparametric way. This leads to various recent techniques such as the influence curve approach, nonparametric methods of regression and the bootstrap techniques.

5.1   Economic Generalizations

Several interesting lines of generalization have been made in recent times on the

Farrell measure of technical efficiency. First of all, Fare and Lovell [1] noted that Farrell measures technical efficiency relative to an isoquant rather than to an 'efficient subset' and his measure is a radial measure of technical efficiency in the sense that it gives the maximum amount by which an input vector x yielding the single output y can be proportionately reduced while still producing output y. Thus the function $F(y,x)$ defined by

$$\text{Min } \{\lambda \mid \lambda \cdot x \in L(y)\}, \quad x \in L(y)$$

and (5.1)

$$F(y,x) = \infty, \quad x \notin L(y), \text{ for } y > 0$$

is called the Farrell (input) measure of technical efficiency, where the production technology is modeled by a production function $\phi(x)$, or inversely by the input correspondence $L(y)$, where $\phi(x)$ is the maximal output obtainable from an input vector x and $L(y)$ denotes all input vectors yielding at least the output y:

$$\phi(x) = \max \{y \mid x \in L(y)\}, L(y) = \{x \mid \phi(x) \geq y\} \tag{5.2}$$

Fare and Lovell introduced two other subsets of the input correspondence $L(y)$:

Isoquant: $\text{Isoq } L(y) = \{x \mid x \in L(y), \lambda \cdot x \in L(y),$

$\lambda \in [0,1) \}$ for $y > 0$

and $\text{Isoq}(0) = 0$

Efficient Subset: $\text{Eff } L(y) = \{x \mid x \in L(y), z \leq x$ (5.3)

implies that $z \notin L(y)\}$ for $y > 0$

and $\text{Eff } L(0) = 0$

The efficient subset Eff $L(y)$ helps to identify production functions whose isoquants are not contained in their Eff $L(y)$. If the production function $\phi(x)$ is continuous and satisfies a strong free disposability property i.e., $\hat{x} \geq x$ implies $\phi(\hat{x}) > \phi(x)$, then the Farrell efficiency measure satisfies the condition Eff $L(y)$ = Isoq $L(y)$. clearly the family of CES production functions with strictly positive elasticity of substitution satisfies this property but there exists functions like the Leontief-type production function and the subfamilies of variable elasticity of substitution and weak input disposability where Eff $L(y) \neq$ Isoq $L(y)$. Fare and Lovell proposed some nonradial mesures for which Eff $L(y) \neq$ Isoq $L(y)$. However in an applied sense the choice between a radial and nonradial measure is decided by the empirical data and as our discussion in chapter 4 shows the probelms of robust estimation is very critical.

One of the most useful and fundamental extension of Farrell efficiency is provided by the DEA model discussed before. Recently Charnes et al. [2] have extended the DEA model in several directions e.g., by providing for tests for Pareto-efficiency. On reaching a non-Pareto-efficient point their method calculates all the optimal observed points in its facet, hence, implicitly all the convex combinations which form the facet. Thus for m inputs x_i and s outputs y_r let $f(x_1,...,x_m; y_1,...,y_s) = 0$ be the linear equation of the facet. Suppose we want to test if the point $(\bar{x}, \bar{y})$ is efficient. Assuming sufficient differentiability in the neighborhood of the interior point $(\bar{x}, \bar{y})$, we compute

$$\partial y_r/\partial x_i = - (\partial f/\partial x_i)/(\partial f/\partial y_r) \tag{5.4}$$

where each partial derivative is evaluated at $(\bar{x}, \bar{y})$ then the optimal dual variables corresponding to the input $\bar{x}_i$ and output $\bar{y}_r$ are respectively $(\partial f/\partial x_i)_{(\bar{x},\bar{y})}$ and $(\partial f/\partial y_r)_{(\bar{x},\bar{y})}$. It is clear from (5.4) that the rate of change of output y_r with respect to input x_i is simply the negative of the ratio of the optimal dual x_i constraint variable to the optimal dual y_r constraint variable. More specifically all Pareto-efficient points (X_j,Y_j) of the facet for the points $(\bar{x}, \bar{y})$ satisfy

$$\mu^{*'}y - \upsilon^{*'}x - \phi^* = 0$$

where (μ^*, υ^*) are the dual vector evaluators at an optimal basic solution. By the Charnes-Cooper test criterion, it follows that

$$f(x,y) = \mu^{*'}y - \upsilon^*x - \phi^* = 0$$

where we have clearly $\mu_r^* = \partial f/\partial y_r$ and $-\upsilon_i^* = \partial f/\partial x_i$.

A second aspect emphasized by them deals with the geometry of the empirical Pareto-efficient production functions determined by the multi-output DEA model. For instance in many practical situations a decision maker tries to choose inputs and outputs with the thought that the empirical production frontier should be isotone or order-preserving in the sense that if $x^a \le x^b$, then $f(x^a) \le f(x^b)$. They showed that in the single output case (s=1) the empirical frontier function (i.e. the Pareto-efficient function) is always isotone. But the multiple output case however satisfies only a weaker property that the frontier function is only 'cone-directional isotone' i.e. there always exists a cone of directions in output space on which the outputs' projection is isotone. This is a fundamental result, since it may subsume both radial and nonradial measures of efficiency we discussed before. Also the choice of directions may provide the policymaker some further scope for optimization e.g. the theory of the second best in public goods literature.

A third aspect in the DEA model is the distinction between discretionary and non-discretionary inputs. In many practical applications inputs such as unemployment rate or median salary are not subject to discretionary change by the decision makers. These are called non-discretionary inputs. If sufficient data are available, then these inputs have to be incorporated through additional constraints to obtain the efficiency rating by DEA principle.

Very similar to the non-discretionary inputs is the fixed or, semi-fixed factors in production theory in economics which distinguishes a static or short-run production frontier from a dynamic one. Johansen has consistently emphasized the relevance of this distinction for studying technical progress and its impact on the dynamic shift of the production frontier. Recently, Forsund and Jansen [3] have explored the problem of interaction between sectoral models of efficiency based on microdata and the economy-wide models of growth. Besides aggregation and the micro-macro linkage, there remain important problems of characterizing the dynamic components of efficiency and also empirically estimating them. The empirical estimation of the capacity distribution in the multiple output case, the determination of the utilization region and the specification of 'learning by doing' phenomena in technical progress are some of the major problems which remain yet to be tackled.

5.2   Extensions of Data Envelopment Analysis

Since the DEA model is so widely applicable, it is important to consider its extra-economic aspects for the purpose of generalization.

The method of data envelopment analysis (DEA) can be viewed in two ways: as a method of deriving envelopes out of a set of data points, or as a technique of estimating efficiency in the input-output space. In both cases we have to assess the influence of individual data points and detect the most influential cases where the sensitivity may be high. In situations where predictions are needed it may be necessary moreover to circumvent partially the effects of sensitive data points by isolating stable regions, or regions where the influence is minimal or insignificant. The influence curve approach of statistical regression theory [4,5] utilizes the residuals from the regression curve for various diagnostic searches and robustness issues e.g., outlier tests, robust estimates and variate transformations to handle non-Gaussianity. We may now discuss some aspects of the empirical influence curve (EIC) approach in the context of the DEA model, when the data points are subject to a stochastic generating mechanism. Specifically we would discuss the following issues:

(1)   develop a method of EIC approach by analyzing the residuals of the DEA model,

(2) compare linear versus nonlinear statistical transformations of the data points as measures of efficiency, and finally,

(3) explore some methods of nonparametric regression in the DEA models, which does not assume any specific functional form for the production frontier.

These applied aspects are intended to make the DEA model more operational particularly in control environments and non-market contexts where the traditional assumptions of economic theory as to the competitive equilibrium may fail to hold.

A. Analysis of Residuals

Consider a set of n decision-making units (DMUs) each producing one output $y = (y_j)$ with m inputs $X = (x_{ji})$, $j=1,2,...,n$ and $i=1,2,...,m$ such that

$$y_j = x'_j \beta - \varepsilon_j, \varepsilon_j \geq 0; \quad j = 1, 2, \dots , n \qquad (5.5)$$

i.e.,

$$y = X\beta - \varepsilon, \quad \varepsilon \geq 0$$

where ε_j is the nonnegative error component. If ε_j's were unconstrained and distributed independently of x_j's with a zero mean, then we would have the standard linear regression model:

$$y = X\beta + e, e \sim N(0,\sigma^2 I) \qquad (5.6)$$

where the vector $\tilde{e}$ of estimated residuals and the estimates $\tilde{y}, \beta$ would satisfy:

$$\tilde{e} = y - \tilde{y} = (I - M)e, \tilde{y} = X\beta$$

$$\beta = (X' X)^{-1} X' y, M = X(X' X)^{-1} X' \qquad (5.7)$$

By using the specification (5.5) one could specify two versions of the DEA model. One assumes that output alone (i.e., ε_j) is random, so that by minimizing the sum $\sum_{j=1}^{n} |\varepsilon_j|$ one obtains the estimates $\hat{\beta}$ of the efficiency frontier. This leads to the least absolute value (LAV) estimator $\hat{\beta}$ as we have seen before:

$$\underset{\beta \in C(\beta)}{\text{Min}} \quad \bar{g} = \beta' \bar{x} \tag{5.8}$$

where

$$C(\beta) = \{\beta \mid X\beta - y \geq 0, \beta \geq 0\}$$

$$\bar{x} = (\bar{x}_i), \bar{x}_i = (1/n) \sum_{j=1}^{n} x_{ji}$$

The second version compares each DMU relative to the overall constraint set $C(\beta)$ by solving n LP models one for each DMU i.e.,

$$\underset{\beta(k) \in C(\beta)}{\text{Min}} \quad g_k = \beta' x_k = \beta'(k) x_k \tag{5.9}$$

where $k = 1,2,...,n$ and $x_k = (x_{ki})$ is the m-element input vector for k-th DMU. By varying k in the index set $I_n = \{1,2,...,n\}$ the whole efficiency surface in piecewise linear forms is characterized by the set $B^* = \{\beta^*(k) \; k \in I_n\}$, where $\beta^*(k)$ is the optimal solution of the LP model (5.8). Here we have at most n sets of efficiency vectors $\beta^*(k)$ which can be interpreted as the shadow prices of the m inputs. For any fixed $k \in I_n$ the residuals $\tilde{\varepsilon}_j = \tilde{\varepsilon}_j(k)$ can be computed here as

$$\tilde{\varepsilon}_j(k) = x_j' \beta^*(k) - y_j \geq 0, \quad j \in I_n \tag{5.10}$$

Clearly this formulation differs from the sepcifciation (5.8) in two basic respects. First of all, the first version is closely related to the standard regression model except that the LAV method (or L_1-norm as it is usually called in statistical literature) is followed here instead of the least squares (LS) but the second version (5.10) is more akin to the random parameter model, where the variations in $\beta^*(k)$ are induced in part by the random input vector x_k. Secondly, the impact of additions (deletions) of new (existing) data points e.g., (x_s, y_s) may be very different in the two cases. If $P_s = (x_s, y_s)$ is a new data point, it would have no influence on the efficiency frontier of (5.8) if it satisfies

$$x_s'\beta^* > y_s \text{ i. e., } \hat{e}_s = x_s'\hat{\beta} - y_s > 0 \tag{5.11}$$

but for the case (5.11) this would be true if it satisfies not one but k strict inequalities i.e.,

$$\tilde{\varepsilon}_s = \tilde{\varepsilon}(k) = x_s'\beta^*(k) - y_s > 0, \quad k \in I_n \tag{5.12}$$

Clearly, if $\beta^*(k)$ equals β^* for some $k \in I_n$, the new point P_s would have no impact if the condition (5.9) holds but for other k's, $k \neq k_0$ the point P_s may have substantial impact. Thus the specification (5.9) is more general in that it can allow for random variations in both inputs and output. At a practical level this specification has several advantages. First of all, it allows a strictly data-based measure of the distribution of efficiency across the observed units. Thus for a given data set $D_n = \{d_j = (x_j, y_j) \mid j \in I_n\}$ we could classify the observed set of n units into three groups: (i) group S_1 where none satisfied the efficiency condition, (ii) group S_2 where each unit satisfies the efficiency condition p percent of the times or less, and (iii) group S_3 where each unit satisfies the efficiency condition by more than p percent of the times, where $p = r/n$ with r denoting the number of times a unit turns out to be efficient. Let n_1, n_2 and n_3 be the number of units in the three groups S_1, S_2, S_3 respectively where $n_1 + n_2 + n_3 = n$. Clearly if the proportion n_1/n equals 1.0, then the entire data set D_n fails the consistency test, whereas for $n_1 = 0$ and $p > 0$ the entire data set would satisfy the requirement of consistency with the efficiency hypothesis at some positive probability level however small it may be. Secondly, if it were possible to screen the data set and classify them into three groups as above, then one could estimate the efficiency frontier statistically either separately for reach group or as a mixture. In the first case we obtain average estimates of β for each group i.e., $\hat{\beta}^{(k)}$ for group S_k and in the second case we obtain the mixture $\hat{\beta} = \sum_{k=1}^{3} p_k \hat{\beta}^{(k)}$ where p_k is estimated from the sample proportions $p_k = n_k/n$. In large sample situations the sample proportions would provide consistent estimates of the population proportion p_k and the mixture $\hat{\beta} = \sum \pi_k \hat{\beta}^{(k)}$ could be given an optimum interpretation in terms of the maximum likelihood (ML) principle. Before we suggest this interpretation, we must provide a caution here. Once the groups S_k (k=1,2,3) are formed here from the LP models generating the vectors $\{\beta^*(k), k \in I_n\}$, we treat each group as a subpopulation; then we pose the problem of estimating a single vector β from k different subpopulations. This estimate $\hat{\beta}$ say may be obtained for example by the ML principle if a distribution can be postulated or, by a nonparametric statistical procedure. To fix ideas let us assume that a distribution can be postulated, where the density of an observation $d_j = (x_j, y_j)$ from subpopulations k is $f_k(\beta,d)$, k=1,2,3. Denote the proportion of units in the population belonging to group S_k by p_k and let $\pi = (\pi_1, \pi_2, \pi_3)$. We use a random sample $d_1, d_2,...,d_n$ of size n from the population and the ML principle to estimate the parameter vector β and the proportions π_k. In the mixture ML method the values of π_k and β are chosen to maximize

$$L_n = \prod_{j=1}^{n} f(\beta, \pi, d_j) \qquad\qquad (5.13)$$

where $f(\beta, \pi, d_j) = \sum_{k=1}^{3} \pi_k f_k(\beta, d)$ is the mixed distribution generating the population. Clearly, maximizing the log of L_n in (5.13) would entail a nonlinear programming problem even when the densities $f_k(\cdot)$ are normal.

In the separate group case, one applies the ML approach by choosing both β and $k(\beta,d_j)$ so as to maximize

$$l_n = \prod_{j=1}^{n} f_k(\beta, d_j) \qquad (5.14)$$

where $k(\beta,d_j) = k$ whenever observation d_j is from group S_k. Here the observations are assigned to groups or subpopulations as part of the procedure and the maximization is over all assignments as well as over values of β. The population proportions π_k are usually estimated by the sample proportions $p_k = \hat{\pi}_k(n)$ i.e., the proportion of observations in the sample assigned to group S_k. One disadvantage of this approach is that if the number of groups increases say k=1,2,...,s then the parameters (β, π_k) increase in number and it is known that the usual ML estimates need not be consistent in this case [6].

A third aspect of generality of the DEA model (5.10) is that it allows a method of clustering the data points $P_s = (x_s, y_s)$ into efficiency subsets. Let $C^*(s)$ denote the convex hull of n points $z_s = x_s/y_s$ in m dimensions (assuming y_s to be positive) in the nonnegative orthant of the input space. Consider a new point P_j, $j \notin I_n$. If it belongs to the convex hull $C^*(s)$, then it must satisfy the dual of the LP model (5.9) for some $k \in I_n$. Select two representative values of k, e.g., typical units, or units appearing to be efficient on an a priori basis. Let A and B be the two facets of the convex hull $C^*(s)$ for these values of $k = k_1, k_2$. Thus for every new data point four cases can arise: (a) if the new point falls in the A-hull but not in the B-hull, we assign it to A, (b) if it falls in B-hull but not to A we assign it to B, (c) if it falls in both hulls we may not assign it to either and finally (d) if the new point does not belong to $C^*(s)$ we ignore it for efficiency analysis. Several practical cases can be handled if we interpret the A and B hulls suitably. For example the A-hull may represent the LAV model (5.8) and B-hull may be for any unit very close to the mean input levels $\bar{x}$. The degree of closeness may be suitably defined in terms of a statistical distance function. Another example would be two sets of cross-section data of similar firms and our objective is to estimate the efficiency gap.

One of the most important points in the clustering technique using the DEA approach is that one could define a set of hierarchical clusters as the facets of the convex hull $C^*(s)$ and then develop the notion of a robust cluster. Let $\tau = 1, 2, ..., t$ be a sequence of hierarchical clusters determiend by a suitable distance function or by the score function g_k in (5.9). Then for a given set $\tilde{D}$ of new data points, a particular cluster $C_\tau^*(s)$ can be defined to be robust if there exists no subsequent clustering τ_1 such that an element from $C_\tau^*(s)$ is clustered together with an element outside it. Let $C_\tau^*(s \mid \tilde{D})$ denote the robust cluster. By considering various partitions of the data set one could develop a probabilistic measure of robustness, that can be used to statistically test the degree of coarseness or fineness of the cluster. Two important open questions here are: how to define an optimal clustering in the stochastic data space and how to incorporate different types of prior informations. Several heuristic attempts have been made by Farrell [7], Timmer [8] and Nunamaker [9] to develop ad hoc measures of clustering, none of which specify the conditions of what may be called 'optimal custering'.

Now we consider the LP model (5.8) and the LAV method of estimation and analyze its residual as a linear regression model. But before we do that we assume that the error component εj has been replaced by its deviation from the mean i.e., $(\varepsilon_j - \bar{\varepsilon})$ and the intercept term is included in the parameters β. As we have seen in earlier chapters, that this is usually done in the parametric theory of the frontier. After this adjustment the residuals ε_j has a zero mean and one of the m parameters β_i is in the form of a deviation from $\bar{\varepsilon}$. Now let $\hat{\beta}$ be the optimal solution of the LP model (5.8) and X_B be the associated optimal basis and it is assumed for simplicity that it is nonsingular and of rank m and y_B be the associated vector of outputs. Then we obtain

$$\hat{y} = X\hat{\beta} = XX_B^{-1}y_B = XX_B^{-1}Dy \tag{5.15}$$

$$-\hat{\varepsilon} = y - \hat{y} = (I - H)y, \ H = XX_B^{-1}D \tag{5.16}$$

where

$$y_B = Dy, \ E(y_B) = DE(y) = DX\beta$$

$$E(\hat{\varepsilon}) = 0, \ Var(\hat{\varepsilon}) = (I - H)'(I - H)\sigma_\varepsilon^2 \tag{5.17}$$

It is clear that the behavior of the residual $\hat{\varepsilon}$ is controlled by H which depends on X_B and D. Since H maps y into $\hat{y}$, one could analyze the correlation of y_j and $\hat{y}_j$ values. If the correlation is very high i.e., close to unity, then the corresponding residuals will have relatively small variances; otherwise the residuals will have large variances.

For diagnostic analysis the estimated residuals can be utilized in several ways. First of all, one could use the size of the predicted residual as a measure of goodness of fit. For data perturbation it may be used to select a new data subset which has an optimum degree of goodness of fit. Thus let $\hat{\varepsilon}_{(s)}$ be the predicted residual based on the data set with the s-th case excluded and $\hat{\beta}_{(s)}$ be the LAV estimate obtained from the LP model of the form (5.8):

$$-\hat{\varepsilon}_{(s)} = y_j - x'_j\hat{\beta}_{(s)} \qquad j=1,2,...,n \tag{5.18}$$

$$j \neq s, \ s=1,2,...,n$$

The sum $C = -\sum_s \hat{\varepsilon}_{(s)}$ may be used as a criterion of selection of data points. If this procedure is applied to the second version (5.9) of the DEA model it would identify one or two facets of the efficiency surface as optimal in the sense of least sum of errors. Likewise the addition of new data points may be handled. It is clear that so long as the optimal basis X_B remains invariant to data perturbations whether deletions or additions, we would have robustness of the efficiency measure. As a matter of fact one could distinguish between four types of robustiness: (a) the optimal basis X_B remains invariant, (b) the parameter vector $\hat{\beta}$ remains insensitive, (c) the optimal basis X_B or, the estimator $\hat{\beta}$ remains invariant with a high probability against data deletions or additions, and (d) the invariance holds against specified departures from the exponential distribution of errors.

A second use of the estimated residuals $\hat{e}$ in (5.16) is in the influence curve approach and its empirical version. To define the population influence curve let T_n be a vector valued statistic of length m based on samples $\varepsilon_1, \varepsilon_2, ..., \varepsilon_n$ assumed to be independently distributed from a population with cumulative distribution function (cdf) F and let $\hat{F}$ be the empirical cdf such that there exists a statistical functional $T = T(\hat{F})$ with the property $T(\hat{F}) = T_n$. The influence curve (IC) approach analyzes the properties of the statistic T_n by examining the behavior of T(F) or $T(\hat{F})$ when F or $\hat{F}$ is perturbed. Consider a new point d for which the residual is $\varepsilon = \varepsilon(d)$ and let λ_d be the cdf giving mass 1 to the vector point d. The vector-valued influence curve $IC_{T,F}(d)$ of T at F is then defined pointwise by

$$IC_{T, F}(d) = \lim_{\delta \to 0} \frac{T[(1 - \delta)F + \delta\lambda_d] - T(F)}{\delta} \tag{5.19}$$

assuming the limit to exist. Thus the influence curve provides a measure of the influence on the statistical function T[•] of adding an observation at d as n becomes large. As a data based method two uses of the influence curve approach are important. One is that we can compare alternative estimators of efficiency e.g., $\hat{\beta}$ of (5.8) and $\beta^*(k)$ of (5.9), just as Andrews et al. [10] and Hampel [11] have used influence curves to compare the stability properties of alternative estimators and to suggest robust modifications of the existing estimation technique in terms of the so-called M-estimators. A second practical use of the influence curve approach is in detecting how individual data points affect the sample average. Thus consider the estimate $\hat{\beta}$ of the LAV model (5.8) based on a sample of size n. Assume that a single additional point is added giving a new sample cdf of $\bar{g}$ as:

$$\hat{F}_+ = \frac{n\hat{F}}{n+1} + \frac{\lambda_d}{n+1} \qquad (5.20)$$

or

$$\bar{g}_+ = \bar{g} + \frac{g - \bar{g}}{n+1}$$

where $\bar{g}_+ = T(\hat{F}_+)$ and $g = g_d$ corresponds to the objective function for the new data point. Alternatively, the influence of the s-th point on $\bar{g}$ can be evaluated by removing this point from the sample and writing

$$\bar{g} = \bar{g}_{(s)} + \frac{1}{n}\,(g - \bar{g}_{(s)}),\ s = 1,\, 2,\, \ldots,\, n \qquad (5.21)$$

where $\bar{g}_{(s)}$ denotes the sample average computed without the s-th case. Thus (5.21) specifies a collection of n influence curves obtained by deleting each case in turn. The influence of any point $d = d_j$ on $\bar{g}$ is obtained by evaluating the j-th curve at $g_j = g_d$, $d = d_j$ in terms of the n case statistics:

$$\bar{g} - \bar{g}_{(j)} = \frac{g_j - g_{(j)}}{n-1}$$

It is clear that any point with a sufficiently large residual would influence the sample average estimate $\hat{\beta}$ of the mean model (5.8).

The empirical influence curve (EIC) which is more useful can be obtained from the theoretical curve (5.18) by substituting the sample cdf $\hat{F}$ for F. This can be done in two different ways. One is to derive the empirical cdf $\hat{F}$ from the set $B^* = \{\beta^*(k), k \in I_n\}$ of efficient units determiend by the DEA model (5.9) and use it in (5.19).

A second way is to incorporate points which are close to the efficiency frontier in some sense and then reestimate β as in linear regression theory. Thus from (5.5) and (5.8) we know that at the optimal basis X_B associated with the estimate $\hat{\beta}$ we have $\varepsilon_j = 0$ for $j \in B$ and $\varepsilon_j > 0$ for $j \notin B$. Select a level $\varepsilon_0 > 0$ such that all points ε_j's satisfying $0 < \varepsilon_j \leq \varepsilon_0$ are considered ε_0-close to the efficiency frontier. On using these additional points we obtain the empirical influence function as

$$EIC(x, y) = n_1 (\tilde{X}' \tilde{X})^{-1} x(y - x' \tilde{\beta}) \tag{5.22}$$

where n_1 is the total number of points ($m < n_1 < n$) on or ε_0-close to the efficiency frontier, $\tilde{X}$ is the design matrix after enlarging the optimal basis X_B, due to the addition of ε_0-close points and $\tilde{\beta}$ is the least squares estimate defining the error vector $\tilde{\varepsilon} = y - x' \tilde{\beta}$. Let S_0 be the set of poitns which are either ε_0-close to or, on the frontier. Then we obtain from above:

$$EIC_j = EIC(x_j, y_j) = n(\tilde{X}' \tilde{X})^{-1} x_j \tilde{\varepsilon}_j \text{ for } j \in S_0$$

In ordinary linear regression large residuals tend to make the influence curve unbounded, and this has led to the development of robust regression methods which downweight cases with large residuals. Here we start with the LAV estimate $\hat{\beta} = X_B^{-1} y_B$ of the mean model (5.8) and then construct a set S_0 of points which are either ε_0-close to, or on the efficiency frontier and then derive the least squares estimate $\tilde{\beta}$ where the influence curve is always bounded. Thus the estimate $\tilde{\beta}$ is a two-stage estiamte, implicitly depending on the LAV estimate $\hat{\beta}$.

B.   Minimax Estimation

The influence of individual data points on the estimates of the parameter vector β in the mean LP model (5.8) may also be analyzed through a minimax approach presented before. We consider a two-person zero-sum game transformation of the model as follows:

$$\underset{\beta \in C(\beta)}{\text{Min}} \; \underset{\gamma \in C(\gamma)}{\text{Max}} \; (\beta' X' - y') \gamma = \sum_{i=1}^{m} \sum_{j=1}^{n} (\beta_i X_{ij} - y_j) \gamma_j \qquad (5.23)$$

where

$$C(\beta) = \{ \beta \mid X\beta - y \geq 0, \beta' e_m = 1, \beta \geq 0 \}$$
$$C(\gamma) = \{ \gamma \mid \gamma' e_n = 1, \gamma \geq 0 \}$$

Here the DM is player I who has to estimate the vector β, whereas the second player is Nature who selects the vector γ from the compact set $C(\gamma)$. In the language of the theory of statistical games, player II maximizes the cost of inefficiency measures by the residual $\hat{e}' = \beta' X' - y'$, where player I chooses β to minimize it. This can be seen more clearly by dropping the term $y'\gamma$ from the objective function and writing the payoff function as $\phi(\beta,\gamma) = \gamma' X\beta$, which is the loss function or cost for player I, if γ is given. Clearly if $\gamma_j = 1/n$ for all j, we get back the mean LP model (5.8). But this means that either the second player is passive or, player I lacks information to guess the value of γ_j in any other way i.e., the principle of insufficient reasons. The minimax principle provides more flexibility as a safety-first or cautious decision rule for the DM, since for each i he considers the worst risk (i.e., most unfavorable distributions of γ_j's) and then chooses the best of the worst. We may state some theoretical resulls by noting that the vectors β and γ may now be treated as probability vectors i.e., mixed strategies. Since the n data points may be grouped into r subsets (r < n) the dimension of γ may be smaller than n.

Theorem 1

For every optimal solution $\hat{\beta}$ of the LAV model (5.8) there exists a Bayes solution $\hat{\gamma}$ where $\hat{\gamma}_j = 1/n$ for all j. Furthermore, if the data set (X,y) have all positive elements then there must exist a Nash equilibrium point (β^0, γ^0) defined as a pair of strategies satisfying

$$\gamma^0(X\beta^0 - y) = \max_{\gamma \in C(\gamma)} \{\gamma(X\beta^0 - y)\}$$

$$(5.24)$$

$$\gamma^0(X\beta^0 - y) = \min_{\beta \in C(\beta)} \{\gamma^0(X\beta - y)\}$$

Proof

The first part follows from the fact that the objective function of (5.8) can also be writtren as $\bar{g} = \sum_i \sum_j \beta_i x_{ij} \gamma_i - \sum_j y_j \gamma_j$ with $\gamma_j = 1/n$ for all j. For the second part we note that there always exists a nonzero feasible and hence optimal vector $\hat{\beta}$ of the LP model (5.8) when the data set (X,y) have all positive elements. Moreover the stragegy sets $C(\beta)$ and $C(\gamma)$ defined in (5.23) are compact, where the strategies of the two players are finite. Since the payoff function $\phi(\beta,\gamma)$ is continuous, the existence of the Nash equilibrium point (β^0, γ^0) follows.

Theorem 2

A necessary and sufficient condition that the point (β^0, γ^0) is a Nash equilibrium point is that there exist scalar vaues u^0, v^0 and a vector λ^0 such that they satisfy the following conditions

(i) $X'\lambda^0 + u^0 e_m \leq X'\gamma^0$

(ii) $\gamma^{0'} X\beta^0 - \lambda^{0'} X\beta^0 - u^0 = 0$

(iii) $X\beta^0 \le y + v^0 e_n$ (5.25)

(iv) $\gamma^{0'}(X\beta^0 - y) - v^0 = 0$

(v) $\beta^0 \in C(\beta), \gamma^0 \in C(\gamma)$

Proof

The proof follows by a direct application of the necessary and sufficient conditions of the Kuhn-tucker theorem on nonlienar programming, where the Lagrangian function is

$$L = \gamma'(X\beta - y) + \gamma'(y - X\beta) + u(1 - \beta'e_m) + v(1 - \gamma'e_n)$$

From these conditions it follows that the equilibrium point (β^0, γ^0) is a solution of the following LP problem:

$$\text{Min } v - u \qquad (5.26)$$

s.t. (i) through (v) of (5.25)

Theorem 3

Let γ be fixed at $\bar{\gamma} \in C(\gamma)$ and let $\beta^0(\bar{\gamma})$ be the conditional solution of the model (5.23) for given $\bar{\gamma}$. Then $\beta^0(\bar{\gamma})$ is the conditional minimax solution of the LP model

$$\text{Min } v$$
$$\text{s. t. } X\beta(\bar{\gamma}) \le y + ve_n \qquad (5.27)$$

and

$$\beta(\bar{\gamma}) \in C(\beta) \text{ in } (5.23)$$

Proof

For a given $\bar{\gamma} \in C(\gamma)$ the Langrangian function is:

$$L = \gamma'(y - X\beta) + u(1 - \beta' e_m).$$

Again by applying the necessary and sufficient conditions of the Kuhn-Tucker theorem we get the desired result.

Remark 5.1

So long as v^0 associated with $\beta^0(\bar{\gamma})$ is not zero, it would indicate a perturbation of the production frontier defined by the LAV model (5.8). We would have increasing, constant or diminishing returns to scale for any unit according as v^0 is positive, zero or negative.

Remark 5.2

So long as v^0 is positive, the estimates $\beta^0(\bar{\gamma})$ would be more robust than those obtained from the LAV model (5.8). Some implications of this robustness are analyzed elsewhere [12]. For the standard version (5.9) of the DEA model one may define the extended constraint set

$$C = C(\beta(k)v_k) = \{(\beta,v) \mid X\beta(k) \le y + v_k e_n; \beta'(k)e_m = 1$$
$$X\beta(k) \ge y; \beta(k), v_k \ge 0, k \in I_n\}$$

and the minimax procedure as

$$\min_{(\beta(k),\, v_k) \in C} J_k = \beta'(k)x_k + v_k \tag{5.28}$$

Clearly a second stage choise is available e.g., $\min\limits_{k \in I_n} J_k^0$ where J_k^0 is the minimum value of the objective function in (5.28). Let (β^0, v^0) denote the second stage solution, whereas the first stage solutions are $(\beta^0(k), v_k^0, k \in I_n)$.

Theorem 4

For any data set (X,y) with positive elements, there exists at least one optimal solution $(\beta^0(k), v_k^0)$ for every $k \in I_n$. Hence there exists the solution (β^0, v^0). Furthermore if v_k^0 is zero for any k, then this reduces to the standard solution $\beta^0(k)$ of the DEA model.

Proof

For the data set with positive elements, the feasible set is nonempty and since it is compact and the objective function is linear there must exist at least one optimal solution $(\beta^0(k), v_k^0)$. Hence the result.

Remark 5.1

So long as v^0 is positive, the associated solution (β^0, v^0) is robust in the sense of minimax and it indicates the existence of potential increasing returns to scale.

Remark 5.2

One could interpret the model (5.28) as a "composed error version" of the stochastic production frontier proposed by Jondrow, Lovel et al. [13]. Thus the variations in $\beta^0(k)$ may be viewed as $\beta^0 + \eta(k)$ where the composed error could be defined as $\varepsilon = \eta'(k)x_k + v_k$ where v_k is nonnegative but $\eta(k)$ is symmetric with zero mean.

5.3 Combining Parametric and Nonparametric Models

One way to combine the parametric aspects in a nonparametric framework of the DEA model is by nonlinear frontiers. There are two motivations for specifying nonlinear production frontiers in the DEA setup e.g., whether it gives a better fit than a linear frontier and whether it can better tackle the problem that the residuals may have distributions departing from normality. The first aspect has been already discussed in section 4 of Chapter 4, where e.g., it is shown that the following two nonlienar specifications

(a) $y_j = \prod_{i=1}^{m} x_{ji}^{\beta_i} \epsilon_j, \quad 0 \le \epsilon_j \le 1$

(b) $y_j = x'_j \beta - x'_j B x_j - \epsilon_j, \quad \epsilon_j \ge 0$

which are log-linear and quadratic respectively, perform better than the linear specifications in terms of goodness of fit. One reason for this result is that the nonlinear objective function does not have the restriction of dimensionality of the optimal basis of an LP model as in (5.8), hence a nonlienear frontier can include many more points than a linear frontier. Secondly, in the stochastic case the nonlinear frontier may permit more flexibility in the stochastic coverage of data points.

The problem that the residuals from a linear DEA model depart from normality in distribution raises two different issues e.g., linearity of the model and heteroscedasticity, where the latter may depend on the units selected as efficient. One way to handle the problem is to specify a general class of transformations first for both the dependent and independent variables and then incorporate one-sided errors for estimating the transformed efficiency frontier. Such a general class of transformation is provided by the Box-Cox class of transformations [14]. First, we describe the method and then indicate how it can be incorporated in the DEA model. The basic motivation for Box-Cox transformations is that in some specifciations the dependent variable may not be normally distributed but there may exist a transformation such that the transformed observations are normally distributed. For example, consider the nonlinear model

$$y_t = \exp\{x'_t \beta\} \cdot \exp(e_t) \tag{5.29}$$

$t = 1,2,...,T$ where y_t is the t-th observation on a dependent variable, x_t is a K-element column vector containing the t-th observation on some explanatory variables, β is a vector of K parameters to be estimated and the errors e_t are normally independently distributed $N(0,\sigma^2)$ with mean zero and fixed variance σ^2 Clearly the dependent variable y_t is log normally distributed and heteroscedastic with variances $V(y_t)$:

$$V(y_t) = [\exp\{x_t'\beta\}]^2 \cdot [\exp(\sigma^2) - 1], \ t = 1, 2, \ldots, T$$

However on taking logarithms one obtains:

$$\ln y_t = \{x_t'\beta\} + e_t \qquad (5.30)$$

where the transformed dependent variable $\ln y_t$ is normally distributed, homoscedastic and a linear function of β and hence the application of least squares (LS) to (5.30) yields a minimum variance unbiased estimator for β. Box and Cox consider a more general case of finding a transformation of the dependent variable y that simultaneously linearizes the model, corrects heteroscedasticity and normalizes the distribution of errors. Thus one type of transformation is of the following form:

$$y_t^{(\lambda)} = \{x_t'\beta\} + e_t \qquad (5.31)$$

where

$$y_t^{(\lambda)} = \begin{cases} y_t^\lambda - 1, \lambda \neq 0 \\ \ln y_t, \lambda = 0 \end{cases} \qquad (5.32)$$

and e_t is $N(0,\sigma^2)$, i.e. normally independently and identically distributed. Here it is assumed that there exists a transformation of the dependent variable, of the form given in (5.32), such that the transformed dependent variable has three properties, i.e., it is normally distributed, homoscedastic and has an expectation that is lienar in β. Clearly if

$\lambda = 1$ we get the familiar linear model

$$y = X\beta + e \tag{5.33}$$

and the value $\lambda = 0$ yields the nonlinear model (5.30). In a more general case the dependent variables may also be transformed e.g.,

$$y_t^{(\lambda)} = \beta_1 x_1^{(\lambda)} + \beta_2 x_2^{(\lambda)} + \ldots + \beta_K y_K^{(\lambda)} + e_t \tag{5.34}$$

Two general features of this class of transformations are particularly useful in applied econometric work. First of all, it provides an important method of generalizing functional forms; thus e.g., a linear and log-lienar production frontier can be generated by this transformation and only the best empirical fit with the observed data would determine the optimal value of λ, which can then be used to discriminate between the two specifications. Secondly, given the optimal value of λ the conditional maximum likelihood (ML) estimates of the parameters β can be used along with the standard statistical tests. For example, in the case of (5.31) and (5.32) the probability density function $p(y)$ of the observations can be written as

$$p(y) = J \cdot \left(2\pi\sigma^2\right)^{-T/2} \exp\left[-2\left(\sigma^2\right)^{-1} \sum_{t=1}^{T} \left(y_t^{(\lambda)} - x_t'\beta\right)^2\right] \tag{5.35}$$

where $J = \prod_{t=1}^{T} \left|\partial y_t^{(\lambda)}/\partial y_t\right|$ is the Jacobian of the transformation from y_t to e_t. For a given value of λ the conditional ML estimator of β is the LS estimator

$$b_\lambda = (X'X)^{-1}X'y^{(\lambda)}$$

and the maximized log-likelihood can be written as:

$$\ln L(\lambda) = - (T/2)(1 + \ln 2\pi) - (T/2)\ln \hat{S}_E^2(\lambda) + (-T/2) \sum_{t=1}^{T} \ln \hat{S}_E^2(\lambda)$$

$$+ (\lambda - 1) \sum_{t=1}^{T} \ln y_t \tag{5.37}$$

where $\hat{S}_E^2(\lambda) = e'_\lambda e_\lambda / T$ is the residual sum of squares from a fit using the transformed responses since e_t is the vector of residuals from the regression of $y^{(\lambda)}$ on X. Box and Cox use the following iterative method for computing the optimal value of the unknown parameter λ. First, we compute $\ln L(\lambda)$ for a range of values of λ say between -2.5 to +2.5. By plotting $\ln L(\lambda)$ against λ one can locate the approximate value of λ that maximizes $\ln L$ (i.e. the ML estimate of λ). Let $\hat{\lambda}$ be the ML estimator of λ and suppose we wish to test the null hypothesis $H_0: \lambda = \lambda_0$ (e.g.... $\lambda_0 = 1$ may be a null hypothesis i.e. no transformation is required). Then the likelihood ratio test statistic for the hypothesis

$$G_0^2 = - 2[\ln L(\lambda_0) - \ln(\hat{\lambda})] \sim \chi^2(1, \alpha) \tag{5.37}$$

is asymptotically distributed as a chi-squared variate, where $\chi^2(v,\alpha)$ is the $100(1-\alpha)$ percentile of a chi-squared distribution with degrees of freedom v equal to the number of components in λ. One can also use the asymptotic normality of the ML estimate $\hat{\lambda}$ to construct a confidence interval. However one note of caution is in order for the iterative method of finding the optimal value of λ, where we start with a reasonable range of values for λ, then use OLS to find b_λ and then select that set of estimates for which $\hat{S}_E^2(\lambda)$ is a minimum. However this is a conditional method and as Spitzer [15] points out, these standard errors will underestimate the more relevant unconditional ones.

Hence one should select a wider range of values for λ before the search procedure is applied.

There are two ways in which the general class of Box-Cox transformations may be incorproated in the framework of the DEA model. One is to make the error term e.g., e_t in (5.30) one-sided. The second, and a simpler way is to estimate the total number of efficient units by the DEA model (5.9) and then apply the Box-Cox class of transformations. As an empirical illustration we apply this approach to the same cross-section sample of 25 school districts in California used in earlier chapters. The results reported in Tables 1-2 estimate the linear regression of the transformed variable Z on W_i where

$$Z = \begin{cases} y^\lambda - 1/\lambda, \lambda \neq 0 \\ \ln y \quad , \lambda = 0 \end{cases} \quad \text{and} \quad W_i = \begin{cases} (x_i^\lambda - 1/\lambda, \lambda \neq 0 \\ \ln x_i \quad , \lambda = 0 \end{cases}$$

Z transforms output (y) and W_i transforms the four inputs (x_i, i=1,2,3,4). Two sample groups S_1 (n=9) and S_2 (n=12) are used when the Box-Cox transformation is applied to the efficient units only i.e., those units out of n which are found to be efficient by the DEA method (5.9), S_1 containing units which are efficient at least 33% of the time and S_2 containing units which are at least once efficient. It is clear from the tables that the estimate of the production frontier is much better than that of the average production response in terms of higher R^2-value and lower standard error of regression. Thus the identification of the efficient units found efficient by the DEA method helps improve the regression fit. This result confirms the finding in Chapter Four of an alternative method whereby the entire data set were first stratified into efficient and nonefficient points by the DEA method and then a dummy variable regression model was computed. Secondly, one notes that for this example the higher the value of λ above 1.0 the worse the empirical fit; also lower values of 0.9, 0.8 did not improve the result. Thirdly, for the optimum value of $\lambda = 1.0$ we tested the residual for normality by the Shapiro-Wilk statistic and the null hypothesis was not rejected at 5% level. Furthermore, the null hypothesis that $\lambda^* = 1$ for all data points was strongly rejected for both specifications in Tables 1-2 by the chi-squared statistic (5.37) at 1% level of statistical significance. This implies that nonlinearity (i.e., approximate log-linearity) still provides a better specification than a linear function. This suggests two fundamental issues about the DEA model. First, should we use a linear or nonlinear form when we apply the DEA model (5.9) to observed data points. Afterwards when the data points are screened into efficient and nonefficient subsets, should we again apply Box-Cox transformation to estimate the production frontier? Secondly, how could one interpret in meaningful economic terms an econometric production frontier, where the outputs and inputs are all transformed in order to satisfy certain optimality properties of the error statistics?

Table 1. Estiamtes of the Observed Production Response by Box-Cox Transformation
(Sample group S_2)

C	W_1	W_2	W_3	W_4	R^2	$\hat{S}_E$
			$\lambda = 1.0$			
61.12*	0.129E-2*	-0.815	-0.480	0.022	0.73	4.18
(4.71)	(2.57)	(-1.56)	(-0.88)	(1.12)		
			$\lambda = 1.15$			
100.99*	0.593E-3*	-0.911	-0.599	0.015	0.71	8.15
(4.78)	(2.54)	(-1.65)	(1.02)	(1.21)		
			$\lambda = 1.50$			
335.44*	0.950E-3*	-1.059	-0.934	0.56E-2	0.64	38.57
(4.69)	(2.46)	(-1.64)	(-1.18)	(1.24)		
			$\lambda = 2.0$			
1987.2*	0.684E-5*	-1.089	-1.671	0.111E-2	0.56	346.78
(4.28)	(2.39)	(-1.37)	(-1.35)	(1.07)		

Note

1. Asterisk indicates significance in terms of t-values in parenthesis at least at 5% level.

2. E-n denotes 10^{-n}.

3. $\hat{S}_E$ denotes the estimated standard error of regression.

5.4   Nonparametric Regression and Bootstrap Methods

Since the DEA model is nonparametric, it is quite natural to ask if a nonparametric regression approach could be applied to estimate the parameters. On writing the DEA model (5.9) as

$$y_j = \mu(x_j) - \tilde{\varepsilon}_j, \quad \tilde{\varepsilon}_j \geq 0, j \in I_n \tag{5.38}$$

we note that a parametric regression model assumes that the form of $\mu = \mu(x_j)$ is known e.g., $\mu = x_j' \beta$ except for finitely many unknown parameters; hence in such models the inference about μ is equivalent to inference about β. A nonparametric regression model however assumes only that μ belongs to some collection of functions e.g., μ may be assumed to be only differentiable or concave i.e., it may be assumed to have only specified qualitative properties. Thus for the nonparametric regression model the model-builder has to rely more heavily on the observed data points, since he has to choose an appropriate function space to which μ is believed to belong. Motivation for such choice in efficiency analysis is usually provided by smoothness, concavity and other properties of generalized substitution among inuts as in translog and CES production functions. From an applied viewpoint there are two important uses of the nonparametric regression model [16,17]. First of all, it may be used as a diagnostic techinque for choosing an appropriate parametric model of regression; thus using a nonparametric regression model does not preclude the use of a parametric model. Secondly, the parametric regression model usually looks at the conditional density f(y|x), which in the normal case admits a linear representation as the conditional mean $E(y|x) = x'\beta$. However if the normality hypothesis does not hold, one may still apply the condition

$$f(y|x) = f(y,x)/g(x) \tag{5.39}$$

Table 2. Estimates of the Production Frontier by Box-Cox Transformation

Sample Group	C	W_1	W_2	W_3	W_4	R^2	$\hat{S}_E$
			$\lambda = 1.0$				
S_1	51.93*	0.002*	-0.576	-0.311	0.017	0.89	3.18
	(2.51)	(2.86)	(-0.57)	(-0.27)	(0.44)		
S_2	39.93*	0.001*	0.072	0.480	-0.008	0.89	2.61
	(3.47)	(3.64)	(0.14)	(0.94)	(-0..43)		
			$\lambda = 1.15$				
S_1	90.17*	0.0008*	-0.810	-0.602	0.016	0.87	6.48
	(2.64)	(2.86)	(-0.70)	(-0.46)	(0.59)		
S_2	66.29*	0.64E-3*	0.095	0.502	-0.006	0.87	5.50
	(3.28)	(3.37)	(0.15)	(0.82)	(-0.41)		
			$\lambda = 1.50$				
S_1	316.40*	0.14E-3*	-1.299	-1.310	0.009	0.84	32.0l
	(2.81)	(2.90)	(-0.81)	(-0.72)	(0.74)		
S_2	220.77*	0.11E-3*	0.312	0.622	-0.003	0.82	28.72\
	(2.94)	(3.04)	(0.36)	(0.69)	(-0.56)		
			$\lambda = 2.0$				
S_1	1868.45*	0.11E-4*	-1.757	-2.349	0.002	0.81	293.60
	(2.73)	(2.84)	(-0.70)	(-0.79)	(0.66)		
S_2	1317.59*	0.79E-5*	0.868	0.920	-0.001	0.78	266.91
	(2.70)	(2.98)	(0.78)	(0.64)	(-0.92)		

Note: All comments in footnote of Table 1 apply here also.

where $f(y,x)$ is the mutivariate density and $g(x)$ the marginal density and derive from the observed data points a nonparametric estimate of the conditional density function $f(y|x)$ and test if its expectation can be approximated by a linear function of x. Taking the simplest case first when y and x are both scalar random variables the simplest form of nonparametric density estimator of $f(y|x)$ is the histogram, which has two major disadvantages i.e., it has discontinuities at cell boundaries and it is zero outside a certain range. To remove these disadvantages Rosenblatt [18] introduced a kernel estimate of $f = f(y|x)$ as

$$\hat{f} = \frac{1}{n} \sum_{j=1}^{n} K_1(x - x_j)/2h$$

where

$$K_1(u) = \begin{cases} 1, & \text{if } |u| < h \\ 0, & \text{otherwise} \end{cases}$$

As we saw in Chapter three that one way of looking at the kernel estimate is that $\hat{f}$ is an average of n values, one corresponding to each of the design set points. Data points near x (which are within distance h) contribute a value $1/(2h)$ while points further from it contribute a value zero. Clearly the jump from $1/(2h)$ to zero is the source of discontinuity. Hence we could replace $K_1/(2h)$ by another function $K_2(x-x_j)$ which decreases more gradually with increasing $|x - x_j|$. The estimate $\hat{f}$ then becomes

$$\hat{f} = \frac{1}{n} \sum_{j=1}^{n} K_2(x - x_j) = \frac{1}{n} \sum_{j=1}^{n} K^*(x, x_j)$$

By writing $K_2(x-x_j)$ as $K^*(x,x_j)$ one easily obtains the multivariate kernel estimate of $f = f(y|x)$. As in the univariate case each design set (vector) point x_j contributes towards the estimate f at x an amount inversely related to the distance between vector points x and x_j.

Again an average of these contributions is taken in the estimate $\hat{f}$. Note that the kernel function K may also be chosen as a density in which case the asymptotic distribution of $\hat{f}$ itself may be specified and hence asymptotic statistical tests performed. Although for large samples most of the evidence suggests that the choice of the form of the kernel function K is not very important, yet it is still an open question for small samples and more so in DEA models where the errors are constrained to be one-sided.

It is clear that the DEA model (5.9) can be viewed as a two-stage estimation procedure, where the nonparametric regression can be applied at second stage after $r \leq n$ efficient units are determined at the first stage of the DEA model. The errors in the first stage (i.e., $\tilde{\varepsilon}_j = \tilde{\varepsilon}_j(k)$) are one-sided but in the second stage when the expectation function $\mu(x_j) = \mu(x_j(k))$, k = 1,2,...,r has to be estimated on the basis of r efficient units one could apply nonparametric regression theory or nonparametric estimation of the conditional density. Note that in the second stage the errors may be assumed to be symmetric or nonsymmetric, thus 'the composed error' version of a stochastic production frontier proposed by Jondrow, Lovell *et al.* [13] would be a special case.

Even from a parametric viewpoint the second stage of the DEA model (5.9) may be interpreted in terms of the "the interpretive search procedure" suggested by Leamer [19] in his diagnostic procedures.

Leamer applied this procedure to modify the classical least squares estimates by imposing suitable additional constraints so that jointly they imply an adequate interpretation of the data evidence. Assume that the random vector y in (5.38) has an n-dimensional probability density function $h(y;\theta)$ depending on an m-dimensional parameter vector θ and let $H(\theta)$ be an m-dimensional cumulative distribution function of θ. Then one can write for the continuous case

$$f(y) = \int h(y;\theta)dH(\theta)$$

as the mixing density with $H(\theta)$ viewed as the mixing proportion. In the discrete case of a finite mixture, this becomes

$$f(y) = \sum_{\tau=1}^{c} p_\tau h_\tau(y; \theta_\tau)$$

where the mixing proportions $H_\tau(q_\tau)$ are denoted by p_τ. To fix ideas suppose the data set $D = (X,y)$ could be grouped into two clusters C_τ ($\tau=1,2$) where the density $h(y;\theta)$ depends on two parameters θ_1, θ_2 e.g., θ_τ may be the mean parameter when $D \in C_\tau$ ($\tau = 1,2$). If p_τ and θ_τ are known then the LP model corresponding to (5.9) becomes

$$\text{Min } g_\tau = \beta'_\tau \bar{x}_\tau$$
$$\text{s. t. } X'_\tau \beta_\tau \geq \theta_\tau; \quad \beta_\tau \geq 0; \quad (\tau = 1, 2) \tag{5.40}$$

Let β^*_τ be the optimal solution of (5.40). Then an "interpretive-search estimator" due to Leamer may be defined as a weighted average of points β^*_τ thus:

$$\beta^* = \sum_{\tau=1}^{2} p_\tau \beta^*_\tau, \quad \Sigma p_\tau = 1 \tag{5.41}$$

where β^*_τ is a constrained estimate and p_τ is a weight function. However in most cases these parameters p_τ, θ_τ have to be estimated, since they are not usually known. Denoting the likelihood function associated with $f(y)$ by

$$L = \prod_{j=1}^{n} \left[\sum_{\tau=1}^{2} p_\tau h_\tau(y_j; \theta_\tau) \right] = L(p, \theta, \beta)$$

we have to transform the LP model (5.40) into a nonlinear problem

$$\text{Min } g = (\sum_{\tau=1}^{2} p_\tau \beta_\tau)' \bar{x} - \ln L(p, \theta, \beta)$$

$$\text{s.t.} \sum_{\tau=1}^{2} p_\tau = 1, \, p_\tau \geq 0, \, \beta \geq 0 \tag{5.42}$$

$$\text{Prob} \, [\tilde{y}_j \geq \sum_{i=1}^{m} \beta_i x_{ij}] = F_j(\sum_{i=1}^{m} \beta_i x_{ij}) > 0$$

Special computational algorithms are available for solving these nonlinear problems e.g. in cases when y_j is distributed like a normal or exponential distribution [20]; otherwise numerical approximation methods have to be followed.

Two aspects are to be noted in this approach. First, it combines the individual estimates β_τ^* into a single weighted average estimate $\beta^* = \sum_{r=1}^{c} p_r^* \beta_t^*$ rather than an efficiency surface $B^* = \{\beta_t^*, r=1,2,...,c\}$ defined in the approach before. But if the proportions p_τ can be interpreted as probabilities then one can order these in an ascending order $0 < p_{(1)} < p_{(2)} < ... < p_{(c)}$ taking only distinct and positive probabilities and select the one with "the maximum probability" to represent the "most probable cluster" i.e. $p_{(c)}$ with the estimate $\beta^*_{(c)}$ satisfying

$$X_{(c)}^{-1} \beta^*_{(c)} = \theta_{(c)}, \, \beta^*_{(c)} \geq 0$$

yields the cluster $C_{(c)}$ which may then be called "the maximum probability cluster." Similarly the other clusters $C_{(c-1)}, C_{(c-2)},...,C_{(1)}$ can be identified. Secondly, we note that in some cases the nonlinear programming problem (5.42) can be explicitly solved by convex programming algorithms, e.g., the case when y_j is exponentially distributed. Note that Farrell [7] found for his frontier estimation that the empirical distribution of efficiency takes one of two forms: J-shaped or bimodal. It is clear that if the clusters C_τ are dissimilar, the mixture model above could easily generate these distributions. One could therefore test such hypothesis statistically.

   A natural extension of the nonparametric regression approach is to apply the bootstrap techniques to estimate the distribution of the residuals. To fix ideas consider the LAV model (5.40) for a particular efficient facet and write it as

$$\theta = X'\beta + e \tag{5.43}$$

where we assume the error vector e has components that are independently and identically distributed with a density function f(e). Let $\hat{\beta}$ be an LAV estimator of an efficient facet, then the corresponding estimator $\hat{\theta}$ of θ must satisfy

$$X'\hat{\beta} = \hat{\theta} \tag{5.44}$$

Let Ω be the column space of X' and let M be the median of e_1, the first component of e and we define the scale parameter s as $s = [2f(M)]^{-1}$. We seek to test hypotheses of the form:

$$H_0: Z\beta = 0 \text{ versus } Z\beta \neq 0$$

where Z is a specified design matrix (of order q by m say) such that $Z\beta$ forms a set of m linearly independent estimable functions. Let $w = \{X'\beta \mid Z\beta = 0\}$ denote the reduced model defined in a proper subspace of Ω. The respective sum of absolute errors (SAE) is then defiend for both the full and reduced models as:

$$SAE(\Omega) = \min_{\beta} \sum_{j} |\theta_j - x'_j\beta| \tag{5.45}$$

$$SAE(w) = \min_{(\beta \mid Z\beta \in w)} \sum_{j} |\theta_j - x'_j\beta|$$

Preceeding by analogy with ordinary least squares, Schrader and McKean [21] have used a test statistic $F(L_1)$ as follows

$$F(L_1) = \{SAE(w) - SAE(\Omega)\}/q(\hat{M}/2) \qquad (5.46)$$

where $\hat{M}$ is any consistent estimate of the median M. They used the asymptotic theory which states that under suitable regularity conditions the above statistic $F(L_1)$ has asymptotically a central chi-squared distribution under the null hypothesis H_0. But since this result may not hold for small sample sizes, they followed the bootstrap algorithm developed by Efron and Tibshirani [22] and Hardle and Bowman [23]. One such bootstrap algorithm for the above test statistic (5.46) proceeds as follows:

1. Compute the full model L_1-norm estimate $\hat{\beta}(L_1)$, the full model residuals $e_1, e_2, ..., e_n$ and the test statistic $F(L_1)$ above.

2. Select $\tilde{e}_1, \tilde{e}_2, ..., \tilde{e}_n$ the (n-m) nonzero residuals.

3. Draw a bootstrap random sample $e_1^*, e_2^*, ..., e_n^*$ with replacement from $\tilde{e}_1, \tilde{e}_2, ..., \tilde{e}_n$. Calculate $\hat{\beta}^*(L_1)$ and $F^*(L_1)$ from the model $e^* = X'\beta + e$.

4. Independently repeat step 3 a large number of times, say N times. The bootstrap probability value P^* is the number of $F^*(L_1)$ greater than or equal to $F(L_1)$ divided by N.

5. Reject H_0 at level α if $P^* \leq \alpha$.

Other types of bootstrap algorithms developed by Hardle and Bowman show their versatility in application. It is no doubt that these techniques would open up new issues of robustness in the DEA framework, since we would no longer be tied down to the asymptotic theory of distribution based on large samples.

5.5   Distribution of Technical and Price Efficiency

The distribution of the parameters β in the DEA models (5.8) and (5.9) has two basic implications: one for technical efficiency and the other for price efficiency. The latter may affect β either directly through demand constraints and observed market prices of inputs and outputs, or indirectly through shadow prices.

The distribution of technical efficiency parameters has already been discussed in earlier chapters. In the current literature two aspects of the distribution issue have been analyzed in some detail. One is the characterization of the overall distribution [24] of the efficiency ratio generated by the efficient solutions of the DEA model (5.9). This was done both parametrically and nonparametrically and it was found on the basis of our educational example for the public elementary school districts in California that the empirical shape of the efficiency distribution is J-shaped and highly asymmetrical. This has the implication that the small sample behavior is most likely to be skewed. Hence the need for robustness studies is all the greater. The second point is that the real world situation which generates the input output data may be subject to significant degrees of reisk aversion and also noncompetitive elements. Some methods of incorporating risk aversion are indeed called for. It is true that the concept of 'risk averse efficiency' developed by Peleg and Yaari [25] could be applied here if we view the DEA model (5.9) as the industry manager's problem, where he is maximizing his utility function. The game-theoretic models we discussed in earlier sections provide a second alternative. Recent econometric research into the estimation of risk aversion parameters from observed input-output data seem to be relevant here and need to be explored further.

There is another aspect of the DEA model (5.9) which is related to the censored regression model, where Powell [26] has applied the LAV method of estimation. Under certain regularity conditions he proved that such estimators are consistent and asymptotically normal for a wide class of error distributions and are also robust to heteroscedasticity. Clearly the small sample behavior of such LAV estimators may be established by the bootstrap technique, so that the results would have wider applicability. Besides the estimation problem, the censored model in the normal distribution case has

interesting features in terms of output variance in a heteroscedastic framework. To see
the implications consider the output response model

$$y = \beta'x - \varepsilon, \quad \beta'x \geq 0$$

where the errors $\varepsilon = (\varepsilon_j)$ are assumed to be continuously distributed such that they are
statistically independent with a constant mean and constant variance and $\mu(x,\beta) = \beta'x$ is
assumed to be nonnegative with x being nonrandom. The constrained or limited
dependent variable $\hat{y}$ is then defined by $\hat{y} = \{\max(0,y), \text{ with } y \geq 0\}$. It is clear that the
mean $\hat{\mu}$ and variance $\hat{\sigma}^2$ of $\hat{y}$ are related to the mean μ and variance σ^2 of the
unconstrained variable y by

$$\hat{\mu} \geq \mu, \quad \hat{\sigma}^2 \leq \sigma^2$$

and hence the constrained model is more stable in terms of the coefficient of variation
i.e., $\hat{\sigma}/\hat{\mu} \leq \sigma/\mu$. Clearly the output response $\hat{y}$ in the constrained model has a mixed
probability distribution with a point mass of the probability $\text{Prob}(y \leq 0)$ at zero. For a
given data set $D = \{x,y\colon (x_j,y_j), j \in I_n\}$ suppose there exists a subset $\hat{D} = \{x,y\colon (x_j,y_j),$
$j \in I_s, s \leq n\}$ for which the probability $\text{Prob}(y \geq 0) = u_0$ holds for some $u_0, 0 < u_0 \leq 1,$
then the following results can be stated:

Theorem 4

There exists a maximum probability level u^* and the associated efficiency vector β^*
which solve the following program for some $j \in \hat{D}$

$$\text{Max } u \qquad \text{s. t. } \sum_i \beta_i x_{ij} > q\sigma, j \in \hat{D}$$

$$u \geq u_0, \quad q = F^{-1}(u)$$

Proof

Since u_0 exists and y has a continuous distribution, $\text{Prob}(y \geq 0) = u_0$ implies

$$\text{Prob }(\frac{\varepsilon}{\sigma} \leq \frac{\beta' x}{\sigma} = F(\frac{\beta' x}{\sigma}) = u_0$$

Since the cumulative distribution $F(\cdot)$ is continuous and increasing we get $\dfrac{\beta' x}{\sigma} = F^{-1}(u_0)$.

Now the domain $u_0 \leq u \leq 1$ of u is compact and the inverse function $F^{-1}(u)$ is continuous in this domain. Hence there exists a maximum probability level u* and the associated efficiency vector β*.

Two implications of the above result are to be noted. First of all, it provides a method of analyzing data sensitivity e.g., if for the entire data set D the above result holds for u* = 1, then the data set j ∈ D may be said to be insensitive to stochastic variations. Thus it is helpful in data screening and clustering. Secondly, the linear and nonlinear efficiency measures may be directly compared in terms of their associated maximum probability levels.

Theorem 5

For every positive level c there exists a unique optimal soultion β* = β*(c) which minimizes the variance σ^2 of the constrained output $\hat{y}$ under the restrictions R = {β | μ = β'x ≥ c, Σ β_i = 1, β ≥ 0}, if the error ε is normally distributed with mean zero and a constant variance. Furthermore there exists some subset $\hat{D}$ for which the LP model:

Min $\mu = \beta' x$, β ∈ $\hat{R}$ = {β | $\sum\limits_{i} \beta_i x_{ij} \geq y_j$, j ∈ $\hat{D}$, Σβ_i = 1, β_i ≥ 0, all i} has an

optimal solution β* such that μ* = β*'x would also minimize the variance σ^2 of the constrained output μ* = c.

Proof

On setting $\sigma = 1.0$ without any loss of generalization the mean $\hat{\mu}$ and variance $\hat{\sigma}^2$ of the constrained output $\hat{y}$ can be written as:

$$\hat{\mu} = f(\mu) + \mu F(\mu)$$

$$\hat{\sigma}^2 = \hat{\mu}(\mu - \hat{\mu}) + F(\mu)$$

where $f(\cdot)$ is the probability density of a unit normal variate and $F(\cdot)$ is the corresponding cumulative distribution. By direct differentiation it can be easily verified that the second derivative $\hat{\sigma}^2$ with respect to μ is negative for any positive μ; also $\hat{\sigma}^2$ is an increasing function of μ such that $\hat{\sigma}^2$ tends to σ^2 as $\mu \to \infty$. Thus the unique optimal solution $\beta^* = \beta^*(c)$ exists for every fixed level of positive c. Moreover the subset $\hat{D}$ is not empty and hence the LP model: $\{ \text{Min } \mu = \beta'x, \beta \in \hat{R} \}$ has an optimal solution β^* for some $j \in \hat{D}$. Let $c^* = \beta^{*\prime}x$. Then β^* is feasible in R and since $\hat{\sigma}^2$ is a strictly concave function of c, it attains its minimum value at $c = c^*$.

It is useful to point out that the mean constrained output $\hat{\mu}$ is a strictly convex function of μ for every positive level of μ, hence the optimal solution β^* of the LP model can be used to compute the associated value of $\hat{\mu} = \hat{\mu}(\mu^*)$, $\mu^* = \beta^{*\prime}x$. By varying the sample sizes in the subset $\hat{D}$, one can thus observe how $\hat{\mu}$ and $\hat{\sigma}^2$ change as μ and hence β^* change. This would be of great value in sensitivity analysis. For example one may consider the mean LP model (5.8) considered before for a subset $j \in \hat{D}$ of data points and examine how robust is the optimal parameter vector β^*.

Two interesting attempts at characterizing the impact of price distribution on productive efficiency have been recently made. One is due to Moene [27] who studied the Johansen concept of efficiency and asked the question: does the anticipation of price fluctuations induce employers to choose plant sizes which are more robust or adaptable to such fluctuations? The second attempt is by Fare and Grosskopf [28] who assume that the micro units or firms face noncompetitive environments and hence they may minimize costs but relative to shadow prices which deviate from the observed market prices. These authors assume that the inputs have been chosen correctly and we have to find the correct or optimal shadow prices.

Starting from a two factor model with one output (Y) and two inputs, capital (K) and labor (L) the *exante* choice-of-technique function at full capacity level is viewed by Moene as:

$$Y = F(K,L)$$

Expost however the plant design is frozen in the sense that the production capacity is fixed and there is no substitution possibility between L and K, so that the *expost* production function of the plant is

$$Y(t) = \min \left(\frac{1}{a} N(t), Y \right), \quad a = L/Y \tag{5.47}$$

or, equivalently, $Y(t) = h(t)Y$; $N(t) = h(t)L$ where $Y(t)$, $N(t)$ are output and employment in period t and $h(t)$ indicates the degree of capacity utilization ($0 \le h(t) \le 1$, all t). When future prices are known with certainty the optimal rule of capacity utilization is very simple i.e. to produce up to the full capacity level as long as the quasi-rent (s) per unit

$$s = p - aw$$

is positive, where p is output price and w is the wage rate. Thus the optimal strategy is

$$h = \begin{cases} \frac{1}{Y} \min (D, Y) & \text{when } s \ge 0 \\ 0 & \text{when } s < 0 \end{cases} \tag{5.48}$$

where D is future demand or sales.

Now consider the case of price uncertainty and assume the producer to be risk neutral. The optimal plant design is then determined by those values of K and L which maximize the expected present value of the project i.e.

$$\text{Max } J = E \left[\sum_{t=1}^{T} h \, s \, Y(1 + r)^{-t} \right] - q \, K$$

$$= \beta(T) \, E(hs) \, Y - qK \tag{5.49}$$

subject to (5.47) and (5.48)

where r is the discount rate exogeneously given, $\beta(T) = \sum_{t=1}^{T} (1 + r)^{-t}$, T is the technical lifetime of the equipment and q is the price per unit of K. The expectation E is taken with respect to D, p and w. Moene defined two events:

R: {the event that $s \geq 0$ and $D \geq Y$}

Q: {the event that $s \geq 0$ and $D < Y$}

where R indicates the capacity constraint and Q the demand constraint. The optimality conditions turn out to be

$$B \, F_K = q; \quad B \, F_L = C \tag{5.50}$$

where

$$B = [P_r(R) \, E(p|R) + P_r(Q) \, a \, E(hw|Q)] \, \beta(T)$$

$$C = [P_r(R) \, E(w|R) + P_r(Q) \, E(hw|Q)] \, \beta(T)$$

Here Pr(•) denotes probability, B is the expected present value of revenues associated with a marginal increase in capacity and C is the expected present value of the expost costs associated with a unit increase in L. The impact of uncertainty or fluctuations may thus be analyzed in terms of the optimal decision rule (5.50). His major finding is that the supplier will choose a plant design, which is more flexible than the certainty case in the sense that it involves relatively less fixed costs and more variable costs. Furthermore, if it is a flexprice market in the Hicksian sense (i.e., prices adjust instantaneously to balance supply and demand) then the increased variance of output prices and wages for given mean values would tend to increase the expected gain, just as it is true in a competitive market model with price uncertainty.

The implications of different types of price distributions and of asymmetry in information offer an interesting line of future research here.

For calculating price efficiency Fare and Grosskopf propose two approaches: a nonparametric or programming approach similar to that used in the DEA model and a distance function approach based on the distance between the observed and optimal shadow prices. If the input quantities and their prices are denoted by vectors x and q,

then for a given output vector y, the firms are assumed to minimize costs $C = \sum_{i=1}^{m} q_i^* x_i$ where q* is the shadow price vector. The quotients of q_i^* and q_i, i=1,2,...,m are used to define various forms of price efficiency.

However this approach hinges on the critical assumption that the inputs have been chosen correctly, although the (optimal) shadow prices deviate from the observed market prices. The task before the decision maker is to find the correct shadow prices i.e. the efficient prices. The stochastic aspects can be introduced in this framework in two ways: (a) by introducing the probabilistic criterion of consistency with the efficiency hypothesis as discussed in Chapter 3, and (b) by a parametric search procedure where the empirical distribution of observed prices is used as a filtering device. However in most practical cases it is difficult to uphold the assumption that the inputs have been chosen correctly. Maybe one could invoke either the theory of rational expectations or the theory of the second best to put the assumption in a more generalized perspective.

References

1.   Fare, R., Measuring the technical efficiency of production, Journal of Economic Theory, 19 (1978), 150-162.

2.   Charnes, A., Cooper, W.W., Golany, B. and Seiford, L., Foundations of data envelopment anaysis for Pareto-Koopmans efficient empirical production functions, Journal of Econometrics, 30 (1985), 91-107.

3.   Forsund, F.R. and Jansen, E.S., The interplay between sectoral models based on micro data and models for the national economy, in Production, Multi-Sectoral Growth and Planning, Amsterdam: North Holland, 1985.

4.   Cook, R.D. and Weisberg, S., Residuals and Influence in Regression, London, Chapman and Hall, 1982.

5   Nelder, J.A., Iterative weighted least squares: an algorithm for many occasions, in Data Analysis and Informatics, Amsterdam: North Holland, 1980.

6.   Bryant, P. and Williamson, J.A., Asymptotic behavior of classification maximum likelihood estimates, Biometrika, 65 (1978), 273-281.

7.   Farrell, M.J., The measurement of productive efficiency, Journal of Royal Statistical Society, Series A, 125 (1957), 253-290.

8.   Timmer, C.P., Using a probabilistic frontier production to measure technical efficiency, Journal of Political Economy, 79 (1971), 776-794.

9.   Nunamaker, T.R., Using data envelopment analysis to measure the efficiency of nonprofit organizations: a critical evaluation, Managerial and Decision Economics, 6 (1985), 50-58.

10.   Andrews, D.F. et al., Robust Estimates of Location, Princeton: University Press, 1972.

11.   Hampel, F., The influence curve and its role in robust estimation, Journal of American Statistical Association, 69 (1974), 383-393.

12.   Sengupta, J.K., The measurement of productive efficiency: a robust minimax approach, Managerial and Decision Economics, 9 (1988), 153-161.

13.   Jondrow, J., Lovell, C.A.K., Materov, I.S. and Schmidt, P., On the estimation of technical efficiency in the stochastic frontier production function model, Journal of Econometrics, 11 (19820, 233-238.

14.   Box, G.E.P. and Cox, D.R., An analysis of transformations, Journal of Royal Statistical Society, Series B, 26 (1964), 211-243.

15.   Spitzer, J.J., A Monte Carlo investigation of the Box-Cox transformation in small samples, Journal of the American Statistical Association, 73 (1978), 488-495.

16. Eubank, R.L., <u>Spline Smoothing and Nonparametric Regression</u>, New York: Marcel Dekker, 1988.

17. Hand, D.J., <u>Kernel Discriminant Analysis</u>, New York: Research Studies Press, 1982.

18. Rosenblatt, M., Remarks on some nonparametric estimates of a density function, <u>Annals of Mathematical Statistics</u>, 27 (1956), 832-835.

19. Leamer, E.E., <u>Specification Searches: Ad Hoc Inference with Nonexperimental Data</u>, New York: John Wiley, 1978.

20. Everitt, B.S. and Hand, D.J., <u>Finite Mixture Distributions</u>, London: Chapman and Hall, 1981.

21. Schrader, R.M. and McKean, J.W., Small sample properties of least absolute errors analysis of variance, in Y. Dodge ed., <u>Statistical Data Analysis Based on the L_1-Norm and Related Methods</u>, New York: Elsevier Science Pubishers, 1987.

22. Efron, B. and Tibshirani, R., Bootstrap methods for standard errors, confidence intervals and other measures of statistical accuracy, <u>Statistical Science</u>, 1 (1986), 54-77.

23. Hardle, W. and Bowman, A.W., Bootstrapping in nonparametric regression: local adaptive smoothing and confidence bands, <u>Journal of American Statistical Association</u>, 83 (1988), 123-127.

24. Sengupta, J.K., Data envelopment anaysis for efficiency measurement in the stochastic case, <u>Computers and Operations Research</u>, 14 (987), 117-129.

25. Peleg, B. and Yaari, M.E., A price characterization of efficient random variables, <u>Econometrica</u>, 43 (1975), 283-292.

26. Powell, J.L., Least absolute deviations estimation for the censored regression model, <u>Journal of Econometrics</u>, 25 (1984), 303-325.

27. Moene, K.O., Fluctuations and factor proportions: putty clay investments under uncertainty, in <u>Production, Multi-Sectoral Growth and Planning</u>, New York: Elsevier Science Publishers, 1985.

28. Fare, R.G. and Grosskopf, S., Measuring shadow price efficiency, in A. Dogramaci and R. Fare (eds.), <u>Application of Modern Production Theory</u>, Dordrecht: Kluwer Publishing, 1988.

Chapter 6

APPLICATIONS OF NONPARAMETRIC THEORY

Recent developments in the nonparametric approach to efficiency have led to an upsurge of empirical and illustrative applications. Although Farrell started the nonparametric approach in the context of agricultural production data, the data envelopment analysis (DEA) initiated it as a tool for evaluating managerial efficiency. Since it has shadow price implications, it has important role in resource allocation models for economic development and international trade. The stochastic aspects of nonparametric theory, which are currently under intensive research efforts have important connections with the parametric and nonparametric models in the theory of stochastic programming. Treatment of risk and uncertainty, efficiency under incomplete information and the specification of the dynamic efficiency frontier under conditions of uncertainty regarding future demand are some of the major research areas where more applied work is forthcoming. Finally, the DEA approach through its emphasis on the data structure and their heterogeneity has opened up the broader question: how to integrate other data-based techniques with the nonparametric theory of the DEA model? We have already discussed in earlier chapters the use of such data-based techniques as nonparametric regression, influence curve approach and the bootstrap techniques. The use of entropy as an information-theoretic measure of data analysis comes readily to mind in this connection. Although entropy maximization has been related to statistical estimation theory, through Fisher's information matrix, Kullback's discrimination information and Akaike's information criterion, its role in DEA model has yet not been explored.

6.1 Production in Quasi-Market and Non-Market System

In competitive markets production to be efficient must satisfy the conditions for both technical efficiency and price efficiency. In quasi-competitive markets only a few prices are market determined e.g. teacher salaries in educational systems, while nonmarket systems

224

do not have their resource allocation processes determined by optimizing objectives. Reasons for the latter may be the lack of any well defined criterion like profits, which is not definable due to the absence of prices e.g., some sort of notional or accounting mesure like prices may be used for services but these are of very little value, since these are determined by administered rules. Thus if one wants to compare several training programs run by an organization in terms of their relative efficiency, salaries may be fixed for all the programs yet their performanc e may differ in efficiency.

The applications of the DEA model to measure technical efficiency have been made in several quasi-market and non-market fields [1-4] such as (a) educational institutions, (b) hospital services, (c) comparison of private and public universities and (d) comparison of different training programs in the defense field. As a pioneering study one may refer to the work of Charnes, Cooper and Rhodes [1] who utilized the extensive data from Program Follow Through (PFT), which was a large scale social experiment in U.S. in the late 1960's to provide remedial assistance to educationally disadvantaged primary school students. Their objective was to test the advantages of PFT programs relative to the designated NFT (i.e. Non-Follow Through) counterparts in various parts of the U.S. From a set of 11 output measures some of which are only qualitative the following three were chosen: y_1 for total reading score as measured by the Metropolitan Achievement Test, y_2 for total Mathematics score and y_3 for Coopersmith Index of Self-esteem Inventory. Five inputs were selected from among a set of 25 as follows: x_1 for the education level of mother, x_2 for the highest occupation of a family member according to a prearranged rating scale, x_3 for the parental visit index representing the number of visits to the school site, x_4 for parent counseling index calculated from data on time spent with child on school-related topics such as reading together and x_5 for the number of teachers at a given site. Their application of DEA technique showed that in terms of efficiency the PFT programs failed to be superior to the NFT programs for the sample sites selected; also they located several sources of relative inefficiency which would be ordinarily missed by the standard regression approach.

As a second important application we may refer to the comparative application of data envelopment analysis and translog methods to hospital production data made by Banker, Conrad and Strauss [4]. Their applied study provides interesting insights into the relative strengths of the estimation performed by the above two methods. From the cost and production data for the fiscal eyar 1978 of 114 North Carolina hospitals which were submitted to North Carolina Blue Cross-Blue Shield and the Duke Endowment, the following four aggregated inputs were considered: (1) nursing services, (2) ancillary services such as room, laboratory work, x-ray, etc., (3) administrative services and (4) capital. Furthermore, to examine the impact of utilization of the hospital services by patients of different age groups, three output measures were chosen: (1) patient days for inpatients below age 14, (2) patient days for inpatients aged between 14 and 65, and (3) patient days for inpatients aged above 65. Their estimates showed that the translog cost function displayed constant returns, whereas the DEA LP models suggested the prevalence of both increasing and decreasing returns to scale in different segments of the hospital productoin correspondence, suggesting by implication that the translog model may be averaging diametrically opposite behavior.

Next we describe an educational study [5] we performed on the school production functions in California. The question of how to minimize school costs is of great importance considering the large magnitude of resources flowing into public education. Recently, Kenny [6] has developed a model of optimal school size which predicts that schools minimize total instructional costs by operating in a region of increasing returns to school inputs. He divides the total cost of schooling into two components: the transportation cost for students getting to and from school and the cost of instructing students at school. Whereas the first component cost tends to increase as the school enrollment rises, the second tends to decline. Kenny's model can be generalized in two directions that are consistent with modern economic theory. One is to introduce scale economies through Arrow's concept of 'learning by doing' e.g., the traditional production function $y = f(K,L)$ is modified to $y = F(K,AL)$, where y is output K capital, L labor and

AL is labor augmented in efficiency due to knowledge and experience. The augmenting variable A is assumed to depend on the stock of capital and time, if the time-series data are available. The production function f(K,L) exhibits increasing returns to scale but with augmented labor, the modified function f(K,AL) shows constant returns to scale as in neoclassical theory. For school systems, the production function may be written as

$$y = f(q,As)$$

where q is a quality variable, s is size measured by enrollment and A is an augmenting variable depending on quality and time. Since the cost of increasing quality is an increasing function of q and s, it is clear that the total cost of a given quality of schooling would be minimized by expanding the school until the increase in quality improvement cost associated with adding one more student is just offset by the decrease in average instructional costs due to adding one more student.

The second aspect of generalizing the scale economies argument calls for the distinction between the average and the efficient production function, where the latter is also called a production frontier. If the overall scale economies tend to vary with the size of schools, the standard regression methods would only estimate an "average" production function, while what we need may be the frontier production function. If the scale effects of small and large schools are significantly different, the econometric estimates of the parameters of the frontier production function must be able to capture the distinction and to that extent the optimal school size model would vary from a small school to a large school.

We tested these two generalized aspects of scale economies in schooling over the statistical data on public elementary schools (grade 6) in California for the years 1976-77 and 1977-78. The production function regression (e.g. log-linear and translog functions) and frontier estimation by linear programming include numerous variables like enrollment statistics, teacher salaries and other expenditures, average class size, proportion of minority students and standardized test scores in reading, writing, spelling and mathematics. These empirical estimates support three broad conclusions. first, the schools operate in a region of increasing returns to school inputs, when the inputs include teacher salaries, average class size and minority enrollmeent. Second, the production frontier estimates, on average, differ significantly from the average production function regressions. This implies that an optimal school size model based on average regressions may not always be unbiased and representative. Third, the overall economies of scale estimated by the frontier production function differ significantly between schools which are either close or coincident with the frontier curve and those which are not. This implies in particular that the second group of schools which do not belong to the frontier have much less scale economies than the first. These conclusions seem to imply that holding the cost of teachers and other instructional inputs constant, schooling may be much more expensive for small schools than the large ones.

6.2   Managerial Models in Operations Research

We have already noted that unlike Farrell's and Johansen's efficiency models, the DEA model was developed essentially for comparing and evaluating managerial efficiencies across the decision making units. Thus the DEA model specifically distinguishes between (1) program versus managerial efficiency, and (2) discretionary versus nondiscretionary inputs. Thus when the implicit cost function of the k-th unit i.e., $g_k = \beta'(k)x_k$ is minimized we use a reference set or cluster k, corresponding to which we can determine the efficient and nonefficient units. For fixed k, this involves the comparison of managerial efficiency. But when k is varied we obtain the matrix $B^* = \{\beta_i^*(k); \ i=1,2,...,m;$ k=1,2,...,N\} for the single output case. The comparison of $\beta^*(k)$ for different k involves program efficiency. For this comparison the DEA model requires common outputs and inputs for the reference sets. Then one may think of this comparison between k=1,2,...,N "technologies" as a method of comparing their varying degrees of efficiency for converting common inputs into common outputs. Charnes, Cooper and Rhodes [1] applied these two measures of efficiency to the data from Program Follow Through already mentioned. The distinction between discretionary and nondiscretionary inputs is important because the latter inputs are generally fixed in the short run. Banker and Morey [7] appied these concepts to measure their influence in DEA efficiency evaluations. A similar distinction is drawn by Johansen between short run and long run production frontiers and he emphasized in particular that the productive inefficiency may be reflected in part in the distribution of unutilized capacity across firms. Several empirical estimates [8] of the capacity distribution have been recently made for Norwegian industries and they show the extent of underutilization at the sectoral and national levels due to demand fluctuations and other uncertainty.

Recently a combination of the DEA and the regression model has been attempted by Charnes, Cooper and Sueyoshi [9] to analyze the court decision to break up Bell (i.e. American Telephone and Telegraph Co.). They propose the following nonlinear programming model:

$$\text{Min} \sum_{t=1}^{n} \delta_t$$

$$\text{s.t. } f(p_t, q_t, T_t) + \delta_t = \ln C_t; \ \delta_t \geq 0; \ t=1,2,...,n$$

where $f(\cdot)$ is the translog cost function and $\ln C_t$ is the natural logarithm of cost C_t, the observed total cost in year t:

$$f = \alpha_0 + \sum_i \alpha_i \ln p_i + \sum_k \beta_k \ln q_k + \mu \ln T + \frac{1}{2} \sum_i \sum_j \gamma_{ij} \ln p_i \ln p_j$$

$$+ \frac{1}{2} \sum_k \sum_r \delta_{kr} \ln q_k \ln q_r + \sum_i \sum_k \rho_{ik} \ln p_i \ln q_k$$

$$+ \sum_i \lambda_i \ln p_i \ln T + \sum_k \theta_k \ln q_k \ln T + \tau [\ln T]^2$$

Here p_i = price of input i=1,2,3 for capital, labor and mateirals, q_k = quantity of k-th output k=1,2 for local and long distance service and T = an index of technological change. On solving the nonlinear model above they obtain estimates of total cost which possesses a frontier property relative to the observed cost with $f(p_t, q_t, T_t) \leq \ln C_t$. They compare this estimate with a straightforward regression estimate previously made by Evans and Heckman [10] and found the latter to be deficient in several respects e.g., (i) it assumes the data to be uncontaminated by managerial errors or other sources of inefficiency, (ii) it cannot easily incorporate the implicit constraints on the share of factors in total costs and (iii) its statistical tests are specific to average measures of central tendency. However this debate raises very many fundamental issues on the relation between parametric and nonparametric frontier estimates. First of all, the method followed above is parametric and certainly the standard statistical criteria for evaluating the efficiency or quality of estimates are not applicable. Secondly, the consistency of the observed data set with any kind of efficiency hypothesis, linear or nonlinear may need be tested separately before any regression estimates are performed. Since this was not done by Evans and Heckman, it is doubtful if their results are comparable.

6.3   Economic Development and International Trade

In empirical studies on economic development two types of approach have been followed with regard to the sources of economic growth. One approach emphasizes the production function studies in the agricultural sector of the less developed countries (LDC) and points out the various sources of technical and allocative (price) efficiencies. For example, Lau and Yotopoulos [11] analyzed the agricultural sector in India in several studies and argued that the observed costs may be nonoptimal relative to obtainable input prices due to government controls. Several parametric studies [12,13] have also been made on the price distortion in the agricultural sector at the national and international level, thus resulting in technical and allocative efficiencies.

A second approach seeks to identify the scale economies or, increasing returns as a strategic factor in dynamic growth, which is sometimes called the Verdoorn law. The neoclassical theory of comparative advantage and gains from trade is then applied to explain the rapid emergence of newly industrializing countries of south-east Asia e.g., Taiwan,

Korea, Singapore, Hong Kong as leaders of export-led growth. Other countries were also identified by OECD as newly industrializing on the basis of the three criteria: (a) their rapid penetration of world markets of manufactures, (b) a rising share of industrial employment and (c) a sharp increase in real gross domestic product per capita relative to the more advanced industrial countries. Since increasing returns and price flexibility which can facilitate growth in competitive markets are merely the two aspects of the efficiency analysis: the technical and allocative efficiency, it is no wonder that the nonparametric approach has great scope of application here. The interplay between sectoral and national models of dynamic efficiency, which has been studied by Forsund and Jansen [14] in respect of Johansen's concept of efficiency is very important here. An interesting study in this area about the role of multinational firms in importing new technology to a less developed country has been made by Joshi [15] who applied the theory of stochastic production frontier to the machine tools industry in India over 1974-82 to compare the relative technical efficiencies of the indigenous and the foreign collaborating firms. His study showed that the efficiency differences between these two groups of firms were statistically insignificant before 1980 but since 1980 the foreign collaborating firms showed an impressive growth up to an average 90% level of full capacity utilization, whereas the indigenous firms did not show any such dramatic rise at all. However this study has been parametric, aggregative and mainly econometric. Various facets of the efficiency frontier have not been investigated and the impact of the market forces not at all analyzed. The scope of application of the nonparametric approach here is very wide.

6.4   Stochastic Programming and Markov Process Models

The DEA model where we vary the objective function: min $g_k = \beta'x_k$, (k=1,2,...,n) over the n sample units to measure their relative efficiencies, can be interpreted as a stochastic linear programming (LP) model, by considering the input-output data (x_j,y_j), j=1,2,...,n as the realizations of a stochastic process. If the stochastic process evolves over time as in a Markov process then the DEA model can be viewed as a dynamic stochastic program. In neoclassical models of economic growth the Markov process models have been frequently applied to specify the optimal growth profile of an economy consisting of two or more sectors. In the two sector case, sectors are usually those producing consumer goods and capital goods, or those comprising backward and growing sectors.

Consider the DEA model above where we solve n LP problems to obtain n_1 units as efficient (i.e. $n_1 \leq n$) and assume that n_1 is not too small i.e. greater than 8 say. We consider then the statistical distribution of the minimand $g_k^* = \min g_k$ for k=1,2,...,n. Let F(z) be the cumulative distribution function (cdf) of the random variable $z = g_k^*$ and $F_N(z)$ be the step function

$$F_N(z) = \begin{cases} 0, z < z_{(1)} \\ i/N, z_{(i)} \leq z \leq z_{(i+1)} & 1 \leq i \leq N-1 \\ 1, z_{(N)} \leq 1 \end{cases}$$

where $z_{(1)} \leq z_{(2)} \leq ... \leq z_{(N)}$ are the ordered values of g_k^* with $N = n_1$. One type of statistical distance of the empirical distribution function from the unknown population cdf F(z) is given by the Kolmogorov-Smirnov statistic:

$$D_N = \text{least upper bound of } |F_N(z) - F(z)|$$

which is tabulated at 1 and 5% levels of significance. From this statistic one can easily calculate the probabilities

$$\text{Prob } (D_N < c/N) \text{ for } c = 1,2,...,N$$

for any finite N. These results have been utilized by Birnbaum [16] to compute numerically the probability distribution of D_N for finite N and for large N. The empirical distribution agrees with the original Kolmogorov-Smirnov formula as follows:

$$\lim_{N \to \infty} \mathrm{Prob}(D_N < \frac{t}{N}) = 1 - 2 \sum_{j=1}^{\infty} (-1)^{j-1} \exp(-2t^2 j^2)$$

Thus it is possible to use the statistic D_N above for finite N for three major purposes, e.g., (1) for testing the hypothesis that a large sample was obtained from a random variable z with a distribution function $F(z)$ explicitly given as a truncated normal (or, half normal) distribution, (2) for testing the null hypothesis that the two distributions of z are identical, where the first one is derived from the set of minimand values $\{g_k^*, k=1,2,...,N\}$ and the second one from the mean LP model with the objective function min $\bar{g} = \beta'x$ and finally (3) for constructing a confidence interval about the empirical distribution function $F_N(z)$, so that it can be asserted on a preassigned probability level that the unknown 'true' distribution function $F(z)$ is essentially contained in that interval. Recent techniques of kernel estimation and bootstrap methods [17] discussed in eariler chapters can also be applied.

For a dynamic stochastic programming version of the nonparametric efficiency model, we may consider two examples, one from the short run production scheduling model in operations research known as the HMMS model and the other from the theory of optimal growth and investment planning.

The HMMS model is basically an optimal control model in the class known as linear quadratic and Gaussian (LQG) class and it solves for an optimal linear decision rule of a single plant (or unit) in terms of one output, two inputs and inventories, when the demand pattern is stochastic. We modify the model in terms of the DEA framework as follows. Let x_{ijt} denote input i=1,2, for plant j at time t, x_{3jt} are inventories, y_{jt} is the single output of plant j at time t. To test if the plant k is efficient in an intertemporal sense we set up the following intertemporal optimization model, where $\bar{d}_{jt} = \bar{d}_t$ is the mean demand assumed to be identical for each plant:

$$\mathrm{Min} \ g_k(T) = \sum_{t=1}^{T} C_{kt}$$

$$C_{kt} = \sum_{i=1}^{2} \beta_i x_{ikt} + \beta_3 \, | \, x_{3kt} - x^o_{3kt} \, |$$

$$\text{s. t.} \sum_{i=1}^{2} \beta_i x_{ijt} \geq y_{jt}, \; t = 1, 2, \ldots, T$$

$$x_{3jt} - x_{3j, t-1} = y_{jt} - \bar{d}_{jt}$$

$$\text{all } j = 1, 2, \ldots, n; \; x_{ijt}, y_{jt}, \bar{d}_{jt} \geq 0$$

Here x^o_{3jt} is the desired or target level of inventory for plant j and the last equation is the state space equation for inventories which are subject to a first order Markov process when $d_{jt} = \bar{d}_t + \varepsilon_t$ specifies the demand pattern with ε_t being a white noise process. Clearly if the inventory equation is dropped, we get back the standard DEA model for one output and two inputs. But in this case we have observed data in the form of $(x_{ijt}, y_{jt}, \bar{d}_{jt}, x^o_{3kt})$ and ask if the k-th plant is efficient in meeting the mean demand. If it is, then we must have

$\sum_i \beta^*_i x_{ijt} = y_{jt}$ for all t=1,2,...,T where $\beta^* = (\beta^*_i)$ is the optimal solution vector. Clearly the myopic case occurs when T = 1.Several interesting issues arise when we introduce stochastic considerations into the above formulation e.g., (1) the parameters β_i may be made time-dependent as β_{it} and it is quite possible for plant k to be efficient but only for some t values not all. Thus one could define a plant to be strongly efficient of order τ if it remained efficient for all earlier times t=1,2,...,τ-1; (2) the inventory equation would be probabilistic as soon as the demand process admits of stochasticity and this can be studied by different types of linear and nonlinear decision rules [18] as in the theory of chance-constrained linear programming, and finally (3) the optimal solutions of the LQG model may be easily compared with the DEA optimal soutions with partricular regard to data sensitivity.

Note however that in the traditional HMMS model the parameters β_i are estimated first by ordinary regression methods on the basis of observed input output data and then given these values of β_i and an estimtae of mean demand, one computes the optimal levels of the two inputs x_{ijt} (i=1,2), inventories (x_{3jt}) and output (y_{jt}). There is no reason why the two methods would produce mutually compatible results.

Next consider an optimal growth model in the neoclassical tradition [19] where the economy is assumed to have a number of sectors, each of which produces a single output which can be used in part as input for the next period. Denote by $y_j(t)$ the output produced by sector j at time t and let $x_{ij}(t)$ be the amount of output of sector i needed for production of output j i.e.,

$$x_{ij}(t) \le \lambda_{ij}(t) \, y_i(t\text{-}1); \qquad\qquad\qquad 0 \le \lambda_{ij}(t) \le 1$$

where $\lambda_{ij}(t)$ is the allocation ratio and one period time lag is assumed here. Furthermore we have the production frontier conditions:

$$y_j(t) \le \sum_{i=1}^{n} \beta_{ij} \lambda_{ij}(t) y_i(t-1)$$

$$i,j=1,2,...,n; \quad t=1,2,...,T$$

In the traditional models of optimal growth we assume the parameters β_{ij} to be given along with the initial output vector y(0) and then we solve for an optimal time profile of the allocation matrices $\lambda_{ij}^{*}(t)$ and the associated output vectors y*(1),y*(2),...,y*(T) which maximizes a social welfare function e.g., one such function is

$$u(T) = \sum_{t=1}^{T} (1+\delta)^{-t} (\sum_{j=1}^{n} w_j y_j(t))$$

where w_j are fixed nonnegative weights and δ is the discounting rate. But in case of dynamic efficiency frontier in Farrell and DEA versions, we would assume that the observed data are given in the form of $\{y_j(t), x_{ij}(t), \text{ and } \lambda_{ij}(t), i,j=1,2,...,n; t=1,2,...,T\}$.

We would then solve for the optimal values of β_{ij} and ask if they are consistent with the efficiency hypothesis.

A special case of this model may be specified in terms of the open-dynamic Leontief-type input-output model which has the equilibrium balance equation:

$$x_i(t) = \sum_{j=1}^{n} a_{ij} x_j(t) + \sum_{j=1}^{n} b_{ij} \Delta x_j(t) + d_i(t) \qquad i,j=1,2,...,n$$

Here $x_i(t)$ is gross output of sector i, $d_i(t)$ is the final demand and the matrices $A = (a_{ij})$, $B = (b_{ij})$ are the current and capital input coefficients where $\Delta x_j(t) = x_j(t+1) - x_j(t)$. Full capacity utilization is assumed here for the capital and current account coefficients. Following Johansen's concept of efficiency one may assume A and B to be given and then introduce actual rates of capacity utilization by $\theta_j(t)$, $0 \le \theta_j(t) \le 1$ so that $\theta_j \Delta x_j(t)$ is the actual realized output for sector j. One may then set up a Johansen-type efficiency model as follows:

$$\text{Max} \sum_{t=1}^{T} \sum_{j=1}^{n} \theta_j(t)$$

$$\text{s. t. } x(t) - Ax(t) - B\hat{\theta}(t)\Delta x(t) \ge d(t)$$

$$x(0) > 0 \text{ given}$$

where $\hat{\theta}(t)$ is a diagonal matrix with $\theta_j(t)$ in the diagonal satisfying the capacity constraint $0 \le \theta_j(t) \le 1$ for all j. The close similarity of this approach with the DEA model has been analyzed by Sengupta [20] to show that the latter's efficiency concept can be related to the concept of 'dominant technology' of a dynamic Leontief model. As before the efficiency of order τ with $\tau \le T$ can be characterized for any sector, thus generalizing the static concept of efficiency of the DEA model. Furthermore, the stochastic aspects of this type of model can be introduced through variations in the demand vector $d(t)$, or through the capacity utilization and distribution functions as in Johansen's approach.

6.5   Multivariate Data Anaysis and Information Theory

For the single output DEA model we have already seen that one has to solve n LP models to find out if r of them ($r \leq n$) are efficient by the DEA criterion. Thus we have the problem of comparing more than one efficient LP problem whenever $n_1 \geq 2$. So far we have discussed two types of approaches. One is the method of Timmer [21] based on the least absolute value (LAV) technique of estimation, which takes the arithmetic mean of the n LP models in the objective function and sets up one mean LP model. Clearly by replacing n by r where r units are found to be efficient one would obtain a more representative unit amongst the efficient units by this procedure. A second approach is to follow the clustering method and apply a dummy variable regression procedure as discussed in Chapter 3.

We now consider a third method based on information theory e.g. an entropy measure which is also nonparametric. To fix ideas we first start from a parametric procedure. Suppose we have a set $D^r = ((x_1,y_1), (x_2,y_2),....,(x_r,y_r))$ of input-output data where each x_j is an m-tuple vector with an associated parameter vector β_j for j=1,2,...,r. Furthermore assume that for each subset j we could define the maximum likelihood (ML) estimate of β_j by maximizing the log likelihood function $\log f_{s(j)}$ where s(j) are the sample observations for each j. Then to select an approximate model we adopt the criterion of maximum expected value of the log likelihood function

$$\max E\{\log f_{s(j)}\}$$

where E denotes the expectation with respect to the known distribution $f_s(\cdot)$ derived from the sequence of probability densities $\{f_{s(j)}, j=1,2,...,r\}$. Recent applications [22] of the criterion of maximizing the expected likelihood function of the sample observations have shown that it has many desirable properties e.g., insensitivity to extreme data variations.

The above criterion is easily modified to Akaike's information criterion (AIC) for discriminating among the r submodels found to be efficient by the DEA model. This latter criterion is

$$\text{Min AIC} = -2 \log \text{ML} + 2k$$

wehre ML denotes the maximum likelihood function and k is the number of parameters (here k = m) within the model. This is called MAICE i.e. minimum of AIC estimation, which has two advantages: (1) it can be used to determine the order of a polynomial function for the production frontier and (2) it can be easily related to the entropy measure. To see the second implication consider the problem of choosing among the r submodels once again. For each submodel the data variations (d) around a particular facet of the efficiency surface may be specified by a distribution $P_s(d)$ say, where s=1,2,...,r. We need the best approximation to the true distribution q(d) of the entire data set d. One may here use the entropy of the true distribution q with respect to any assumed distribution p_s defined as

$$B(q; p_s) = - \sum_{i=1}^{N} q_i \ln(q_i/p_{is})$$
$$= E_d \ln p_s(d) - E_d \ln q(d)$$

assuming discrete distributions. Since the expected value of ln q(d) is common to all the values $B(q;p_s)$, the best approximation can be obtained by searching for the maximum of E_d ln $p_s(d)$. Clearly this procedure is very general and can be easily extended to data sets involving multiple outputs and multiple inputs and also $p_s(d)$, q(d) may be replaced by continuous densities. Several useful applications of the approach above may be briefly referred to. First of all, the quantity $I(q; p_s) = -B(q;p_s)$ which is called discrimination information by Kullback and expected weight of evidence by Good is basically related to the entropy measure $H_q = -\Sigma q_i \ln q_i$; hence maximizing $B(q; p_s)$ over s=1,2,...,r is equivalent to minimizing $I(q;p_s)$ which can be interpreted as the cost of divergence of p_s from the true distribution. Since the DEA model minimizes the cost $g_k = \beta'x_k$, it would be quite compatible. Secondly, the probbility distributions $p_s(d)$ associated with a given facet of the efficiency surface can be generated by the bootstrap technique [23] by using a theorem of stochastic programming [24]. This theorem says that for any efficient facet determined by the LP method using the observed input-output data (all positive), there exists a neighborhood around the frontier for which data variations preserve the frontier under certain mild regularity conditions. Random samples can be generated from this neighborhood when the bootstrap technique is applied. Finally, it would be of great interest to compare the max $E_d \ln p_s(d)$ criterion of information theory with the maximum likelihood criterion, when the latter assumes a specific distribution e.g., a truncated normal distribution or, a composed error structure. There exists a large scope for such comparative studies, which would provide additional insights into the nonparametric approach to efficiency estimation.

References

1.   Charnes, A., Cooper, W.W. and Rhodes, E., Evaluating program and managerial efficiency: an application of data envelopment analysis to program follow through, Managment Science, 27 (1981), 688-697.

2.   Bowlin, W.F., Charnes, A., Cooper, W.W. and Sherman, H.D., Data envelopment analysis and regression approaches to efficiency estimation and evaluation, in R.G. Thompsòn and R.M. Thrall eds., Normative Anaysis in Policy Decisions: Public and Private, Basel: Baltzer, A.G. Publishers, 1985.

3.   Dogramarci, A. (ed.), Studies in Productivity Analysis, Dordrecht: Kluwer Academic Publishers, 1988.

4.   Banker, R.D., Conrad, R.F. and Strauss, R.P., A comparative application of data envelopment analysis and translog methods: an illustrative study of hospital production, Management Science, 32 (1986), 30-44.

5.   Sengupta, J.K. and Sfier, R.E., Production frontier estimates of scale in public schools in California, Economics of Education Review, 5 (1985), 297-307.

6.   Kenny, L.W., Economies of scale in schooling, Economics of Education Review, 2 (1982), 1-24.

7.   Banker, R.D and Morey, R., Efficiency Analysis for exogeneously fixed inputs and outputs, Operations Research, 34 (1986), 89-98.

8.   Forsund, F.R., Hoel, M. and Longva, S. (eds.), Production, Multi-Sectoral Growth and Planning, New York: Elsevier Science Publishers, 1985.

9.   Charnes, A., Cooper, W.W. and Sueyoshi, T., A goal programming-constrained regression review of the Bell system breakup, Management Science, 34 (1988), 1-26.

10.   Evans, D.S. and Heckman, J.J., Multiproduct cost function estimates and natural monopoly tests for the Bell system, in D.S. Evans ed., Breaking Up Bell, Amsterdam: Elsevier Science Publishers, 1983.

11.   Lau, L. and Yotopoulos, P., A test for relative efficiency and application to Indian agriculture, American Economic Review, 61 (1971), 94-109.

12.   Kalirajan, K., On measuring absolute technical and allocative efficiencies, Sankhya: the Indian Journal of Statistics, 47 (1985), 385-400.

13.   Bale, M.D. and Lutz, E., Price distortions in agriculture and their effects: an international comparison, American Journal of Agricultural Economics, 63 (1981), 8-22.

14.   Forsund, F.R. and Jansen, E.S., The interplay between sectoral models based on microdata and models for the national economy, in Production, Multisectoral Growth

and Planning, Amsterdam: North Holland, 1985.

15. Joshi, H., Productive efficiency of the Indian machine tools industry: a comparative study of collaborating and indigenous firms, unpublished PhD dissertation, Indian Institute of Technology, Kanpur, 1988.

16. Birnbaum, Z.W., Distribution-free tests of fit for continuous distribution functions, Annals of Mathematical Statistics, 24 (1953), 1-8.

17. Silverman, B.W., Density Estimation for Statistics and Data Analysis, London: Chapman and Hall, 1986.

18. Sengupta, J.K., Decision Models in Stochastic Programming, Amsterdam: North Holland, 1982.

19. Radner, R., Efficiency prices for infinite horizon production programs, Review of Economic Studies, 34 (1967), 51-66.

20 Sengupta, J.K., Efficiency measurement in nonmarket systems, in Stochastic Optimization and Economic Models, Dordrecht: D. Reidel Publishing, 1986.

21. Timmer, C.P., Using a probabilistic frontier production function to measure technical efficiency, Journal of Political Economy, 79 (1971), 776-794.

22. Akaike, H., Statistical inference and measurement of entropy, in G.E.P. Box, T. Leonard and C. Wu, Scientific Inference, Data Analysis and Robustness, New York: Academic Press, 1983.

23. Efron, B. and Tibshirani, R., Bootstrap methods for standard errors, confidence intervals and other measures of statistical accuracy, Statistical Science, 1 (1986), 54-77.

24. Sengupta J.K., Data envelopment anaysis for efficiency measurement in the stochastic case, Computers and Operations Research, 14 (1987), 117-129.

AUTHOR INDEX

242

SUBJECT INDEX

THEORY AND DECISION LIBRARY

SERIES B: MATHEMATICAL AND STATISTICAL METHODS

Already published: